Segmentation in Social Marketing

Timo Dietrich · Sharyn Rundle-Thiele
Krzysztof Kubacki
Editors

Segmentation in Social Marketing

Process, Methods and Application

Springer

Editors
Timo Dietrich
Griffith University
Brisbane
Australia

Krzysztof Kubacki
Griffith University
Brisbane
Australia

Sharyn Rundle-Thiele
Griffith University
Brisbane
Australia

ISBN 978-981-10-1833-6 ISBN 978-981-10-1835-0 (eBook)
DOI 10.1007/978-981-10-1835-0

Library of Congress Control Number: 2016948622

Printed on acid-free paper

This Springer imprint is published by Springer Nature
The registered company is Springer Nature Singapore Pte Ltd.
The registered company address is: 152 Beach Road, #22-06/08 Gateway East, Singapore 189721, Singapore

Contents

Segmentation in Social Marketing: Why We Should Do It More Often that We Currently Do

Krzysztof Kubacki, Timo Dietrich and Sharyn Rundle-Thiele

Abstract The assumption underpinning use of the market segmentation process is the belief that consumers have different wants which cannot be satisfied by a single one-size-fits-all marketing program. In this book we show that market segmentation is a crucial element of social marketing. This chapter serves as an introduction to the book and provides an overview of its main parts. In the first part—Segmentation in Social Marketing—we have four chapters reviewing the current state of knowledge on the use of segmentation in social marketing and we place market segmentation's role within a wider social marketing context. In the second part—Segmentation process, methods, and application—in three chapters we introduce a five-step segmentation process for social marketing programs, describe different approaches to segmentation, and provide key resources for social marketers seeking to employ the methods described. And in the final part—Segmentation in practice—we have four chapters presenting different case studies detailing how segments have been derived in social marketing in a broad range of contexts including healthy lunches, alcohol and adolescents, and recycling.

K. Kubacki · T. Dietrich (✉) · S. Rundle-Thiele
Menzies Health Institute Queensland, Griffith University, Nathan, Australia
e-mail: t.dietrich@griffith.edu.au

K. Kubacki
e-mail: k.kubacki@griffith.edu.au

S. Rundle-Thiele
e-mail: s.rundle-thiele@griffith.edu.au

K. Kubacki · T. Dietrich · S. Rundle-Thiele
Department of Marketing, Griffith University, 170 Kessels Road, Nathan QLD 4111, Australia

T. Dietrich
Faculty of Medicine and Biomedical Sciences, Centre for Youth Substance Abuse, University of Queensland, Herston, QLD 4029, Australia

T. Dietrich et al. (eds.), *Segmentation in Social Marketing*,
DOI 10.1007/978-981-10-1835-0_1

Introduction

Market segmentation is nothing new to commercial marketers. In 1912 Arch Shaw described market segmentation as the strategy of identifying economic and social boundaries of different markets to meet consumer wants better than the competitors. Over the last century market segmentation has evolved into one of the fundamental principles of marketing in both the industrial and consumer markets (for reviews, see Beanne and Ennis 1987; Wedel and Kamakura 2002). A homogenous, measurable, accessible and substantial market segment has been perceived as an important business opportunity that allows a company to maximise the use of their limited resources (Beanne and Ennis 1987). The assumption underpinning use of the market segmentation process is the belief that consumers have different wants which cannot be satisfied by a single one-size-fits-all marketing program. People have different product preferences and requirements, they engage differently with different communication tools, access products and services in different locations, and have different sensitivities to price. The implication is that by identifying differences and similarities between potential market segments, marketers can design programs appealing to a broader proportion of consumers by thinking of markets in more ways than one or narrowing focus to one type of consumer only and, as a result, enhance their market performance.

Based on the earlier success of market segmentation in commercial marketing, Alan Andreasen included segmentation in his set of six social marketing benchmark criteria (1994), later adopted and extended to eight benchmark criteria by the National Social Marketing Centre (NSMC 2012) in the United Kingdom. According to the NSMC (2012) social marketing segmentation should identify segments with common characteristics within a program's target audience and tailor the marketing program to the specific requirements of each segment. The goal of the social marketing benchmark criteria is to increase the impact of social marketing programs, and given that behaviour change and positive outcomes are more likely when more of the Andreasen's social marketing benchmarks are used (Carins and Rundle-Thiele 2014), full use of all six social marketing benchmarks is recommended.

The case for segmentation in social marketing would appear to be compelling. In July 1956, Wendell Smith wrote in the *Journal of Marketing* that 'market segmentation may be regarded as a force in the market that will not be denied' (p. 6). Although much has changed in the last seventy years, some of Smith's arguments resonate with today's social marketing practitioners and academics. As much as technological changes in the mid-twentieth century allowed for increased efficiency of mass production, the social media revolution over the last ten years has enabled social marketers to target smaller market segments efficiently and engage in a dialogue with audiences who have traditionally seemed hard-to-reach. Social marketers can finally truly engage citizens in a full spectrum of programs, from one-to-one marketing (which is not covered in this book), targeting a segment of one, two or many more, to an overall strategy delivering a one-size-fits all approach.

With new technologies the ability for mass-customisation of social marketing programs has also arrived. While self-service and similar technologies reduced marketing costs in the 1950s, digital technology now facilitates consumer co-creation of marketing mixes tailored to the needs of individual consumers. However, markets are saturated with attractive products and services, of which many are in direct competition with social marketing offerings. For example, manufacturers of alcohol, tobacco, and fast food develop sophisticated segmentation, targeting and positioning strategies to better satisfy their customers' wants. They are in direct competition with many social marketing programs, and social marketers have to develop more competitive and attractive offerings that aim to outweigh the bundle of benefits provided by the products and services they are competing against. Concentrating thinking on the different segments present in the market helps social marketers to understand how their offering can remain relevant in a constantly evolving landscape. As Smith (1956) argued, 'It is the obligation of those responsible for sales and marketing administration to keep the strategy mix in adjustment with market structure at any point in time and to produce in marketing strategy at least as much dynamism as is present in the market' (p. 7). Seventy years later, customer-focused and competitively-minded social marketing programs often require segmentation to resonate with different audiences. Or as Smith put it, market segmentation is a condition or cost of growth.

In this book we show that market segmentation is a crucial element of social marketing. This book is divided into three main parts. In the first part—*Segmentation in Social Marketing*—we have four chapters reviewing the current state of knowledge on the use of segmentation in social marketing and we place market segmentation's role within a wider social marketing context. In the second part—*Segmentation process, methods, and application*—the next three chapters introduce a five-step segmentation process for social marketing programs, describe different approaches to segmentation, and provide key resources for social marketers seeking to employ the methods outlined. And in the final part—*Segmentation in practice*—we have four chapters presenting different case studies detailing how segments have been derived in social marketing in a broad range of contexts including healthy lunches, alcohol and adolescents, and recycling.

In Chap. 2, Kubacki and colleagues describe and analyse the use of segmentation in social marketing programs. The Social Marketing @ Griffith team provides evidence from a series of five systematic literature reviews in social marketing where a total of 93 interventions were assessed. This review indicates that segmentation is rarely reported in peer-reviewed journal articles describing social marketing programs, and when segmentation is reported it is often limited to the adaptation of communication materials to different segments without considering other essential elements of the marketing mix: product, price and place. The chapter concludes that restricting social marketing programs to social advertising may limit their effectiveness, and more research is urgently needed to assess the effectiveness of segmentation in achieving the behavioural goals of social marketing programs.

Jeff French's chapter, 'The importance of segmentation in social marketing strategy' considers the segmentation process in the broader context of social marketing. Although developing several social marketing programs for different segments requires additional resources, Jeff argues that segmentation can add value to social marketing as it increases program effectiveness and efficiency, increases the responsiveness of the program, and ensures its relevance. Supporting the findings of Kubacki et al.'s umbrella review (Chap. 2), Jeff also shows that segmentation is not widely adopted in social marketing and health communication programs, provides a compelling list of reasons why segmentation if often neglected, and continues by concluding that in the future segmentation will become an important part of social marketing.

Sally Dibb's chapter entitled 'Changing times for social marketing segmentation' suggests that social marketing academics and practitioners need to be more proactive in adapting segmentation approaches from commercial marketing. While generation of segments is an important first step in the segmentation process, the decision of which segment(s) to target then needs to occur to inform program design, implementation and evaluation. Sally introduces a social marketing targeting tool, a set of targeting criteria used in commercial marketing adapted to the social marketing context. The tool can support social marketers in the process of identifying the most attractive segments to target with social marketing programs. The chapter concludes with identification of several important opportunities for social marketing segmentation that stem from technological advances in data availability, data capture and analytics.

Calculating and reporting on return on investment remains uncommon for social marketing programs. That is why Nancy Lee's chapter entitled 'How and why segmentation improves ROI' concludes the first part of our book—*Segmentation in Social Marketing*. Using a series of case studies, Nancy explores how selecting and appealing to a priority target audience segment through various elements of marketing mix—including product, price, place, promotion, messages, messengers, creative execution, media channels, media timing and frequency—can influence the ROI (return on investment) of social marketing programs. The chapter concludes with in illustration of how ROI can be calculated following a five-step process.

Timo Dietrich's chapter on the five-step segmentation process starts the second part of our book—*Segmentation process, methods, and application*. Arguing that one of key barriers to the use of segmentation in practice is lack of relevant expertise and sufficient guidance for social marketing practitioners, Timo proposes a five-step social marketing segmentation process specific to social marketing research contexts. Using the Blurred Minds social marketing program that is currently being designed for an upcoming Queensland school intervention, Timo shows that even a very narrowly-focused program (in this case for 14–16 year-olds students attending Queensland Catholic High Schools) can benefit from the application of the five-step market segmentation process.

Chapter 7 explores different market segmentation methods. Sara Dolnicar and Bettina Grün introduce two approaches to market segmentation: *a priori* or *common sense segmentation* and *a posteriori* or *data-driven segmentation. A priori or common sense segmentation* occurs when the key characteristics of the segments to be targeted are known and research is required to inform the design of marketing programs and/or the market size is too small to permit data-driven segmentation to occur. *A posteriori* or *data-driven segmentation* occurs when segments are not known in advance and research is needed to identify attractive target segments. The authors provide a set of steps to be followed by researchers undertaking data-driven segmentation focusing on metric measurement methods.

In the final chapter of the second part of the book, Aaron Tkaczynski explains TwoStep cluster analysis, a market segmentation method that permits use of non-metric measures to be used to identify segments. This chapter commences by outlining the TwoStep clustering procedure and four validation techniques that are recommended before accepting a TwoStep cluster analysis solution. Next a review of social marketing studies that report use of TwoStep cluster analysis is provided. The chapter concludes with a case study describing the use of TwoStep cluster analysis to identify potential segments for a walking to school social marketing intervention that is currently being developed in Queensland.

Starting the final part of the book—*Segmentation in practice*—Melanie Randle and Sara Dolnicar focus on a fascinating and important issue of civic participation. Non-profit and community organisations rely on volunteers donating their time and skills to help them to achieve their goals. This chapter uses three case studies to showcase how segmentation was used to encourage civic participation in a community-based pro-environmental program to identify barriers to becoming a foster carer as perceived by individuals who had never considered becoming one, and to identify segments among volunteers focusing on different volunteering motivations. As the recruitment of volunteers remains one of the key issues for non-profit organisations and community groups, this chapters shows how market segmentation can help non-profit organisations to become more rigorous and effective in their marketing efforts.

Childhood obesity is one of the most pressing social issues in developed and developing countries. Chapter 10 provides an insight into a segmentation of carers of primary school-aged children that can inform the design of a targeted social marketing program implementation aiming to increase healthful eating for primary school aged children. Using TwoStep cluster analysis, the method discussed earlier by Aaron Tkaczynski in Chap. 8, Francisco Crespo Casado and colleagues identified three segments of carers. Carers' attitudes towards their children's lunchboxes marked the key differences between segments and differences in the number of fruits and vegetables packed were evident between segments.

Chapter 11 provides a segmentation study of young adults in the Netherlands focusing on their values and attitudes towards alcohol. The attitudes of young people towards alcohol consumption have been the subject of many studies in the last two decades, but Jolanda Mathijssen, Sandra Kuiper and Meriam Janssen extend the topic by exploring the main characteristics of the five segments that emerged in their study: Moderates, Party animals, Unconcerned, Embarrassed, and Bingers. Since the key focus of social marketing is on behaviour change, it is important to note that apart from the differences in values, attitudes, expectancies and motives, the five segments differed in drinking behaviour.

Responsible waste management behaviours are the focus of the final chapter in Part III of the book. Using focus groups and data from a survey exploring the attitudes towards the environment and behaviours such as recycling and composting commissioned by RECYC-QUÉBEC, a recycling company in Quebec, Canada, Maxime Boivin, Emmanuelle Gagné and Champagne Saint-Arnaud identified seven distinct market segments. Taking composting behaviour as an example and using the Theory of Planned Behaviour, the authors explored the unique characteristics of each segment and provided recommendations for targeting and positioning strategies for a future social marketing program. It is an excellent case study of social marketing being used as a transitional stage in preparation for future legislative changes introducing a ban on organic waste in landfill sites.

In the final chapter of our book, we consider a series of social marketing examples to show how social marketers can embrace marketing thinking by applying segmentation to understand response to programs at a segment level, employing theory to inform segmentation, and using personas to simplify complex multivariate data output generated from segmentation approaches.

We hope that this identification of the benefits of segmentation for the process of social change, guidance on how segmentation can be undertaken, and the numerous examples of segmentation being utilised in social marketing contained within this book will inspire the growing adoption of segmentation in social marketing practice. Increased application of segmentation throughout the full social marketing process is expected to improve the effectiveness and efficiency of social marketing programs.

References

Andreasen, A. (1994). Social marketing: Its definition and domain. *Journal of Public Policy & Marketing, 13*(1), 108–114.

Beane, T. P., & Ennis, D. M. (1987). Market segmentation: A review. *European Journal of Marketing*, *21*(5), 20–42.

Carins, J., & Rundle-Thiele, S. R. (2014). Eating for the better: A social marketing review (2000–2012). *Public Health Nutrition, 17*(7), 1628–1639.

NSMC. (2012). *Social marketing benchmark criteria.* National Social Marketing Centre. Retrieved from thensmc.com/sites/default/files/benchmark-criteria-090910.pdf. Accessed on May 16, 2016.

Shaw, A. W. (1912, August). Some problems in market distribution. *Quarterly Journal of Economics*, 703–765.

Smith, W. R. (1956). Product differentiation and market segmentation as alternative marketing strategies. *Journal of Marketing, 21*(1), 3–8.

Wedel, M., & Kamakura, W. A. (2002). Market segmentation. Conceptual and methodological foundations (2nd ed.). New York: Springer Science + Business Media.

Part I
Segmentation in Social Marketing

An Umbrella Review of the Use of Segmentation in Social Marketing Interventions

Krzysztof Kubacki, Sharyn Rundle-Thiele, Bo Pang, Julia Carins, Joy Parkinson, Haruka Fujihira and Rimante Ronto

Abstract Drawing on evidence from a series of five systematic literature reviews, this umbrella review aims to understand the extent to which segmentation is employed in social marketing interventions. Ninety-three unique social marketing interventions were included in this umbrella review. We identified limited reported use of segmentation in social marketing interventions, with only a handful of social marketing interventions (16 %) reporting the use of segmentation. Further, the majority of social marketing interventions reporting segmentation limited program differences to one P: adaptation of promotional materials. Importantly, interventions reporting using at least four of the social marketing benchmark criteria, at least two out of four Ps, and adapting products rather than just promotional materials to cater to different segments needs and wants were observed to deliver positive behavioural outcomes.

Introduction

Social marketing plays an important role in changing behaviours for the better. Social marketing has been applied across a wide range of different contexts, including (but not limited to) tobacco and other drug consumption (Stead et al. 2007), physical activity (Gordon et al. 2006), environmental protection (McKenzie-Mohr et al. 2012), species conservation (Drury 2009), sport management (Inoue and Kent 2012),

K. Kubacki (✉) · S. Rundle-Thiele · B. Pang · J. Carins · J. Parkinson · H. Fujihira
Department of Marketing, Menzies Health Institute Queensland,
Griffith University, Nathan, Australia
e-mail: k.kubacki@griffith.edu.au

S. Rundle-Thiele
e-mail: s.rundle-thiele@griffith.edu.au

R. Ronto
Menzies Health Institute Queensland, Griffith University, Nathan, Australia

J. Carins
Land Division, Defence Science and Technology Group, Canberra, Australia

T. Dietrich et al. (eds.), *Segmentation in Social Marketing*,
DOI 10.1007/978-981-10-1835-0_2

poverty alleviation (Kotler and Lee 2009), and financial management (Lee and Miller 2012). Segmentation is considered as one of the key components of social marketing, and it has been included in all widely-regarded social marketing planning frameworks (e.g. Andreasen 2002; French and Blair-Stevens 2006; Lefebvre and Flora 1988; Robinson-Maynard et al. 2013). Segmentation describes the process of dividing up a heterogeneous market into homogeneous segments (Donovan and Henley 2010), which are grouped according to similarities to guide strategic planning and decision making. Once segments that are substantial, sustainable and accessible are established, social marketing programs encompassing a marketing mix that includes (but is not limited to) product, price, place and promotion are developed, with differences in programs observable for the segment(s) chosen for targeting. This requires strategic decisions that may involve sometimes ignoring segments which cannot be served effectively using available resources, or do not have the need for the intervention (for example a potential segment consisting of non-drinkers in a social marketing intervention targeting harmful alcohol consumption). Theoretically, application of the segmentation process is expected to optimise scarce financial resources ensuring that social marketers can increase the effectiveness of their programs by identifying segments that include individuals most in need or those where behaviour change and hence campaign success are most likely (Doner Lotenberg et al. 2011).

As social marketing interventions frequently suffer from limited resources (Newton et al. 2013), application of the segmentation process permits social marketers to increase efficacy and to optimise scarce financial and other resources by directing the resources to the most promising segments (McDonald and Dunbar 2012). Research indicates that segments respond differently to social marketing programs (Dietrich et al. 2015a, b). Understanding segment differences permits social marketers to more effectively design programs catering to group differences. For example, in the Dietrich et al. (2015b) study one of the segments, named by the authors as *Bingers*, possessed the lowest alcohol related knowledge score, highest alcohol expectancy score, and the most supportive social environment for binge drinking, indicating a unique approach is warranted to reach this segment. Ideally, social marketers need to target the important others surrounding this segment to reduce support for alcohol drinking.

Regarded as one of the key strategic marketing tools (Dibb et al. 2002), and one of the six social marketing benchmark criteria (Andreasen 2002), a broad understanding of the extent of segmentation use in social marketing is needed. Drawing on evidence from a series of five systematic literature reviews (Carins and Rundle-Thiele 2014; Fujihira et al. 2015; Kubacki et al. 2015a, b, c) this umbrella review aims to understand the extent to which segmentation is employed in social marketing interventions.

Methods

Systematic literature reviews have been growing in popularity in social marketing, with some of the studies published in the last ten years focusing on areas such as alcohol consumption (Kubacki et al. 2015a) and physical activity (Stead et al. 2007), target audiences such as children (Kubacki et al. 2015b) and elderly (Fujihira et al. 2015), the use of social marketing tools such as digital channels (Kubacki et al. 2015c), and the use of the marketing mix, theory and models in social marketing (Luca and Suggs 2010, 2013). Driving those efforts has been the recognition of a growing body of evidence and the resultant need to integrate findings from a rapidly increasing number of studies reporting evaluations of social marketing interventions. The main advantages of systematic literature reviews are their ability to present a vast amount of information about different studies in a succinct manner, focusing on specific research questions, and to reach conclusions based on multiple individual studies (Hartling et al. 2014).

To date, social marketing reviews have been limited to a single behavioural context such as alcohol consumption (Kubacki et al. 2015a) or physical activity (Kubacki et al. 2015b), or a single theoretical problem such as the use of marketing mix or theory (Luca and Suggs 2010, 2013). The extent of application of social marketing benchmark criteria (such as reported use of segmentation) in social marketing interventions described in this chapter can be best measured by conducting an umbrella review. Umbrella reviews, known also as overviews of reviews, are reviews of existing systematic reviews aiming to summarise their results on a selected topic (Whittemore et al. 2014). An umbrella review integrates multiple systematic reviews, synthesising evidence. Recognising the breadth and depth of evidence included in previously published social marketing systematic literature reviews, an umbrella review provides the opportunity to explore the use of segmentation in social marketing across different contexts.

Full details of the literature search processes, data analysis procedures and lists of all articles included in the reviews can be obtained by examining each of the individual reviews (Carins and Rundle-Thiele 2014; Fujihira et al. 2015; Kubacki et al. 2015a, b, c). For the purpose of this umbrella review, previously identified information regarding segmentation, the use of the social marketing benchmark criteria (Andreasen 2002), target audience and behaviour were compiled into a single file, and only interventions reporting the use of segmentation were included for further analysis and discussion.

Fourteen of the interventions identified in the healthy eating review (Carins and Rundle-Thiele 2014) were also included in the review of social marketing interventions targeting children (Kubacki et al. 2015b) and therefore each unique intervention was included in this umbrella review only once. Assessment of segmentation reported in Carins and Rundle-Thiele (2014) was broad, with instances of targeting considered as segmentation. This was not consistent with assessment of segmentation in later reviews where full reporting of segmentation (prior to a targeting decision) was considered as segmentation (Fujihira et al. 2015;

Kubacki et al. 2015a, b, c). To bring assessment of the interventions uniquely identified in the Carins and Rundle-Thiele (2014) review into line with the later assessments, an intervention was deemed to have used segmentation when it reported evidence of dividing a total market into groups with relatively similar needs to design a social marketing intervention that addresses needs by each group (French and Blair-Stevens 2006). As a result, all 34 studies identified in Carins and Rundle-Thiele (2014) were re-analysed by three of the authors to ensure consistency between all social marketing interventions included in this umbrella review.

Results

Table 2.1 provides an overview of the reviews collated in this umbrella review.

In total, across 93 unique social marketing interventions, 15 (16 %) interventions reported the use of segmentation and were included in this umbrella review. All of the included reviews analysed the identified interventions using Andreasen's (2002) social marketing benchmark criteria, including behavioural objectives, audience segmentation, audience research, exchange, marketing mix and competition (Table 2.2). Of the 15 interventions that reported the use of segmentation, only two reported using all six benchmark criteria. Of the ten interventions that reported using at least four benchmarks, eight delivered some positive behavioural change, while only two out of the five interventions that reported using three or fewer

Table 2.1 Segmentation in systematic literature reviews in social marketing

Review	Total number of interventions	Interventions reporting segmentation
Interventions aiming to minimise harm from alcohol consumption (Kubacki et al. 2015a)	23	2 (9 %)
Interventions targeting children under the age of 12 years (Kubacki et al. 2015b)	23	2 (9 %)
Interventions using digital channels for engagement (Kubacki et al. 2015c)	20	8 (40 %)
Physical activity interventions targeting adults 60 years and over (Fujihira et al. 2015)	7	3 (43 %)
Interventions to improve healthy eating behaviour (Carins and Rundle-Thiele 2014)	20 [34[a]]	0 [1 (3 %)[b]]
Total	93	15 (16 %)

[a]Originally 34 interventions were identified in Carins and Rundle-Thiele (2014). Only 20 studies not originally included in Kubacki et al. (2015b) were included in this umbrella review. None of the 20 studies reported the use of segmentation

[b]Levine et al. (2002) was included in two systematic reviews, Carins and Rundle-Thiele (2014) and Kubacki et al. (2015b), and for the purpose of this umbrella review was counted only once

benchmarks reported positive behavioural change. None of the 15 interventions using segmentation reported any negative behavioural outcomes.

The interventions using segmentation reported targeting a wide range of diverse audiences, from specifically defined audiences such as community physicians (Short et al. 2006) to broad audiences such as all of the 34 million inhabitants of the Sao Paulo state in Brazil (Matsudo et al. 2002). There was also a diverse collection of behaviours targeted by the interventions, from flu prevention (Plourde et al. 2008), intimate partner violence (Harris et al. 2009; Short et al. 2006), and alcohol consumption during pregnancy (Glik et al. 2001 and 2008), to broadly defined physical activity (e.g. Huhman et al. 2008) and healthy eating (Levine et al. 2002). Only one intervention reported adapting the entire marketing mix to different segments (Matsudo et al. 2002), and product and promotional activities were different between segments in Purdy et al. (2011). Further, the product element of the social marketing mix was adapted to different segments in five additional interventions (Harris et al. 2009; Kamada et al. 2013; Keihner et al. 2011; Levine et al. 2002; Short et al. 2006), four of which delivered positive behavioural change. Only promotional materials were adapted to different segments in the remaining eight interventions (Dixon-Gray et al. 2013; Glik et al. 2008; Huhman et al. 2008; Justice-Gardiner et al. 2012; Plourde et al. 2008; Reger-Nash et al. 2006; Rotblatt et al. 2013), of which four did not report any positive behavioural change.

Table 2.2 presents the assessment of each of the 15 social marketing interventions which reported using segmentation against Andreasen's (2002) six social marketing benchmark criteria as well as information about their target audiences and targeted behaviours.

Social marketing interventions aiming to minimise harm from alcohol consumption It is noticeable that segmentation is not common in social marketing interventions aiming to minimise harm from alcohol consumption. Kubacki et al. (2015a) identified 23 social marketing interventions that aimed to minimise alcohol harm and found that only two interventions (Glik et al. 2001, 2008) reported any evidence of segmentation. In the study by Glik et al. (2001), in order to increase awareness about the harm of alcohol drinking during pregnancy, the researchers segmented pregnant women in California, United States into two groups: African-American women and Latina adolescent women, and developed two different sets of promotional materials including slogans, languages (English and Spanish), images, and channels (posters and tear-off cards). In Glik et al. (2008), the target audience was segmented into four groups: Caucasian women, African-American women, Latina English-speaking women and Latina Spanish-speaking women. Then similarly, promotional materials were developed accordingly to better suit each group. In both interventions, the variants of promotional materials between each segment were designed and pretested to respond to any differences between groups. For example, in Glik et al. (2008), role models in the posters were chosen based on the majority of the ethnicity in their respective community, and the colour palettes of the posters were tested for each group.

As Donovan and Henley (2010) argued, segmentation can help campaign designers to better develop the marketing mix (4Ps) in order to satisfy different

Table 2.2 Assessment of the use of Andreasen's benchmark criteria in social marketing

Interventions	Target audience	Behaviour	No. of SMBC	Behavioural objective	Audience segmentation	Audience research	Exchange	Marketing mix$^{(4Ps)}$	Competition
Purdy et al. (2011)	Young professionals in Turkey	Sexual health	6	✓(+)	✓	✓	✓	✓(4)	✓
Huhman et al. (2008)	Tweens	Physical activity	6	✓(+)	✓	✓	✓	✓(3)	✓
Kamada et al. (2013)	Adults (40–79 years)	Physical activity	5	✓(*)	✓	✓	✓	✓(4)	✗
Matsudo et al. (2002)	34 million inhabitants of Sao Paulo State	Physical activity	5	✓(+)	✓	✓	✗	✓(3^5)	✓
Short et al. (2006)	Community physicians	Intimate partner violence	5	✓(+)	✓	✗	✓	✓(3)	✓
Harris et al. (2009)	California physicians	Intimate partner violence	5	✓(+)	✓	✗	✓	✓(3)	✓
Justice-Gardiner et al. (2012)	Hispanic cancer survivors	Cancer support	4	✓(*)	✓	✗	✗	✓(3)	✓
Keihner et al. (2011)	Children 9–11 years	Healthy eating (and later increased physical activity)	4	✓(+)	✓	✓	✗	✓(3)	✗
Levine et al. (2002)	Children in kindergarten to 4 years	Healthy eating	4	✓(+)	✓	✗	✗	✓(2)	✓
Reger-Nash et al. (2006)	35–65 y/o in McDowell County; 40–65 y/o in	Physical activity	4	✓(+)	✓	✓	✗	✗ (1)	✓

(continued)

Table 2.2 (continued)

Interventions	Target audience	Behaviour	No. of SMBC	Behavioural objective	Audience segmentation	Audience research	Exchange	Marketing mix$^{(4Ps)}$	Competition
	Broome County, NY; 40–65 y/o in Morgantown; 50-65 y/o in Wheeling								
Rotblatt et al. (2013)	African American, Latina females aged 12–25 years	Sexual health	3	✓(+)	✓	✗	✗	✓(4)	✗
Plourde et al. (2008)	Floridians	Flu prevention	3	✓(+)	✓	✓	✗	✗	✓
Dixon-Gray et al. (2013)	Latinas, 18–29 years, born in the US	Sexual health	3	✗	✗	✓	✗	✗	✓
Glik et al. (2008)	Pregnant women	Alcohol during pregnancy	3	✗	✓	✓	✗	✗	✓
Glik et al. (2001)	Female African American and Latina teenagers	Alcohol during pregnancy	2	✗	✓	✓	✗	✗	✗

* No behavioural change reported
\+ Positive behavioural outcome reported
(4Ps) The number of marketing mix elements reported in the intervention (product, price, place and promotion)

groups within the target audience. It is noteworthy that although segmentation was identified in both studies by Glik et al. (2001, 2008), the researchers only limited their segmented strategies in the communication aspect of their intervention design, by using narrowcasting. As the authors mentioned, narrowcasting refers to "a marketing strategy that uses highly focused messages for specific priority populations" (Glik et al. 2001, p. 223). The authors focused on designing tailored messages and channels for each segment but they did not adapt other marketing mix elements (product, place and price). Both campaigns did not deliver any behavioural change. In Glik et al. (2001) the exposure to campaign materials was quite high, yet knowledge levels had mixed results. Further, knowledge of the dangers of drinking during pregnancy for African-American teenage girls increased sharply after the campaign, while that of Latina girls who already had high levels of knowledge remained the same. In Glik et al. (2008) the campaign had mixed results in different communities. Overall, the exposure rate to the campaign was low; however, the exposure rate was much higher for the clinic-based audience (more than 50 %).

Social marketing interventions targeting children under the age of 12 Of 23 social marketing interventions reported in Kubacki et al. (2015b), only two reported using segmentation and both of them delivered positive behavioural outcomes (Keihner et al. 2011; Levine et al. 2002). Keihner et al. (2011) used ten grade-specific lessons for Grade 4 and Grade 5 to provide stronger links to the arts and/or mathematics subjects of the California Content Standards. In addition, English and Spanish language brochures were used for parents. In both grades, students showed improvements in requests for fruit and vegetables and shopping self-efficacy.

Similarly, Levine et al. (2002) also used grade-specific activities catering to age differences for three different groups of children: pre-kindergarten and kindergarten, first and second grades, and third through fifth grades. The grade-specific activities were designed to build children's skills and motivate them to make healthy food choices. The intervention also included strategies designed for secondary audiences. Teachers and school canteen staff were educated as part of the intervention. Training and technical advice were provided to school nutrition staff to assist with motivation and skills-based knowledge. Classroom education was provided through curriculum modules to address behavioural goals and to enable children to practice to make and assess their food choices. In addition, parents were also targeted in the intervention period, and participated by getting involved in take-home activities, contributing to classroom events (e.g. sending in a recipe), or attending school and community events. Overall, students showed improvement in their food choices.

Social marketing interventions using digital channels for engagement Kubacki et al. (2015c) identified 20 social marketing interventions using digital channels for engagement, and seven of them reported the use of segmentation. In the most comprehensive of those interventions, a commercial enterprise was established in Turkey to promote two brands of condoms, both targeting young adults (Purdy et al. 2011). Fiesta and Kiss respectively targeted the premium and budget segments of the market: Fiesta condoms were aimed at more affluent consumers, at a higher price point and with more variants, than Kiss condoms. Fiesta condoms were marketed using an extensive digital campaign, whilst Kiss condoms were not promoted using any social marketing tools. Overall, more than 4.3 million Fiesta condoms were sold with a higher than average proportion of online condom sales for a middle-income country (8 % sold online). In comparison, 2.6 million Kiss condoms were sold.

Two further interventions, Short et al. (2006) and Harris et al. (2009), developed online continuing medical education programs aiming to inform physicians about intimate partner violence. The interventions developed four separate sets of cases tailored to health professionals' different clinical areas: family/internal medicine, obstetrics/gynaecology, paediatrics, and mental health. Three to four unique cases were developed for each clinical speciality area. Both interventions reported positive changes in physicians' intimate partner violence management practices.

In Huhman et al. (2008), an intervention developed to address the public health problem of sedentary lifestyles among American children, specialised messages and media strategies were developed for different segments, including Native Americans, African Americans, Asian Americans and Hispanic/Latino tweens, through extensive formative and message-testing research. The interventions also offered specialised messages for parents, the intervention's secondary target audience, to encourage them to support their tweens' physical activity. The results of this intervention reported a significant increase in physical activity for the entire target audience following a two-year intervention period.

Finally, four interventions adapted the intervention materials into at least one other language: Justice-Gardiner et al. (2012), Dixon-Gray et al. (2013) and Rotblatt et al. (2013) into Spanish and English, and Plourde et al. (2008) into Spanish, Creole and English. No intervention outcomes were reported by Dixon-Gray et al. (2013) and Justice-Gardiner et al. (2012). In Rotblatt et al. (2013) during the first 12 months following the introduction of the online program, providing the self-administered chlamydia and gonorrhoea home testing kit increased the testing volume four times in comparison to the per-clinic average chlamydia testing volume in the same time period. In Plourde et al. (2008) heavier exposure to the intervention was associated with larger increases in behaviour change.

Social marketing physical activity interventions targeting adults 60 years and over Three out of seven interventions reported in Fujihira et al. (2015) reported using segmentation. However, only one of those interventions targeted solely people 60 years and older and segmented this primary target group—women 60–79 years of age—into two smaller segments with different needs and abilities, both of which had lower back or knee pain and were to be targeted with different social marketing offerings including different types of physical activities (Kamada et al. 2013). The first offering targeted women who were either not engaged in or insufficiently engaged in regular walking behaviour, and the second offering targeted women who engaged in flexibility and/or muscle-strengthening activities, either occasionally or daily. However, when comparing each intervention group with the control group for regular physical activity, pain outcomes, and each different activity, no significant changes were observed.

People over 60 were one of several different segments, including students and workers, targeted in Matsudo et al. (2002), a community-wide intervention aimed at all inhabitants of the Sao Paulo state in Brazil. The intervention included programs and materials developed specifically for each of the segments. The intervention successfully increased people's physical activity levels: 54.8 % of the total population reached the recommended minimum 30 min' physical activity level after four years of the program.

Finally, the intervention reported in Reger-Nash et al. (2006) included segmentation that did not focus specifically on people over 60; however, the intervention provided advertisements for the African American community by featuring African American actors to appeal to the regional minority population. An increase of walking behaviour was observed during the intervention, and was maintained for 12 months following the intervention.

Social marketing interventions to improve healthy eating behaviour Only one of the thirty-four interventions reported in Carins and Rundle-Thiele (2014) was deemed to have used segmentation. This was the Levine et al. (2002) study that also appeared in the Kubacki et al. (2015b) review. As mentioned in the section above, the Levine (2002) study segmented children into three different age groups, providing activities specific to each group, after which students showed improvement in their food choices.

Discussion

The aim of this umbrella review was to understand the extent to which segmentation was used in social marketing interventions identified in five systematic literature reviews completed between 2013 and 2015 (Carins and Rundle-Thiele 2014; Fujihira et al. 2015; Kubacki et al. 2015a, b, c). Umbrella reviews provide an integrated overview of primary studies to inform scientific debates and decision-making in practice (Whittemore et al. 2014). Umbrella reviews also synthesise a breadth and depth of evidence where individual systematic reviews may fall short of presenting a bigger picture view (ibid.). This is the first umbrella review focusing on application of benchmark criteria (Andresean 2002) in social marketing, namely segmentation.

This umbrella review identified limited reported use of segmentation in social marketing interventions, with only a handful of social marketing interventions (16 %) reporting the use of segmentation. Further, the majority of social marketing interventions reporting segmentation limited program differences to one P: adaptation of promotional materials. Importantly, interventions reporting using at least four of the social marketing benchmark criteria, at least two out of four Ps, and adapting products rather than just promotional materials to cater to different segments needs and wants were observed to deliver positive behavioural outcomes. Taken together, results of the umbrella review indicate that application of segmentation to inform the design of a product or service offering catering to the unique needs and wants of segments to be targeted may enhance behaviour change outcomes.

This umbrella review shows that the use of segmentation in social marketing interventions aiming to minimise harm from alcohol consumption (9 %), targeting children under the age of 12 years (9 %), using digital channels for engagement (40 %), social marketing physical activity interventions targeting adults 60 years and over (43 %) and interventions aiming to improve healthy eating behaviour (3 %) is low: only 15 out of 93 (16 %) interventions reported the use of segmentation. Given that behaviour change is more likely when more of the social marketing benchmarks are applied (Carins and Rundle-Thiele 2014) social marketers are encouraged to use segmentation in future. While further empirical examination is recommended to confirm this finding (Rundle-Thiele 2015), evidence does indicate that application of segmentation needs to become part of everyday social marketing practice.

Very few interventions provided detailed descriptions of their segmentation strategy (see for example Kamada et al. 2013; Purdy et al. 2011). Segmentation procedures differ and reporting of procedures used is recommended to evaluate the quality of the work undertaken. The overwhelming majority of studies focused on reporting key differences in social marketing mixes used to target different segments (for example Dixon-Gray et al. 2013; Reger-Nash et al. 2006) and, thus, the evidence regarding the use of segmentation in social marketing remains limited.

In addition to the limited use of segmentation in social marketing interventions and restricted descriptions of the examples of segmentation in the identified papers, the most commonly adapted component of the social marketing mix was promotion. Across 15 interventions, eight relied on their segmentation approach to adapt promotional materials to more effectively communicate with and to reach different demographic groups. Translation into different languages was the most common form of adaptation, suggesting considerable room for improvement in adaptation to cater to the unique needs and wants of segments. For example, social marketers could target separate media channels, deliver different appeals, adapt the communication mix to more effectively reach different groups and so on. A narrow focus on communication led to positive behavioural change in 50 % (n = 4) of cases.

There is significant room for improvement in the application of segmentation in social marketing. In the absence of empirical evidence available on the effective use of segmentation in social marketing we outline two recommendations for future testing. First, as 84 % of interventions identified across 5 systematic literature reviews did not report using segmentation, there is a conspicuous gap in social marketing literature and practice. As segmentation has been included in all widely-regarded social marketing planning frameworks (e.g. Andreasen 2002; French and Blair-Stevens 2006; Lefebvre and Flora 1988; Robinson-Maynard et al. 2013) and is recognised as one of the key strategic tools in the marketing toolkit (Dibb et al. 2002), more research is urgently needed to assess the effectiveness of segmentation in achieving the behavioural goals of social marketing interventions (see also Rundle-Thiele 2015). Second, when segmentation is used in social marketing interventions it is often limited to very basic adaptation of communication materials, including translations to different languages. Finally, over-reliance on traditional demographic variables such as age and ethnicity overlooks the importance of other variables such as behavioural and psychographic data (Rundle-Thiele et al. 2015). More research is needed in social marketing to identify segments using a wider range of different segmentation bases and variables (Schuster et al. 2015). Empirical examination of segmentation approaches is recommended to compare and contrast alternatives.

Limitations and Future Research Directions

This umbrella review provides a starting point in order to support future social marketing research on segmentation and the use of segmentation in social marketing interventions. However, results should be treated with caution. First, only studies that self-identified as social marketing were included in the original reviews, therefore it is possible there are more interventions using segmentation that did not explicitly self-identify as social marketing. Second, the interventions presented in this chapter were conducted in very different contexts and used different behavioural measures, therefore our review is limited to descriptive comparisons. We acknowledge the presence or lack of each of the social marketing benchmark criteria (Andreasen 2002) and our inability to follow meta-analytical procedures. Third, this umbrella review focused on social marketing health interventions, and therefore future umbrella reviews should be conducted into the use of segmentation by social marketing interventions influencing other types of behaviours and issues so that a greater evidence base can be established. Fourth, our analysis was limited to information reported in identified studies. It is possible that social marketing interventions used segmentation but did not report it (Aceves-Martins et al. 2016). Further, previous research indicated that more than 70 % of alcohol misuse prevention campaigns did not fulfil any of the benchmark criteria (Wettstein and Suggs 2016). Social marketing studies often focus on reporting intervention outcomes, without paying attention to the process through which such outcomes are achieved. It is therefore important that future studies fully acknowledge the use of social marketing benchmark criteria. This final limitation highlights the importance of providing standardised intervention descriptions (for example following Andreasen's (2002) social marketing benchmark criteria). This would enable future research to integrate results from multiple studies and permit synthesis, thereby extending our understanding of effective social marketing practice. The unique role of segmentation on social marketing effectiveness cannot be empirically examined without an experimental design. An experimental design is needed to isolate the unique effect of segmentation on program outcomes and to test alternate segmentation approaches to understand which approaches optimise outcomes for social marketers. A final opportunity for future research lies in empirically assessing theoretical claims to determine whether segmentation permits financial resources to be optimised.

Acknowledgments The evidence synthesis on which this article was based was funded by the Victorian Health Promotion Foundation (VicHealth) and DST Group. The funders played no role in study design, collection, analysis, interpretation of data, or in the decision to submit the paper for publication. They accept no responsibility for contents.

References

Aceves-Martins, M., Llauradó, E., Tarro, L., Moreno-García, C. F., Escobar, T. G. T., Solà, R., et al. (2016). Effectiveness of social marketing strategies to reduce youth obesity in European school-based interventions: a systematic review and meta-analysis. *Nutrition Reviews, 74*(5), 337–351.

Andreasen, A. R. (2002). Marketing social marketing in the social change marketplace. *Journal of Public Policy & Marketing, 21*(1), 3–13.

Carins, J. E., & Rundle-Thiele, S. R. (2014). Eating for the better: A social marketing review (2000–2012). *Public Health Nutrition, 17*(7), 1628–1639.

Doner Lotenberg, L., Schechter, C., & Strand, J. (2011). Segmentation and targeting. In: Hastings, G., Angus, K., & Bryant, C. (Ed.), *The SAGE Handbook of Social Marketing* (pp. 125–136). London: Sage Publications.

Dibb, S., Stern, P., & Wensley, R. (2002). Marketing knowledge and the value of segmentation. *Marketing Intelligence & Planning, 20*(2), 113–119.

Dietrich, T., Rundle-Thiele, S., Leo, C., & Connor, J. (2015a). One size (never) fits all: Segment differences observed following a school based alcohol social marketing program. *Journal of School Health, 85*(4), 251–259.

Dietrich, T., Rundle-Thiele, S., Schuster, L., Drennan, J., Russell-Bennett, R., Leo, C., et al. (2015b). Differential segmentation responses to an alcohol social marketing program. *Addiction, 49*, 68–77.

Donovan, R., & Henley, N. (2010). *Principles and practice of social marketing: An international perspective.* Cambridge: Cambridge University Press.

Dixon-Gray, L. A., Mobley, A., McFarlane, J. M., & Rosenberg, K. D. (2013). Amor y Salud (Love and Health): A preconception health campaign for second-generation Latinas in Oregon. *American Journal of Health Promotion, 27*(3), S74–S76.

Drury, R. (2009). Reducing urban demand for wild animals in Vietnam: Examining the potential of wildlife farming as a conservation tool. *Conservation Letters, 2*(6), 263–270.

French, J., & Blair-Stevens, C. (2006). Social marketing national benchmark criteria. London: UK National Social Marketing Centre. http://www.snh.org.uk/pdfs/sgp/A328466.pdf. Accessed July 2, 2014.

Fujihira, H., Kubacki, K., Ronto, R., Pang, B., & Rundle-Thiele, S. (2015). Social marketing physical activity interventions among adults sixty years old and older: A systematic review. *Social Marketing Quarterly, 21*(4), 214–229.

Glik, D., Halpert-Schilt, E., & Zhang, W. (2001). Narrowcasting risks of drinking during pregnancy among African American and Latina adolescent girls. *Health Promotion Practice, 2*, 222–232.

Glik, D., Prelip, M., Myerson, A., & Eilers, K. (2008). Fetal alcohol syndrome prevention using community-based narrowcasting campaigns. *Health Promotion Practice, 9*, 93–103.

Gordon, R., McDermott, L., Stead, M., & Angus, K. (2006). The effectiveness of social marketing interventions for health improvement: What's the evidence? *Public Health, 120*, 1133–1139.

Hartling, L., Vandermeer, B., & Fernandes, R. M. (2014). Systematic reviews, overviews of reviews and comparative effectiveness reviews: A discussion of approaches to knowledge synthesis. *Evidence-Based Child Health, 9*, 486–494.

Harris, J. M., Jr., Novalis-Marine, C., Amend, R. W., & Surprenant, Z. J. (2009). Promoting free online CME for intimate partner violence: What works at what cost? *Journal of Continuing Education in the Health Professions, 29*(3), 135–141.

Huhman, M., Bauman, A., & Bowles, H. R. (2008). Initial outcomes of the VERB campaign: Tweens' awareness and understanding of campaign messages. *American Journal of Preventive Medicine, 34*(6 Suppl), S241–S248.

Inoue, Y., & Kent, A. (2012). Investigating the role of corporate credibility in corporate social marketing: A case study of environmental initiatives by professional sport organizations. *Sport Management Review, 15*(3), 330–344.

Justice-Gardiner, H., Nutt, S., Rechis, R., Mcmillan, B., & Warf, R. (2012). Using new media to reach Hispanic/Latino cancer survivors. *Journal of Cancer Education, 27*(1), 100–104.

Kamada, M., Kitayuguchi, J., Inoue, S., Ishikawa, Y., Nishiuchi, H., Okada, S… Shiwaku, K. (2013). A community-wide campaign to promote physical activity in middle-aged and elderly people: A cluster randomized controlled trial. *International Journal of Behavioral Nutrition and Physical Activity, 10*(1), 44.

Keihner, A. J., Meigs, R., Sugerman, S., Backman, D., Garbolino, T., & Mitchell, P. (2011). The power play! Campaign's school idea & resource kits improve determinants of fruit and vegetable intake and physical activity among fourth- and fifth-grade children. *Journal of Nutrition Education and Behavior, 43*(S2), 122–129.

Kotler, P., & Lee, N. R. (2009). *Up and out of poverty: The social marketing solution*. NJ: Pearson Prentice Hall.

Kubacki, K., Rundle-Thiele, S., Pang, B., & Buyucek, N. (2015a). Minimising alcohol harm: A systematic social marketing review (2000–2014). *Journal of Business Research, 68*(10), 2214–2222.

Kubacki, K., Rundle-Thiele, S., Lahtinen, V., & Parkinson, J. (2015b). A systematic review assessing the extent of social marketing principle use in interventions targeting children (2000–2014). *Young Consumers, 16*(2), 141–158.

Kubacki, K., Rundle-Thiele, S., Schuster, L., Wessels, C., & Gruneklee, N. (2015c). Digital innovation in social marketing: A systematic literature of interventions using digital channels for engagement. In: Wymer, W (Ed.), *Innovations in social marketing and public health communication: Improving the quality of life for individuals and communities*. Berlin: Springer.

Lee, N. R., & Miller, M. (2012). Influencing positive financial behaviors: The social marketing solution. *Journal of Social Marketing, 2*(1), 70–86.

Lefebvre, R. C., & Flora, J. A. (1988). Social marketing and public health intervention. *Health Education Quarterly, 15*, 299.

Levine, E., Olander, C., Lefebvre, C., Cusick, P., Biesiadecki, L., & McGoldrick, D. (2002). The team nutrition pilot study: Lessons learned from implementing a comprehensive school-based intervention. *Journal of Nutrition Education and Behaviour, 34*(2), 109–116.

Luca, N., & Suggs, L. S. (2010). Strategies for the social marketing mix: A systematic review. *Social Marketing Quarterly, 16*(4), 122–149.

Luca, N., & Suggs, L. S. (2013). Theory and model use in social marketing health interventions. *Journal of Health Communication, 18*(1), 20–40.

Matsudo, V., Matsudo, S., Andrade, D., Araujo, T., Andrade, E., de Oliveira, L. C., et al. (2002). Promotion of physical activity in a developing country: The Agita Sao Paulo experience. *Public Health Nutrition, 5*, 253–261.

McDonald, M., & Dunbar, I. (2012). *Market segmentation: How to do it and how to profit from it* (4th ed.). Chichester: John Wiley & Sons.

McKenzie-Mohr, D., Lee, N. R., Schultz, P. W., & Kotler, P. (2012). *Social marketing to protect the environment: What works*. NY: SAGE Publications.

Newton, J., Newton, F. J., Turk, T., & Ewing, M. T. (2013). Ethical evaluation of audience segmentation in social marketing. *European Journal of Social Marketing, 47*(9), 1421–1438.

Plourde, C., Cook, L. C., Mitchell, P., & Jennings, C. (2008). Talk to the fifth guy: A lesson in social marketing. *Cases in Public Health Communication and Marketing, 2*, 11–38. www.casesjournal.org/volume2. Accessed July 25, 2014.
Purdy, C. H. (2011). Using the internet and social media to promote condom use in Turkey. *Reproductive Health Matters, 19*(37), 157–165.
Reger-Nash, B., Bauman, A., Cooper, L., Chey, T., & Simon, K. J. (2006). Evaluating communitywide walking interventions. *Evaluation and Program Planning, 29*, 251–259.
Robinson-Maynard, A., Meaton, J., & Lowry, R. (2013). Identifying key criteria as predictors of success in social marketing: Establishing an evaluation template and grid. In: K. Kubacki, & S. Rundle-Thiele (Eds.), *Contemporary issues in social marketing*. Cambridge: Cambridge Scholars Publishing.
Rotblatt, H., Montoya, J. A., Plant, A., Guerry, S., & Kerndt, P. R. (2013). There's no place like home: First-year use of the "I Know" home testing program for chlamydia and gonorrhoea. *American Journal of Public Health, 103*(8), 1376–1380.
Rundle-Thiele, S. (2015). Looking back and moving forwards: An agenda for social marketing research. *Recherche et Applications en Marketing (English Edition), 30*(3), 128–133.
Rundle-Thiele, S., Kubacki, K., Tkaczynski, A., & Parkinson, J. (2015). Using two-step cluster analysis to identify homogeneous physical activity groups. *Marketing Intelligence and Planning, 33*(4), 522–537.
Schuster, L., Kubacki, K., & Rundle-Thiele, S. (2015). A theoretical approach to segmenting children's walking behaviour. *Young Consumers, 16*(2), 159–171.
Short, L. M., Surprenant, Z. J., & Harris, J. M. (2006). A community based trial of an online intimate partner violence CME program. *American Journal of Preventive Medicine, 30*(2), 181–185.
Stead, M., Gordon, R., Angus, K., & McDermott, L. (2007). A systematic review of social marketing effectiveness. *Health Education, 107*(2), 126–191.
Wettstein, D., & Suggs, S. L. (2016). Is it social marketing? The benchmarks meet the social marketing indicator. *Journal of Social Marketing, 6*(1), 2–17.
Whittemore, R., Chao, A., Jang, M., Minges, K. E., & Park, C. (2014). Methods for knowledge synthesis: An overview. *Heart and Lung, 43*, 453–461.

The Importance of Segmentation in Social Marketing Strategy

Jeff French

Abstract This chapter explores the value that segmentation can bring to social marketing projects and programs. The chapter also explores some of the practical and theoretical barriers that are associated with adopting a segmented strategy as part of social marketing program planning and delivery. The rationale for investing in a segmentation based strategy in social marketing is also explored. Questions about the need for and how to justify the investment needed for developing a segmentation informed approach to social marketing are discussed alongside some of the main barriers to segmentation and why it does not always feature as a component in all social marketing programs. As part of this assessment the chapter considers some of the weaknesses and dangers associated with segmentation, including its importance and contribution to the overall program strategy implementation and how it can add value to the evaluation strategy. The latter part of the chapter explores some of the future changes that will be associated with the application of segmentation within social marketing and a world of increasing connectivity, big data and technologies, and methodologies that enable increasing personalised and tailored goods, services and social programs. The chapter also includes a number of checklists and questions that can be used to guide the use and review of segmentation in social marketing.

Introduction

Segmentation is a technique that is often used in both commercial sector marketing and social marketing. The chapters in this book provide a review of the nature of segmentation and how it can be undertaken and many of its strengths and weaknesses within a social marketing context. In essence, segmentation in a social marketing context is driven by a desire to bring about measurable social change by influencing the behaviour of specific groups. Segmentation seeks to develop

J. French (✉)
Strategic Social Marketing, England, UK
e-mail: jeff.french@strategic-social-marketing.org

T. Dietrich et al. (eds.), *Segmentation in Social Marketing*,
DOI 10.1007/978-981-10-1835-0_3

accurate, robust and meaningful understandings of population subsets that share common characteristics. The rationale for this activity is to develop bespoke social interventions designed to influence specific behaviours among specific groups. These segments are internally homogeneous, meaning people in the segment are similar in, for example, their attitudes or beliefs, age, gender, physical location, and most importantly for social marketing, share similarities in their behaviours. Segmentation is underpinned by the assumption that people designated as being within a segment are likely to respond to a set of social marketing interventions in a similar way, but in a way that is dissimilar to how citizens in other segments might respond. Segmentation is driven by concerns that resources are used efficiently, and a need to design interventions that will be capable of influencing the behaviours of the selected target groups. Segmentation is, however, also driven by a concern for a more ethical set of principles related to identifying groups that can be and are generally willing to be influenced, and ensuring intervention programs offered are acceptable and meaningful to the groups they are targeted at. A good example of a sustained and highly effective social marketing program that has used segmentation to both understand and identify subgroups of an at risk population and develop a differentiated and segmented set of interventions to impact the behaviour of different segments is the UK road transport program 'THINK!' 'THINK!' is a multifaceted program that uses information, education, road and vehicle design, legislation, and enforcement to reduce road deaths and accidents. Details of the 'THINK!' program can be found at, http://think.direct.gov.uk/, and a full case study of this program in French et al. (2012).

Respecting Citizens

Segmentation was popularised by marketing theorists such as George Day in the 1970s, with a focus on assisting businesses to satisfy customer needs by tailoring offers while maintaining a focused approach to earning profits through economies of scale. In purely functional terms segmentation helps to ensure efficient use of commercial marketing resources, identifies customer needs and increases impact in terms of product and service uptake and brand value. In addition to its effectiveness and efficiency, this chapter will also explore key reasons why segmentation should be used by social marketers and why it is an important ingredient in successful social marketing programs.

Segmentation is an important technique in social marketing because in addition to helping focus and tailor social marketing intervention strategies, it informs and shapes responses to ethical considerations. Segmentation also has the potential to enhance citizen empowerment and increasingly assists with the co-production of solutions to social challenges. Segmentation is a main—but not the only—technique that provides a direct example of social marketing's commitment to citizen centric planning and delivery. Alongside other techniques for developing an understanding of identifiable population subgroups, such as ethnography and social network analysis, adopting a segmentation strategy indicates that those developing and implementing a social marketing strategy recognise the need for specifically targeted programs and interventions based on a deep understanding and insight about the needs, beliefs, circumstances and behaviours of different subgroups of the population and what influences them. In this sense segmentation is a demonstration of respect for the citizens that social marketing seeks to influence. A good example of how a segmentation strategy is being used to inform a national population-based social marketing program aimed at reducing obesity and engaging citizens in a co-production approach to tackling the problem is provided by the UK Change 4 Life program. Full details of the program can be found at: http://www.nhs.uk/change4life/Pages/change-for-life.aspx. This program has identified six specific subgroups amongst its primary target audience of families with young children. The program has developed a targeted array of interventions tailored to the needs of these segments. The program also seeks to actively recruit and engage citizens from each of these subgroups to inform and promote the program.

The Importance of Segmentation in Social Marketing

Across all areas of government in many countries around the world, there is a growing emphasis on getting closer to citizens, and understanding their wants and needs better. This is leading to more programs designed to reach out and engage citizens in developing solutions to the many complex social challenges we face (Clarke et al. 2007). The basic motivation for this effort is to design and deliver services that are not only effective and efficient, but that also better meet the needs of citizens, rather than the needs of government or the providers of social programs and services. As this book makes clear, at its simplest, segmentation is about classifying a population into different groups, recognising that not all people are the same or need the same things. The purpose of segmentation is to help us understand different people and their varying needs so we can tailor our products, services and social programs to better reflect these needs.

Segmentation can add real value to most social programs and is a common technique that is often, but not always, applied as part of social marketing programs. It seeks to provide a clear understanding about citizens that can inform policy selection, program strategy development, project delivery and the evaluation of programs. Segmentation should usually be one of the first things planners consider when developing a social policy, program or project.

The targeting and positioning of social marketing social offerings, based on representational insight gathered as part of developing segmentation models, is vital to ensure that social marketing interventions are capable of influencing the behaviours of different groups of citizens. However, segmentation is not a universal solution, and the decision to use and invest in segmentation needs to be carefully thought through.

Targeting requires social marketers to utilise segmentation analysis to decide which population segments to target and try to engage in social programs. Target groups need to be large enough to warrant attention and to be viable in terms of allocation of resources. Target groups also need to be accessible and channels of communication and engagement need to exist. The target group also needs to be one that is potentially responsive to social marketing efforts—there is no point engaging groups that do not need, or do not want to be engaged on a given social issue (Hastings and Domegan 2013). For instance, low income smokers are an example of a potentially viable target group, since smoking prevalence is higher in low income populations, but they may be difficult to influence because they are subject to multiple barriers to stopping smoking.

Market segmentation is an approach to identify and manage diverse citizen needs and to target marketing resources (Weinstein 2004; Dibb and Simkin 2009). As stated above, the basic premise of segmentation is that different group preferences and needs can be best managed by grouping similar people together into 'market segments'. Some of the range of groups that are identified as part of this process may become the focus of social marketing efforts (Mahajan and Jain 1978). Segmentation facilitates the development of citizen-oriented social program design and implementation by enabling organisations to develop a deep understanding about the people that they are seeking to understand, serve and help. Segmentations that have predictive utility enable more efficient use and allocation of social marketing resources. Essentially, segmentation recognises that groups of people are different, and often want different things or will respond differently to different forms of engagement and interaction. This is important for social marketing, as we all know that 'one size fits all' responses to behavioural challenges are not often successful. Segmentation can be performed based on a number of different characteristics and profiles (Eagle et al. 2013):

- Demographics such as age, gender, marital status, employment, income, socio-economic status
- Cultures/subcultures including ethnicity, religious beliefs, subcultures of consumption behaviours (e.g. night clubbers, bikers)
- Attitudes such as acceptability towards smoking or drinking
- Psychological, including motivations, personality, interests, and opinions
- Value perceptions such as perceived functional, economic or social value of using energy efficiently
- Psychographics such as lifestyle, knowledge, activities
- Behavioural, for instance people who are gamblers, smokers or drinkers.

To this list, Weinreich (2011) adds geographics, relating to factors such as population size of a city or county, and geographic features such as residential density and climate.

As Lefebvre (2013, p. 125) states: "*segmentation reinforces and builds on the core tenet of marketing that we should be customer or people focused.*" Segmentation within social marketing is essentially about ensuring that social offers in the form of services, products or systems are designed in such a way that they positively influence the social behaviour that is being targeted by the social marketing program. Segmentation is also fundamentally about ensuring, according to Lefebvre, that "*we better tailor and position our value propositions, behaviours, products, and services in relation to peoples existing beliefs and preferences and the behaviours they currently practice*" (p. 125). The rationale for segmentation is then both technical and ethical. It encapsulates the desire for program efficacy with a desire to engage, enable and empower specific groups of citizens in relation to specific behaviours such as stopping smoking, saving for retirement, attending school, or taking up offered social services.

The Added Value of Segmentation Within Social Marketing

Segmentation can add value to every phase of the social marketing process. Specifically, segmentation can add value to the selection of which social marketing programs should be taken forward and what tactical interventions should be included in any program strategy. Segmentation can also add value with regard to the assessment and evaluation of social marketing programs. By adopting a segmented approach, social marketers can evaluate in a more refined way how the groups that are targeted respond to target interventions. This form of tightly defined evaluation is more helpful in distinguishing the optimum social marketing intervention mix, and the positioning of social offers, than a campaign that is undifferentiated and applied in a uniform way across whole populations.

Applying segmentation as part of a social marketing strategy requires balancing the benefits offered against available resources needed to develop and consistently apply a segmented intervention strategy. As stated above, comprehensive segmentation strategies can be expensive, time consuming and involve complexity in implementation. There are a number of additional factors to consider when contemplating investing in segmentation, identifying the following:

- The need to gain organisational buy-into the need for and cost of segmentation
- The need for tracking of implementation, monitoring of performance of the segmentation approach adopted
- The need for a clear allocation of resources
- The need for proactive management of the segmentation process
- The need to engage champions for the strategy and reward progress are key considerations to achieve successful segmentation.

The checklist above can be used in conjunction with Table 1 of benefits that can be associated with the application of segmentation to assess the practicalities as well as the benefits of segmentation within a specific program. Using the above checklist of practical and managerial issues together with a consideration of the benefits of segmentation enables organisations to transparently determine whether segmentation is desirable and/or feasible.

Table 1 Segmentation's contribution to the social marketing process

Segmentation adds value to social marketing in seven ways:
· Summarising and organising in an assessable way a mass of data and insight research about what is known about the citizens who need assistance to cope with, maintain or change a social behaviour · Providing research data that can inform understanding and modelling that enables the development and delivery of a mix of interventions designed to assist target groups adopt or sustain behaviours that produce social value · Segmentation can help to avoid investment in interventions that will not help or are inefficient and potentially counterproductive · Ensuring that limited resources are used effectively and efficiently by identifying where and how to end ineffective and unwanted interventions with minimal impact on citizen satisfaction or negative behaviour · Providing new understanding about under-served and/or vulnerable groups, thereby helping to address inequality and discrimination · Assisting with the analysis of population-based interventions and how they impact on subsets of the population, segmentation enables programs to be evaluated not only by their effectiveness, but also in terms of their return on investment, cost benefit and value for money · Segmentation contributes to forward planning and future forecasting of population needs within social marketing programs. A deep understanding of population segments and their motivations, together with evaluation and tracking data on how each segment is reacting to current social policy interventions, assists, in turn, in the development of scenario planning and future investment modelling to develop forward strategies and budgets to deliver the optimum mix of interventions

While the seven types of added value presented above are not intended as an exhaustive list, they do illustrate why many organisations and agencies choose to invest resources, expertise and time in developing and maintaining segmentations of the target populations they are seeking to serve.

It is widely accepted that the objective of social marketing is to use all the available theories, principles, concepts, techniques and resources to influence human behaviour for social good. However, human behaviour is complex, multifaceted, and subject to both rational decision making and/or more rapid cognition (Kahneman 2011), as well as being influenced by a whole host of environmental, economic and structural factors (Gordon 2013). In order to understand and to then change behaviour, social marketers need to use a wide range of strategies. In the commercial world, the idea that comprehensive and systemic marketing strategies are required to influence human behaviour is well accepted. Now, the need for a more strategic and systemic approach to social marketing is gaining ground. French and Gordon (2015) argue for the development and application of what they call "*strategic social marketing*". Social marketing, the authors argue, should not be seen as a discrete activity that sits alongside other approaches to policy development and implementation (French and Gordon 2015). *Strategic social marketing* is concerned with making a contribution to all social policy development and implementation processes. Conceived in this way, strategic social marketing can be defined as:

> The systemic, critical and reflexive application of social marketing principles to enhance social policy selection, objective setting, planning and operational delivery.

As can be inferred from the above definition, strategic social marketing is concerned with informing policy selection, development and strategic goal setting, selecting effective interventions, assisting with the process of determining how success will be measured, and also ensuring that the mix of interventions selected are managed and coordinated. Social marketing conceived in this way plays an integral role in social policy design and ensures that understanding and insights about the beliefs, values and needs of all relevant segments of the population are captured, analysed and fed into the policy selection and development process. Strategically, social marketing adds value through acting as a voice and facilitator of citizen needs and wants, and contributes to tackling social behavioural challenges. By collecting data and insights, social marketers can help enhance the policy making process by developing segmentation models that can help focus social policy action.

To Segment or not to Segment? that Is the Question

The first fundamental question to consider when contemplating investment in developing and using segmentation to inform social marketing programs is: '*Is a new segmentation really what we need?*' Constructing insightful and predictive segmentation models can be expensive and time-consuming. In some cases, it may be better to use extant data, research and insight to assist with developing targeted interventions.

Commitment to an approach informed by segmentation requires careful consideration of what is really needed. Is there an existing segmentation approach available from the commercial field of social research? Investing in segmentation can be cost-effective, since it can help to target resources to groups who most need help. However, for effective and efficient investment of funds, it is essential to focus on the end result. The point of a social marketing intervention is to have a measurable impact on a selected social behaviour. So it is important to consider the trade-off between spending money on identifying priority segments and the process of developing testing and implementing interventions. Table 2 contains three checklists developed by the UK Cabinet Office (2009) that can help planners think through the key decision of whether investment in segmentation is necessary and plausible.

A key aspect of segmentation's added value is that it increases program effectiveness and efficiency because it enables the development of interventions that are more responsive and relevant to the target group's needs, wants, beliefs and behaviours. Segmentation is not just a process of categorising subgroups of the population into sets that share similar characteristics and behavioural patterns; it is also the process of developing the right mix of interventions that are relevant and valued by such subgroups. The development of segmented interventions is undertaken with the desire to increase the responsiveness of identified subgroups of the population which, in doing so, makes a contribution to improving wellbeing across whole communities. The development of data sets that inform the

Table 2 Segmentation review questions (The Cabinet Office 2009)

(1) Do you have a clearly defined objective that's driving your plan to do segmentation? (2) Do you understand how segmentation will help you achieve this? (3) Do you know the parameters you are working within (e.g. the scope of your project/number of people affected)? (4) Do you know the deadlines you are working to and broad budget you are working within?
You should be able to answer all of these questions positively; if not, you probably need to do more to explore and define your program aims and objectives before committing to segmentation (1) Do you already have a workable segmentation approach that you can use again? (2) Have you already started identifying and selling solutions and actions? (3) Are you already committed to policies or activities that dictate the way ahead?
If you can answer these questions positively it may be unnecessary to produce a new segmentation approach, or too late to consider segmentation for this particular issue (1) Is the target group that you are dealing with quite broad? (2) Are there differences between people or service providers that are likely to affect policy, service delivery or communication? (3) Do you have the ability to tailor what you develop and deliver for different segments once you've identified them? If you answer all these questions positively it is likely that segmentation *will* help you in what you are trying to achieve

Adapted from: The Cabinet Office (2009). Government guide to segmentation, because one size does not fit all. Oxford Strategic Marketing. http://www.cabinetoffice.gov.uk/public_service_reform/delivery_council/workplan.aspx#publications

development of segmentation models describing these characteristics of different subgroups is the core of this process. As discussed above, the types of data that can be used to construct a segmentation model vary in scope, but data relating to actual past behaviour tends to be highly predictive and is, therefore, very useful when developing social marketing interventions. Psychological insight data focused more on attitudinal and belief data is also very useful when constructing segmentation models. Insight data itself can come from a broad range of methodologies and types of data. For example, the UK Department of Transport (2011) identified eight types of insight data needed to understand the main factors that might be influencing behaviour in relation to social programs with a transport focus. These factors are, however, also applicable to most other forms of social challenge. According to the UK Department of Transport (2011) insight data is needed for:

- Structural factors
- Attitudes
- Social and cultural norms
- Knowledge and awareness
- Skills capacity and self-efficacy
- Cost barriers
- Habit
- Transport related behaviour

This list indicates that gathering insight is a complex business. To undertake the development of segmentation models that have predictive power which can help inform the development of social marketing programs clearly requires investment in either in-house expertise or budgets of sufficient size and duration to allow commissioning the gathering, analysis and synthesis of data. A good example of a large-scale and comprehensive segmentation is the Sport England exercise segmentation model and service. This segmentation model of the population of England sets out 19 subgroups of the population according to their understanding, beliefs, social and economic circumstances, and participation in sport and exercise. This comprehensive large-scale segmentation is made available freely for the public and local authorities and sports centres to use to help them understand the populations they seek to encourage to take up more physical activity. Centrally developed, high quality segmentations such as this can be very powerful planning and evaluation tools. Full details of the segmentation and access to its data can be found at: http://segments.sportengland.org/.

The Importance of Segmentation in the Development and Evaluation of Social Marketing

So far, we have discovered three main reasons for investing in a segmented approach to social marketing program development: (1) to increase the effectiveness of the program; (2) to increase the responsiveness of the program; and (3) to ensure the relevance of the program.

There is another key reason, however, that is related to, but distinct from these drivers. This reason relates to the danger of over-focusing or over-committing resources to dominant subgroups in the population. There is a potential risk when developing a segmented understanding of the population of being over-responsive, or giving too much weight to the influence of affluent, well resourced, vocal and assertive minorities at the expense of less well organised and articulate groups. Such minorities often wield disproportionate influence and attract more resources than their relative need requires when it comes to getting access to, or support from social programs. This phenomenon has been called '*the sharp elbowed middle class*' who push their way to the front of the queue and, through their assertiveness, gain more than their fair share of public resources. There are instances where this occurrence, if not directly addressed through a segmented approach that ensures the deliberate targeting of resources to the less empowered and less vocal, can lead to increased inequality of access and provision. Segmentation then, has a role to play in reducing potential inequality and uneven and unfair distribution of social services, goods and resources. Lefebvre (2013) suggests three basic questions to be considered when developing a segmented approach related to this issue: (1) *Who are the people at highest risk?* (2) *Who are the people most open to change?* (3) *Who are the critical-for-success groups?*

These three questions can help those responsible for developing segmentation to orient their efforts and resources towards segments that have relevance, rather than towards models that are comprehensive. In any segmentation there is a further trade-off between completeness and utility, which all social marketers will face, unless they have unlimited budgets. Therefore, segmentation's emphasis, as Lefebvre (2013) suggests, is on focusing attention on those groups that are at risk but open to change, or on targeting the segment that has a key influencing role on the program's primary target group.

Good segmentations, as Yankelovich and Meer (2006) point out, also facilitate the process of deciding which groups to influence. Segmentation models with high levels of utility identify subgroups who are open to being influenced or supported to adopt target behaviours, and also groups who can act as influencers on these primary target audiences. Well-constructed segmentation models can, additionally, identify groups that are strongly resistant to change, and by doing so, provide program managers with options to develop strategies to either address this resistance or to restrict the availability of resources for such groups.

The development of a robust segmentation model to guide the development and selection of social marketing strategy and tactics has the further bonus of helping to identify how specific groups respond to targeted sets of interventions compared either with other groups or with any control groups that have been established to evaluate the efficacy and efficiency of a social marketing program. Hornik and Ramirez (2006) make it clear that by adopting a segmented approach to the implementation of a social marketing program, any process of evaluation of the program will be, in part, focused on the benefits of adopting such an approach, as opposed to a whole population, or undifferentiated, approach. As indicated above, one of the key challenges facing social marketing program developers and implementers is the need to justify the time and cost associated with the application of segmentation in terms of bigger qualitative payback and return on investment. If such gains and benefits cannot be demonstrated, the case for segmentation is obviously weakened.

Why Do Many Social Marketing Programs not Invest in Segmentation?

Eagle and Dahl (2013, p. 170) state "*segmentation is an important and often neglected aspect of campaign development.*" Despite the utility of segmentation within social marketing, many social marketing programs do not always apply a segmented approach. A recent review commissioned by the European Union, the ECOM program (2015), discovered by case study analysis across a number of European countries that segmentation is not a widely used approach when it comes to designing social marketing and health communication programs.

There are many organisational and policy barriers that impact on the application of segmentation. These barriers result in the reality that not all social marketing programs employ segmentation. This has led French and Russell-Bennet (2015) to suggest that segmentation could be viewed as a key technique associated with social marketing, but not one of its unique or defining concepts or principles. Obviously, segmentation is not unique to social marketing since it is also applied in many other social policy and strategy fields. For example, health education programs often develop and apply a segmented strategy.

Doner Lotenberg et al. (2011) have considered a number of the barriers to implementation of segmentation. Some of these factors are technical, such as a shortage of data or a lack of segmentation research and analysis skills. There may also be a lack of clarity or a poorly presented case for the added value of segmentation to a program (Doner Lotenberg et al. 2011). Evidence pushed back in the form of a challenge by those opposed to a proposed segmentation may be associated with an assessment of the costs and benefits of investing in its development. For example, would a segmentation of the types of women who do not breastfeed make any real difference when implementing a program to support breastfeeding rates and duration, compared with a non-segmented approach?

Some social marketing program teams may also lack expertise in four key areas of segmentation: first, an understanding of the theory and application of segmentation as a technique: second, the collection of segmentation data: third, the analysis and synthesis of data to construct segmentation profiles; and last, skills in and understandings of testing and building robust segmentations that are not only representative, but also have explanatory and predictive utility. Another associated barrier may be the lack of specific technical skills and understandings, such as in the use of multivariate analysis.

In addition to the issues raised by Doner Lotenberg et al. (2011), there are at least a further five reasons why segmentation may not be included in a social marketing program. Many of these reasons, rather than being technical in nature, are reflections of existing ideological, managerial, and cognitive biases such as the (expert-knows-best) status quo bias:

- A belief that the social behaviour under consideration is of universal concern and therefore, a segmented approach is not appropriate or necessary. An example might be a social marketing program implemented during a pandemic encouraging people not to shake hands.
- The issue is pressing, time and cash are short and consequently, there is a belief that all available funding should be spent on action rather than research.
- A view that adopting a segmented approach may lead to, or imply negative labelling of some segments of the population which may, in turn, fuel prejudice or unfair treatment.
- The belief that segmentation may lead to perverse social norming, i.e. segmentation may reinforce negative stereotypes which become self-fulfilling. For example, developing segmentations of young men in poor areas to tackle

gang culture may actually reinforce the narrative that it is necessary to join a gang for protection.
- A belief that the perceived return on investment made in segmentation does not warrant the investment of time that is required, nor the financial cost of gathering, analysing and synthesising data.

A further, fundamental criticism of segmentations that focus on individual behaviour is also made. It is argued that segmentations focusing on individual behaviour and personal psychological factors place too much emphasis on what has been called individual agency (Hewson 2010). Such segmentations can underestimate the impact of wider environmental, economic, social and other structural macro-social influences on behaviour and attitudes. For example, an emphasis on individual responsibility for overeating, and consequent obesity, does not take into account the supply of cheap, high-calorie foods promoted by aggressive and pervasive junk food marketing.

It is well known that many other environmental, economic and cultural factors play a significant role in influencing behaviour (Marmot et al. 2008). Gordon (2013) and others have acknowledged the need for social marketing to focus on these wider determining factors when developing programs of action. For segmentation, this implies the development of models that take into account factors under the individual's control, as well as wider factors that impact on individual decision making, such as economic circumstance and other social influences.

Halpern (2015) has made the assertion that the problem with many impressive-sounding segmentations based on values, beliefs and personality types, in both the social and commercial sector, is their track record of not actually predicting much. Halpern asserts that low predictive validity led many psychologists to lose interest in the study of personality types in the 1970s, but does acknowledge that past behaviour is a good predictor of future behaviour. In other words, a person who was regularly late for work last week will probably be late for work next week, regardless of what paper they read, the party they vote for, their preferred flavour of tea, or the type of house they live in. This means that the most helpful data is often behavioural, a view that most social marketers (e.g. Andreasen 1995; Lee and Kotler 2011; French 2011; Hastings and Domegan 2013; Donovan and Henley 2010) would agree with. It is not just what a person says they believe in, but what they actually do that can help us group, target and support people to behave in socially positive ways.

Behavioural segmentations also have the added advantage of indicating explicit sets of evaluation metrics that can be tracked to measure if, when exposed to the social marketing intervention, the target group responded or not and by how much. For example, Halpern (2015) gives the example of trying to persuade a group, identified by its past behaviour, to change using an informational "nudge". The group concerned comprised of people in the UK who owed large amounts of tax to the government. This group, selected for their past behaviour of not filing tax returns, was sent a message emphasising that most people did pay on time. It was found that this group reacted negatively to this kind of approach; in fact, the nudge messages, based on the concept of social norms, actually backfired. It resulted in payment rates dropping further—from about 25 % in the top 5 % of debtors, and from about 35 % in the top 1 % of debtors. This was a real problem, as these groups represented a large proportion of those owing unpaid tax to the UK government. It was subsequently found, however, that messages which emphasised the negative impact on society of people not paying taxes did have a positive impact in encouraging the payment of overdue tax among this behaviourally homogeneous group.

The Future of Segmentation in Social Marketing Programs

As both the conceptual and theoretical development of segmentation continues to develop, as indicated within the chapters of this book, and as new methodologies and technologies make the discovery and targeting of fine-grained subsets of the population more effective and efficient, segmentation should become a more universal aspect of social marketing programs. Segmentation in the future will continue to be increasingly perceived as an ongoing and integral process in the development and delivery of most social marketing (Curtain 2003; Audit Commission 2003; French and Gordon 2015). Ideally, segmentation will be seen as a key component of a more structured and ongoing dialogue between citizens, their governments and the agencies they fund concerning what social challenges need to be addressed, how they should be tackled, and how citizens, non-governmental organisations and the broader not-for-profit sector can work together with governments to address these challenges. As standards of good practice in social marketing are more closely refined and accepted, it is also probable that commissioners and professional social marketing providers will build commissioning systems and quality standards which require segmentation to be included in social marketing programs.

New technologies and approaches to collecting, analysing and synthesising data are already being used to inform segmented strategies in both the commercial and social marketing sectors. The growth, and the ubiquitous, always on, ever-connected nature, of digital communication and social networking, together with the availability of rapidly accumulating personal data and preferences, is enabling more up-to-the-minute segmentations to be developed. The sheer volume of data and the means to rapidly scan and synthesise vast data pools imply, according to Mayer-Schonberger and Cukier (2013), that we are rapidly moving away from the need for selective methodologies that weaken our understanding of populations and their subgroups. Techniques used in segmentation development, such as representative sampling frames, are becoming less important. We are moving to a position where there is less need to seek to represent a target population via sampling because it is becoming possible to include everyone who has an online presence or footprint in the sample. The logical end point is that the data sample size will increasingly become n = all. As data collection and sampling move toward total population inclusion, at the same time digital data storage and analysis is enabling more and more specific targeting of goods, services and information. Segmentation in an era of mass personalisation and customisation means that marketers in both the commercial and social sectors are seeking to target audiences of one. In the social marketing sector, examples such as customised and targeted solutions and online personalised support programs are already emerging (Dooley 2013).

In the future, segmentation within social marketing programs will probably also be characterised as a continuous rather than one-off or sporadic process throughout the life of a program. For example, in the past, at the start of a program the development of a segmentation model was undertaken with one or two exercises to refresh the model over the five-year program life. In the future, it is foreseeable that segmentation will be a more ongoing process of adjustment and refinement, as program evaluation and tracking is strengthened and a commitment to an ongoing dialogue with citizens is developed. Such a continuous process will enable program researchers and planners to continuously refresh their segments. Better process and outcome evaluation will also inform the refinement of the segmentation models. Data collected from evaluations will help to reveal how citizens actually respond to interventions, so that creating a virtuous circle of segmentation models informing good practice and practice evaluation will, in turn, inform their refinement.

Conclusion

Segmentation, as explored in this chapter, is fundamentally about respect for citizens. Its application represents a desire to engage citizens in the process of deciding which mix of intervention approaches should constitute the make-up of social programs that seek to influence social behaviour for the collective good. Segmentation is also a methodology that assists with improving the effectiveness, efficiency and specificity of social programs. Through these twin processes segmentation can add real value to all aspects of social marketing programs and projects, as well as increase their acceptability among both the wider public and targeted subgroups of the population. This chapter has set out some of the key elements of the added value of segmentation within social marketing. On face value, these benefits seem to indicate a compelling case for segmentation to be regarded as an essential part of the social marketing process. However, as this chapter has shown, it is not the case that segmentation is universally applied in the development of social marketing programs. There are a number of barriers, from both methodological and theoretical perspectives, that impact on the adoption and application of segmentation. In the planning of a social marketing program, all these factors require open, informed and transparent consideration to ensure that the case for using or not using a segmented strategy is clearly articulated and can be defended by those making this key strategic decision.

This chapter has argued that while segmentation is not unique to social marketing, it is a powerful technique that has been used in many social marketing programs to improve the efficiency of programs, their impact on social challenges, and the development of better relationships between the providers and consumers of these programs. Segmentation is not, however, without its detractors, and the decision to invest in developing segmentation must be carefully thought through. This chapter has discussed the future of segmentation within social marketing, and concluded that as new, cheaper, more targeted, and faster means of engaging with smaller and smaller subgroups via digital and mobile technology continue to develop, the very notion of segmentation may become anachronistic. Nevertheless, even in a world where interventions can be increasingly tailored and targeted to individuals, it is still the case that subgroups of the population will share similar behaviours, beliefs and attitudes. Segmentation will, therefore remain a powerful tool for delivering similar interventions to those groups. In summary, good segmentation can aid the delivery of tailored social policies in a respectful citizen experience and with better operational efficiency; poor segmentation development can result in mistargeted efforts, wasted resources and ineffectual social programs.

References

Andreasen, A. R. (1995). *Marketing social change*. San Francisco, CA: Jossey-Bass.

Audit Commission. (2003). *Connecting users with citizens*. London: Audit Commission.

Cabinet Office. (2009). Government guide to segmentation, because one size does not fit all. Oxford Strategic Marketing: p. 7 Section 2 the Basics of Segmentation. http://www.cabinetoffice.gov.uk/public_service_reform/delivery_council/workplan.aspx#publications

Clarke, J., Newman, J., Smith, N., Vidler, E., & Westmarland, L. (2007). *Creating citizen-consumers. Changing publics and changing public services*. Thousand Oaks: Sage.

Curtain, R. (2003). How citizens can take part in developing and implementing public policy. Melbourne: Australian Public Policy Research Network. http://curtainrl.pairserver.com/old_site_files/public_policy.html

Department of Transport. (2011). *Behavioural insights tool kit. Social research and evaluation division*. London: Department of Transport.

Dibb, S., & Simkin, L. (2009). Implementation rules to bridge the theory/practice divide in market segmentation. *Journal of Marketing Management, 25*(3), 375–396.

Doner Lotenberg, L., Schechter, C., & Strand, J. (2011). Segmentation and targeting. In G. Hastings, K. Angus, & C. Bryant (Eds.), *The SAGE handbook of social marketing*. London: SAGE.

Donovan, R., & Henley, N. (2010). *Principles and practice of social marketing: An international perspective*. Cambridge: Cambridge University Press.

Dooly, J. (2013). Web 2.0 and its implications for health-related social marketing campaigns. PhD Thesis. University of Wollongong, NSW.

Eagle, L., Dahl, S., Hill, S., Bird, S., Spotswood, F., & Tapp, A. (2013). *Social marketing*. London, UK: Pearson.

Eagle L., Dahl S., Hill S., Bird S., Spotswood F., Tapp. A. (2013). *Social Marketing*. p. 170 London, Pearson.

ECOM Program. (2015). Education and communication program funded by EU review of pandemic communication and behavioural influence. Case Study Review Work Program 3. http://ecomeu.info/

French, J. (2011). Business as unusual. The contribution of social marketing to government policy making and strategy development. In G. Hastings, K. Angus, & C. Bryant (Eds.), *The SAGE handbook of social marketing*. London: SAGE.
French, J., & Gordon, R. (2015). *Strategic social marketing*. London: SAGE.
French, J., Merritt, R., & Reynolds, L. (2012). *Social marketing casebook*. London: SAGE.
French, J., & Russell-Bennett, R. (2015). A hierarchical model of social marketing. *Journal of Social Marketing, 5*(2), 139–159.
Gordon, R. (2013). Unlocking the potential of upstream social marketing. *European Journal of Marketing, 47*(9), 1525–1547.
Halpern, D. (2015). *Inside the nudge unit: How small changes can make a big difference*. London: WH Allen.
Hastings, G., & Domegan, C. (2013). *Social marketing: From tunes to symphonies*. London: Routledge.
Hewson, M. (2010). Agency. In A. Mills, G. Durepos, & E. Wiebe (Eds.), *Encyclopaedia of case study research* (pp. 13–17). Thousand Oaks, CA: SAGE.
Hornick, R., & Ramirez, A. (2006). Racial/ethnic disparities and segmentation in communication campaigns. *American Behavioral Sciences, 49*, 868–884.
Kahneman, D. (2011). *Thinking fast thinking slow*. London: Penguin.
Lee, N., & Kotler, P. (2011). *Social marketing: Influencing behaviours for good*. New York: Sage.
Lefebvre, C. (2013). *Social marketing and social change*. Jossey-Bass, San Francisco: Wiley.
Mahajan, V., & Jain, A. K. (1978). An approach to normative segmentation. *Journal of Marketing Research, 15*(3), 338–345.
Marmot, M., Friel, S., Bell, R., Houweling, T. A. J., & Taylor, S. (2008). *Closing the gap in a generation: Health equity through action on the social determinants of health. Final report of the commission on social determinants of health*. Geneva: World Health Organization.
Mayer-Schonberger, V., & Cukier, K. (2013). Big data: A revolution that will transform how we live, work and think. Houghton Mifflin Harcourt.
Weinreich, N. (2011). *Hands on social marketing: A step-by-step guide to designing change for good* (2nd ed.). Los Angeles: SAGE.
Weinstein, A. (2004). *Handbook of market segmentation*. New York: The Haworth Press.
Yankelovich, D., & Meer, D. (2006). Rediscovering market segmentation. *Harvard Business Review, 84*, 122–131.

Changing Times for Social Marketing Segmentation

Sally Dibb

Abstract Segmentation is one of a number of commercial marketing tools now widely used by governments, policy makers, social marketing practitioners and researchers to address some of the bigger challenges facing society. However, social marketing segmentation has been constrained by ethical concerns and problems with expertise and resources; with the consequence that its use lags behind what happens commercially. There is a pressing need for social marketers to take greater responsibility for developing their own segmentation practices, a change in mind-set which can be achieved in two ways. Firstly, greater effort is needed to tailor commercial segmentation tools for social marketing contexts. A social marketing targeting tool adapted from one routinely used by commercial marketers is presented to illustrate this point. Secondly, more needs to be done to capitalise on technological advance in pursuit of sophisticated segmentation approaches. Focusing on data availability, data capture and analytics, the chapter explores ways in which social marketers can take the lead to develop new methods and practices that capitalise on these advances.

Introduction

Segmentation has been central to commercial marketing practice for over sixty years (Wind 1978), and more recently has become a core pillar of social marketing (Andreasen 2002; French and Gordon 2015). The concept is one of a number of commercial marketing tools that governments, policy makers, social marketing practitioners and researchers increasingly use to address some of the bigger challenges facing society. These problems range from health and well-being concerns such as preventing obesity, reducing alcohol consumption and encouraging

S. Dibb (✉)
The Open University Business School, Milton Keynes, UK
e-mail: sally.dibb@open.ac.uk; sally.dibb@coventry.ac.uk

S. Dibb
Centre for Business in Society, Coventry University, Coventry CV1 5FB, UK

T. Dietrich et al. (eds.), *Segmentation in Social Marketing*,
DOI 10.1007/978-981-10-1835-0_4

smoking cessation, to reducing personal debt, increasing donations to good causes and encouraging more sustainable consumption (French 2011; Johnson et al. 2012). While many of these issues are linked to lifestyle choices, others are the result of broader problems, such as the global economic crisis and global warming. Irrespective of the underlying causes of social marketing concerns, however, the use of segmentation principles in conjunction with behaviour change programs to tackle them is increasingly prevalent (for an example, see https://www.gov.uk/government/organisations/behavioural-insights-team).

For reasons relating to ethics (Newton et al. 2013), expertise and resources (Neiger et al. 2003), the application of segmentation in social marketing settings lags behind its use by commercial firms. Given the recent step-change in technology that has dramatically increased data availability, and with it, the opportunities for more sophisticated segmentation approaches, there is a danger that this gap will widen further. A change in mindset, in which social marketing practitioners take greater responsibility for developing their own segmentation practices (Andreasen 2012), would help to improve the situation. This chapter argues for a more proactive approach in adapting segmentation approaches from commercial marketing. In particular, the opportunities arising from technology and data developments need to be recognised, with social marketers taking the lead in developing methods and practices that capitalise on these advances (Dibb and Carrigan 2013).

After considering some segmentation basics, the reasons why its use in social marketing lags behind commercial contexts are considered, before examining the benefits that can be gained from using relatively simple applications of segmentation ideas. The lessons that social marketers can learn from the application of segmentation in commercial settings are illustrated through the presentation of a new social marketing targeting tool that is adapted from one used by commercial marketers. The opportunities for social marketing segmentation arising from technological advances in data availability, data capture and analytics are then discussed. The chapter concludes with five practical implications for social marketing practitioners embracing the benefits of segmentation.

Market Segmentation Basics

Market segmentation is the process of grouping individuals with similar needs and behaviours into homogeneous segments. A segment is a group of individual consumers or business customers sharing one or more similar characteristics that cause them to have relatively similar product or service needs and buying behaviour. In commercial contexts, the process helps firms to deal with the diverse needs and characteristics of customers in a resource-efficient way (Wells et al. 2010). Segmentation is central to the creation of marketing strategy, deciding which customers to prioritise and which to ignore, ensuring customer retention and the ability to compete effectively. Organisations turn to segmentation for many reasons, including: (1) the need for more effective resource allocation, an issue which became more prominent during the recent global financial crisis (Simkin 2013);

(2) the pursuit of better crafted marketing programs that are more accurately positioned to meet the needs of the target market; and (3) to enable the needs of complex markets to be managed, as shown by the globalisation of marketing that has cemented segmentation's role in supporting different marketing programs in multiple contexts (Hassan and Craft 2012).

In many respects, social marketers face the same kinds of challenges as their commercial cousins. Their work relies on the effective communication and positioning of all sorts of interventions, whether designed to encourage healthy eating, sensible drinking, regular physical activity, more sustainable consumption, or better management of personal finances (Dibb 2014). As in commercial settings, well-crafted segmentation schemes are needed which underpin these programs. Whatever the behaviour to be changed, segmentation can help social marketers tailor interventions so that they closely meet the needs of those they are targeting.

The segmentation process comprises three stages: (1) segmenting, (2) targeting and (3) positioning, and is sometimes referred to as STP. During the first stage, *segmenting*, a number of segments are identified. Segmentation variables, sometimes referred to as base variables, are used to group individuals or entities into segments. Crucially, the individuals or entities that make up a particular segment must have similar needs or behaviours. For businesses, these similarities will relate to the product needs or buying behaviour of consumers or business customers. For example, toy manufacturers can use variables such as age, lifestyle preferences and patterns of play to segment their customers, because these variables drive market needs and preferences. Although motivated by rather different objectives, a public health body developing a fitness intervention for school-aged children might be driven by similar variables. Commercial and social marketers alike have access to a variety of segmentation variables, including those related to demographic, geographic and socio-economic profiles, as well as consumption patterns or other behaviours (Wedel and Kamakura 2000). Advances in technology and the increasing use of the web are giving marketers access to vast data sets, with the consequence that greater numbers of variables can be used and more complex segmentation schemes generated (Liu et al. 2012). These changes are enabling the rapid creation and updating of segments, so that product and service propositions can quickly be modified according to need.

During the second stage, *targeting*, decisions are made about which and how many of the identified segments to target. This is the point at which the organisation must decide how to allocate its resources. For example, an advisory service that offers guidance on managing personal finances and budgeting might opt to concentrate on low income families, even though other segments would also benefit from its services. The reasons might be that the organisation is readily able to access this particular segment or that the needs of low income families are under-served compared with other groups.

The final stage, *positioning*, involves determining how and where to position the offering in the targeted segment. Effective positioning relies on a deep and nuanced understanding of the needs, characteristics and behaviours of those being served, so that appropriate products/services and messages are developed. A particular challenge for charities, public sector bodies and other not-for-profit organisations is to ensure that they are positioned so that their activities are perceived positively among their stakeholders and that their target audiences respond.

Social Marketing Segmentation Lags Behind

Social marketers have for many years borrowed and adapted segmentation ideas from commercial marketing. However, the application of segmentation in social marketing has lagged behind its use in business settings. While commercial firms have capitalised on technological advances that have increased data availability and state-of-the art analytics to create more sophisticated segmentation schemes, social marketers remain more reliant on simple approaches, such as those which use demographics or location-based variables (Dibb 2014).

There are several reasons for this lag. The first arises from concerns about the ethics of using segmentation in social marketing contexts. This issue reflects a reticence among some social marketers to align their activities with those in the commercial sector (e.g. Peattie and Peattie 2003) and the desire to avoid being guilty by association (Hastings 2007, 2013). These concerns take a particular form in relation to segmentation, in which the ethicality of using a non-egalitarian process that prioritises the needs of some groups over others is called into question (Bloom and Novelli 1981; Newton et al. 2013). While some experts advocate that targeting interventions where the need is greatest is justifiable, reaching agreement on which groups to prioritise may not be as straightforward. Some argue that cost effectiveness, and the extent to which outcomes can be realised are key (e.g. Rothschild 2001), while others believe that the more needy should be prioritised (e.g. Donovan and Henley 2003).

A second reason for the lag is that the implementation barriers that impact upon commercial organisations can become magnified in social marketing settings. The most common barrier that social marketers face arises from a shortfall in segmentation skills and expertise among those charged with developing and delivering programs (Neiger et al. 2003). Although this problem is not confined to social marketing (Dibb and Simkin 2001, 2008); the shortage of these capabilities among social marketing practitioners is particularly acute. Many of these individuals, whose backgrounds may be in public health, sustainability, or local government, have not received formal marketing training or had the opportunity to witness marketing practice in commercial situations (Tapp and Spotswood 2013). In this respect, they fit with Gummesson's (1991) description of "part-time marketers".

Shortfalls in other resources required to support the segmentation process also cause difficulties (Dibb 2013). This situation can be compounded by the lack of access to suitable data to drive the segmentation process. Whereas commercial firms routinely gather transactional customer data, social marketers often do not have this luxury. For example, retailers such as Marks & Spencer, Tesco and John Lewis, have ready access to sales data and information gathered from their loyalty programs. A charity aiming to reduce alcohol consumption, or an advisory group trying to cut levels of personal debt, however, often have none of these data collection tools in place. This is further complicated by the fact that individuals with the most need for these services might also be amongst the least likely to seek help, so the ability to develop insights and apply segmentation analysis techniques is much more difficult.

Social Marketing Segmentation in Practice

Social marketing has been criticised for an over-reliance on simple segmentation schemes that fail to reflect the increasing availability of data and methods on which more sophisticated schemes rely (Dibb 2014). Take health interventions as an example—amid cases of good practice, many programs are undifferentiated and broadly targeted. While limited financial resources are as much to blame as a shortage of relevant segmentation expertise, the consequence is that the health interventions being offered do not always meet the public's needs.

A few years ago, a close relative spent a spell in hospital after suffering a heart attack. As part of the UK hospital's discharge process, patients and their immediate family had to watch a National Health Service video designed to help patients recover after they returned home. The video, which then was more than ten years old, offered advice on diet and fitness regimes for those recovering from a heart attack. The narrator was Bill Tarmy, the actor who played Jack Duckworth in the long-running UK television soap opera, Coronation Street. Its content can best be described as a "one size fits all" approach, aimed at the "average" (very unfit and overweight) heart attack patient. As a non-smoking, healthy-eating man, who walked over 25 miles each week, my relative found it impossible to relate to the offered advice or to work out how he could use it to recover his previous level of fitness. His confidence in the material did not improve when shortly afterwards, Bill Tarmey died as a result of his health problems.

The video was, of course, a product of its time and policy makers, health professionals and other service providers have since become increasingly adept at developing more segmented offerings for tackling health and social problems in the UK. The British Heart Foundation website (www.bhf.org.uk) illustrates this trend, with tailored information materials targeting recent heart attack patients, young people, their parents, women, etc. Service providers such as these recognise that behaviour change interventions require excellent insights into how and why particular groups behave the way they do. The benefits of adopting a segmentation mindset alongside social marketing initiatives are therefore readily apparent. An important message is that even relatively simple targeting approaches can yield more effective behaviour change interventions. The example presented in Fig. 1, describes a healthy eating intervention supported by the *British Heart Foundation* and *the Foods Standards Agency* that was tailored to meet the needs of Hindus and Sikhs in the UK. As this example shows, focusing on the needs, attitudes and behaviours of these particular community groups supported the design of a suitable intervention.

The Intervention

The research took place at Hindu Temples and Sikh Gurdwara – communities that have a predisposition to cardiovascular problems and diabetes but can be difficult to reach with health interventions. Individuals from UK South Asian groups are 50% more likely than the average to die prematurely from coronary heart problems. Developing healthy eating interventions within places of worship can be a productive way of accessing individuals who might otherwise be difficult to target. The social life of these places of worship often includes a communal sharing of food in which worshippers donate ingredients for meals that are prepared by on-site cooks and then shared by all. The project reached around 9000 congregants in 15 Sikh gurdwaras and Hindu temples, with the aim of cutting salt consumption and reducing cardiovascular disease. Each gurdwara and temple was visited four times by a dietician. The negative health effects of high salt consumption were explained to the cooks, guidance was offered on how salt and fat levels could gradually be reduced, and alternative spices were suggested. An information event with congregants raised awareness of the effects of eating too much salt and explained the changes being made to the food. Through these visits a better understanding was reached of social imperatives and eating practices. The intervention was evaluated through interviews with 47 cooks, 140 congregants and 19 members of the management committees at the places of worship.

Findings

A number of barriers to the intervention were encountered:

Cultural barriers: special occasions and festivals are associated with fattier and saltier foods. For example, *parsaad* food has to be prepared in a certain way: "*…in parsaad food you can't change anything because it is seen as a gift from the guru. It is made of equal quantity of sugar, butter and flour and you can't change it. It has to be cooked the same way all the time.*"

Social barriers: congregants felt under social pressure to donate high fat foods, while cooks believed those they were feeding preferred rich and salty meals: "*It is because traditionally the more butter and ghee you use, the richer and better person you are.*"

Cooking practices: practices relating to measuring ingredients varied, with some cooks estimating amounts, making it difficult to assess the amount of salt being used. Sometimes the involvement of many volunteers in preparing food created consistency problems: "*We don't know about the morning cooks how much salt they are putting in now and how much they have reduced but we have reduced it by one big spoonful. We also have written all the instructions given by the dietitian and pasted them in front of the kitchen and the food distribution area so that everybody, including the cooks preparing the food and the congregation, knows what we are doing and what is the purpose of this…*"

Impacts

All of the evaluated places of worship achieved a five percent reduction in salt used in the social cooking, with six achieving twice this target. Among the implications were that healthy eating messages delivered after prayers that fit the religious teaching taking place and which are reinforced by religious elders are more likely to be effective. Information materials that use pictures and samples were also seen to make the messages easier for some groups to remember. In some places of worship, the intervention led to further activity, as one of the cooks explained:

> *"We put a stall at the entrance of gurdwara and everybody who comes in sees us and asks us what we are doing. We distributed pamphlets about healthy eating and common diseases like diabetes, blood pressure, heart problems and people take great interest in it. Also [the dietician] brings the blood pressure machine and we check blood pressure of elderly people which they like very much because it gives them idea how good or bad their health is. Many of them have got high blood pressure and they can't go to GP every week. They can worship, eat the langar and get their blood pressure checked, and ask for advice at the same time… The fact that we do it every week is also very helpful because it serves as a constant reminder…"*

Fig. 1 Social cooking project (reproduced from Zaidi et al. 2008)

The social cooking example illustrates what can be achieved by focusing on the needs of a particular segment. However, the continued development of social marketing segmentation requires that a proactive approach is taken to learning from and adapting commercial marketing ideas. The next section features a commonly used commercial targeting approach which is then adapted for social marketing.

Adapting Commercial Approaches: A Targeting Tool for Social Marketers

Following the identification of segments, the *targeting* stage of the STP segmentation process can commence. This stage involves making choices about which segments to target and which not to address or engage. Most commercial and non-commercial organisations do not have sufficient resources to target all of the available segments. Effective targeting involves addressing how many and which segments should be targeted. Even large corporates such as Ford, Barclays, IBM, Marriott or Carrefour make tough decisions to prioritise some segments over others. This prioritisation involves assessing the attractiveness of particular segments, considering their alignment with objectives, and weighing up the opportunities and returns they offer against the available resources and capabilities. The term "target markets" is used to describe the segments which are identified for future sales and marketing activity.

The systematic process that commercial firms use to assess the attractiveness of segments is equally relevant to social marketing interventions. Just as in commercial settings, social marketers make decisions about the number of segments to target according to the resources available, the organisation's capabilities, the needs and expectations of those within the segments, the requirements of other stakeholders, the nature of the environment in which the program will be delivered, and the performance goals of the intervention. While some will become niche specialists, others might choose to target several segments. Organisations responsible for implementing behaviour change interventions must do the same. A charity providing advice on budgeting for those struggling with their personal finances will need to decide where to focus their efforts. An exercise to segment these individuals using variables such as occupational status, life stage, family size, first language, educational attainment and housing variables will likely identify several potential segments. However, limited resources might mean the charity is only able to develop one set of materials and select one engagement plan, requiring a choice to be made about which segment to prioritise.

Deciding which segments to target requires a systematic assessment of the attractiveness of different options. The literature examining targeting typically focuses on a range of commercial criteria for measuring the attractiveness of particular segments. The term "target market attractiveness" is sometimes used to capture this process of assessment. The firm's existing market share within this target market, the nature of the competitive environment, the commercial opportunity in terms of expected revenue or profitability, and the attractiveness of the segment in relation to future growth, are among the considerations. At first sight, the commercial emphasis of this process and the applied criteria might appear a poor fit with the needs of social marketers. However, applying a systematic approach to allocating resources to target segments is just as relevant to social marketers as it is to their commercial counterparts. Such an analytical process ensures clarity in decision making and fairness in the ultimate selections. The criteria that commercial organisations use to assess segment attractiveness also resonate strongly with the social marketing context. For example, in considering where to target its intervention, a public health body seeking to increase breast feeding rates will need to consider the relative impact of targeting resources at different segments of the community. While it is unlikely to regard them as competitors, the body will likely familiarise itself with other programs or interventions already on offer. The likelihood of the intervention meeting the needs of the different segments will also be considered, as will the need to tailor the scale and positioning of the intervention to fit the available resources.

As this example implies, the criteria that are routinely used by the commercial sector can readily be tailored to the social marketing context. Table 1 captures these criteria, explains their commercial relevance and then shows how they can be adapted. Taking as an example the criterion *capability to meet customer needs,* commercial firms will consider the extent to which their expertise will enable them

Table 1 Social marketing targeting tool

Traditional targeting criterion	Social marketing criterion
Current market share and market homogeneity Firm's knowledge of an existing target market will influence its view as to the relative attractiveness of this market versus others	*Segment relevant expertise* The existing knowledge that the body delivering the program has of delivering programs in this or similar segments will influence its views of the potential to change behaviour
Product expertise In related applications or adjacent markets on which to build	*Social marketing/behaviour change expertise* To the relevant problem, behaviours on which the body can build
Production and marketing scale economies Each targeted segment requires a bespoke marketing program. However certain savings in product development, brand building activity, customer service, logistics, or marketing communications may be available between two or more segments, which might not exist if a different set of segments is prioritised	*Intervention design and delivery—scale economies* While targeted segments will require a tailored intervention, certain savings in developing or promoting the program may be available between two or more segments, which might not exist if a different set of segments is prioritised
Competitive environment One segment may already be well served by one or two very strong competitors, whereas there may be greater opportunity to establish a competitive advantage in a separate segment	*Provider environment* The degree to which the behaviour in question is already tackled within a particular segment by other providers, programs or interventions will shape whether further interventions are needed or other segments are preferred

(continued)

Table 1 (continued)

Traditional targeting criterion	Social marketing criterion
Marketing environment and market trends The external opportunities and threats (economic, social, cultural, legal, regulatory, demographic, and technological) that impact/shape the relative attractiveness of different segments	*Social marketing environment and trends* External factors and trends (economic, social, legal, regulatory, demographic, and technological), and their impact alter the desirability of engaging with certain segments
Capability to meet customer needs The extent to which the expertise of the organisation is synergistic with the requirements of customers in particular segments	*Capability to change behaviour* The extent to which the body seeking to implement an intervention has relevant experience in changing the target behaviour in question
Segment size and growth Some segments may be deemed too small, low spending, or volatile to be attractive	*Size and significance of problem behaviour* The degree to which a particular problem behaviour is impacting upon society or affecting a particular group. The extent/scale of that issue in a segment will direct the segment selection
Available resources The sufficiency of time, money, people and skills to address the segments. Some segments are likely to be resourced ahead of others	*Available resources* The extent to which the necessary time, networks and partnerships, money, people and skills are in place shapes which segments are resourced
Expected profitability, revenue and market share The likely tangible outcomes which can be gained. Ultimately firms must satisfy owners, shareholders and investors about profitability and ROI	*Expected outcomes* The likely behaviour change outcomes and other positive consequences for society. Each stakeholder will have particular expectations and goals

to meet the needs of consumers in a particular segment. For social marketers, this criterion is relabelled *capability to change behaviour*, referring to the degree to which the intervening body has expertise that can readily be applied in this domain.

Social marketers can benefit from using this targeting tool in several ways:

- *Resource allocation accountability*: the tool takes a rational and structured approach to the allocation of resources to segments. Adopting a systematic approach can increase the confidence that resources are being appropriately targeted, providing social marketers with a stronger basis for justifying their decisions. As many of the programs being implemented rely either on public or charitable funds, building in this kind of accountability can be crucial. Following a structured approach, using the checklist in Table 1, can enable these tensions to be negotiated more systematically.
- *Better tailored interventions*: the methodical approach that underpins the targeting tool requires a high level of scrutiny of a range of factors, making it possible to design interventions that are more closely tailored to the needs of the selected segment(s).

- *Meeting stakeholders' needs*: social marketing programs often require different stakeholders to work collaboratively. For example, interventions to improve carbon emissions targets typically involve local government bodies working in conjunction with energy suppliers, charities that support community engagement, community energy groups, bodies promoting sustainability, universities and local SMEs (c.f.: http://www.mksmart.org/). While these stakeholders are working towards a common goal, their different needs, expectations and desired outcomes can cause tension. The social marketing targeting tool provides a practical decision-making framework that helps to work through and ease this tension.

Social Marketing in a Period of Technological Change

The technological and social landscapes in which segmentation is applied are rapidly changing. Advances in data capture, the growth of digital and social media, and developments in analytics have underpinned this transformation. More insights can be generated in relation to how people shop, work, communicate and use their leisure time. In commercial settings, these changes are dramatically increasing the availability of consumer and market insights, with consequences for how segmentation is applied (Simkin 2013). The availability of 'in the moment' market insights is increasing responsiveness to consumer needs and trends. With smartphones and tablets giving 24/7 access to people, even when on the move, the opportunity to interact with them as well as tailor offerings has improved. Ready access to vast quantities of data is allowing segments and offerings to be created more quickly. Segmentation schemes with greater granularity are now expected, so that broad segments, which might have been deemed fit for purpose five years ago, are broken down into micro segments. These developments are helping to make the notion of the "segment of one" a reality in which offerings are tailored for individuals using the principles of mass customisation (Arora et al. 2008; Peppers and Rogers 1994, 2011).

These changes have consequences for social marketing, which has much to gain from better access to detailed data relating to people's behaviour and the factors which drive it. This potential is linked to three features of the changing technological environment: (1) increased data availability; (2) new methods of data capture which, together, provide the raw insights needed for segmentation to proceed; and (3) advances in data analytics, that provide the means by which data are transformed. Each of these features is discussed below.

Data availability The changing ways in which individuals live, work and socialise are increasing the data that is available to inform segmentation approaches. In the past, businesses had to commission market research or sift through customer records to gather insights into the market. This process often took many months and the information was quickly outdated. The rise in internet shopping, the penetration of smartphone usage, and the obsession with social media are responsible for an abundance of readily available data in the digital era. The resulting insights reveal every aspect of consumers' lives: what they like to eat, where they shop, how they spend their leisure time, their preferred means of communication, how and where they like to travel, how they pay, where they are, and with whom they network.

Big data refers to "*data of a very large size, typically to the extent that its manipulation and management present significant logistical challenges*" (Oxford English Dictionary). This term describes the extensive array of instantaneous data that is generated from social media, digital and other sources. Big data is characterised by its *volume* or size, its *variety* in terms of the range of different types, and its *velocity*, reflecting the speed and immediacy with which it is generated. Although using big data is challenging, these characteristics offer considerable potential for supporting the generation of more granular segmentation schemes (Mahadevan 2012).

In some cases, readily available 'in the moment' data can be used in conjunction with traditional segmentation schemes to increase their impact. One example is the UK government's *Change4Life* program (http://www.nhs.uk/Change4Life/) which illustrates how the use of a simple segmentation approach based on life stage can be used to improve health and well-being. The initiative features healthy living advice tailored for adults, young people, families and parents, on a number of behaviour-related themes. These themes are: *Eat Well*, *Move More*, *Drink Less*, *Be Healthier*, *Quit Smoking*, and *Parenting*. Visitors to the website are encouraged to take small and simple steps towards better living, such as becoming more active or cutting down on their alcohol consumption. Although the program is targeted at simple segments, its implementation is supported by a range of "smart tools" geared for particular behaviours. For those worried about their smoking, a downloadable app is available to check their consumption and offer tips on cutting back. Users are provided with feedback on how they are getting on and are encouraged to share their progress through social media. Another app, designed to reduce a family's consumption of sugar, uses sugar cubes to show the amount of sugar that is present in a wide range of foods. Figure 2 provides a snapshot of the *Change4Life* sugar smart tools. The tools include an app, promoted through high profile billboard advertisements outside supermarkets, with the aim of encouraging families to use it to identify sugar in products while shopping. This kind of intervention is only possible because of the integration of smartphones and computer tablets into all aspects of our lives.

Data capture The proliferation of interactive technologies, such as hand-held computers, smart phone apps and in-home sensors, has precipitated a step-change in the gathering of behavioural data. For example, the smart phones that inform every aspect of many consumers' lives operate by capturing "in the moment" intelligence about behaviours, preferences and locations. Among the most popular are apps which give directions based on the user's location to local restaurants, shops, bus depots, and points of historic interest; pinpoint local takeaways and enable the ordering of pizza, chicken chow mein or other favourites; and buy travel, concert or movie tickets. Crucially, for social marketers, this capacity to help people organise routine life tasks can just as easily provide an interface for behaviour change interventions.

The dangers of sugar

The website explains the risk of excess sugar in our diets and points out that kids are consuming more than three times the amount of sugar each day than they should. One can of regular coke contains the equivalent of 9 sugar cubes, which exceeds the total recommended daily amount. Daily allowances are illustrated using sugar cubes:

- 4-6 years old, 19g (equal to 5 sugar cubes)
- 7-10 years old, 24g equal to (6 sugar cubes)
- 11+ years old, 30g (equal to 7 sugar cubes)

How to cut back

Ways of cutting back are offered, including advice on portion sizes and on sugar swops. Advice for breakfast sugar swops include the following:

- switch to less sugary breakfast cereals;
- sweeten plain cereals or porridge with chopped banana or berries and low-fat plain yoghurt;
- instead of using jam and chocolate spread on toast, try mashed banana or berries;
- mix porridge oats with fruit and yoghurt, then refrigerate overnight, ready to eat the next morning

At the supermarket

Shoppers are encouraged to check packaging for the colour-coded food labels that show amounts of sugar and to check the ingredients as well. The Sugar Smart app, which is simple enough for kids to use, can be downloaded onto smart phones and used when shopping to scan and show how many sugar cubes products contain.

Fig. 2 Change4Life sugar smart tools (reproduced from https://www.nhs.uk/change4life-beta/campaigns/sugar-smart/sugar-facts)

The commercial potential of these interactive technologies is already being captured through the development of behaviour change apps, including those which promote health and fitness. *RunKeeper* is a smartphone app that measures fitness, enabling individuals to monitor their performance and progress over time. The app keeps track of activities including running, cycling and hiking, monitoring the distance travelled and sets customised goals for users based on their overall fitness aims. Tracking progress towards these goals provides users with positive reinforcement which motivates them to continue with their activities. Similarly, those seeking to lose weight can turn to a host of slimming apps such as *Diet Assistant*, which offers diet plans according to users' weight loss targets, tastes and lifestyles.

Although the commercial health and well-being fields have been quick to exploit these data capture tools, latent potential exists to use these interactive technologies in formative social marketing research and in the design of interventions and evaluations. Those on low incomes, for example, could be supported by tools to better manage their household budget, with immediate feedback showing the effect of unplanned purchases on the weekly budget. Individuals who are worried about their alcohol intake could keep track of their weekly consumption, receiving prompts when they are close to daily or weekly limits, along with suggestions for alcohol-free or low-alcohol alternatives.

Nudge	Drawing on GPS location tracking, an app picks up when an individual enters a shopping area, then nudges a reminder of the household bills that are due for payment or flags if a credit card limit is near to being reached. In segmentation terms, this approach is treating the user as a "segment of one".
Education program	Practical education programs – grounded in the notion of deliberative decision making and delivered via the smartphone – could offer guidance on personal finances, including demonstrating how to set up a household budget or offering information on the rules around personal pensions.
Social norms	Data gathered from particular regional areas or a cultural group is the basis for a social norm intervention that provides consumers with comparative data on spending patterns. Insights could include the spending norms for similar families, for those working in similar occupations or located in similar areas.

Fig. 3 Interventions to manage personal finances

The interactivity of these technologies, which enables social marketers to capture data about behaviour and then intervene, is powerful on several fronts. Firstly, it counters the criticism that social marketing research is over-reliant on self-reported behaviour (Kubacki et al. 2015). Secondly, it embraces a call for researchers to develop more creative methods of data gathering (Gordon and Gurrieri 2014; Lefebvre 2012), providing fertile ground for implementing a wide range of psychological and sociological behaviour change approaches. Interventions designed to reduce personal debt, for example, could be designed around deliberative conscious views of decision making (Ajzen 1991), the use of social norms (Burchell et al. 2013; Thomas and Sharp 2013), or simple "nudge" approaches (Darnton 2008; Thaler and Sunstein 2008). As Fig. 3 shows, the use of segmentation can be tailored to fit the needs of each intervention type. The nudge intervention treats the app user as a "segment of one", responding to his/her location at a particular point in time and personal spending pattern; the education program is likely to adopt simple segmentation based on demographic and socio-economic variables; and the social norms approach will match the user with those with similar demographics and lifecycle profile.

Lifelogging is a more extreme version of this kind of data capture (Roderick 2013), with potential to underpin social marketing interventions. The method uses digital tools to automatically record all aspects of an individual's daily activity (Sellen and Whittaker 2010). Technologies including smart phone apps, wearable sensors and GPS location tracking devices enable the efficient collection of "*... cognitive, behavioural, and affective phenomena as they occur in natural settings and in, or near real-time*" (Cohn et al. 2011, p. 1). The reliability of the gathered data, its cost effectiveness, the immediacy with which it is available, and its ability to relate behaviours to a particular context offer great promise for developing a deeper understanding of behaviour. As data are gathered continuously over a long timeframe, a more holistic view can be achieved and atypical behaviours captured (Cohn et al. 2011). Furthermore, it becomes possible to understand the time-sequencing of behavioural antecedents and the associated outcomes, such as

Mel is 28 and living with her partner in an apartment on the edge of city. Recently she has been on a fitness and healthy eating drive. As part of this plan she has reduced how much she travels by car, is cycling and walking more, and takes the bus to avoid driving. Mel is using a smart phone app to log her movements so that she can assess the progress she is making. The app records how many steps she takes, how far she has walked or cycled, and the distance she has travelled. She also uses it to record what and when she eats, so that she can build up a broader profile of her fitness. Although it was not the reason that Mel subscribed to it, the app also reports the sustainability of her travel and eating choices.

After walking to the bus stop on Monday morning, Mel is soon on board the electric bus that transports her to work. On the way, she uses her smartphone to compare her activity levels with other women in the area of a similar age and socio-economic background. A comparison of the sustainability of her travel choice is also shown. Mel realises that her activity levels are within the top ten per cent for her group and is pleased that her efforts over recent weeks have improved her fitness. She feels satisfied that her decision to stop travelling to work by car means that her travel behaviour is more sustainable.

Spurred on by the positive feedback, when she gets to work Mel decides to take the stairs instead of the lift and even contemplates cycling to work tomorrow. At lunch time, she uses her smartphone to scan her sandwich pack and juice bottle, capturing their nutritional and calorific values. The app instantly offers several healthy suggestions for dessert, showing the impact of each option on Mel's daily calorie consumption. Although Mel decides to skip dessert for now, she knows that the data will be available for her to peruse on her tablet when she returns home. She can always have some ice-cream then instead!

Fig. 4 New technology, new insights, new interventions (reproduced from Dibb 2013)

what triggers an alcoholic to engage in a drinking binge, or the factors which lead someone in debt to seek further credit. The interactive capacity of the technologies used, which enable the gathering and transmission of information, bolsters their potential for delivering social marketing interventions. The profile in Fig. 4 shows how such insights can act as trigger points for intervening.

Analytics The ability to manipulate data sets has been transformed by advances in analytics, which enable complex algorithms and data processing methods to bring together diverse data types (e.g. Haider et al. 2012; Sambandam 2009). For example, developments in sentiment analysis are allowing the emotions behind social media postings to be extracted and characterised. The analysis assesses the "polarity" of the material by gauging whether a positive, negative or neutral opinion is being offered. The emotional states underlying the text, such as whether the source is happy, angry, sad or excited, can also be assessed (e.g. Kiritchenko et al. 2014). Businesses are using this approach to gauge reactions among different market segments to new service offerings, product modifications, or even the redesign of a trusted logo (Henschen 2012). Similarly, there is potential for social marketing practitioners to understand the emotional reactions of different groups to particular kinds of interventions, so that these can be tailored accordingly.

The capacity to draw together multiple levels of data combinations within the city setting, is an exciting development that offers huge potential for tackling urban

Improving Sustainability

Against a backdrop of rising energy bills and concerns about climate change, interest in living more sustainably is growing. Community energy projects are one way of bringing people together to generate or save energy. These projects range from group buying of home insulation to the generation of renewable electricity or heat, using solar panels, wind turbines, or heat pumps (see http://www.roughguide.to/communityenergy/).

The *Community Action Platform for Energy* (*CAPE*) is one of a number of resources that support community energy projects (http://capeproject.co.uk/). The *CAPE* website will provide access to a digital platform that brings communities together with approved local suppliers, the local authority, funding options and the necessary legal advice. By applying advanced urban analytics to energy data, socio-economic data, and satellite and aerial survey data, the website will enable communities to depict how much energy they can save through energy saving or generation projects. Among the benefits users can gain are a reduction in carbon footprint, the generation of income that can be ploughed back into the community, a lessening of fuel poverty, the creation of local jobs and support for local SMEs.

In order to support community energy projects, the website must meet the needs of several different segments of users: communities, individuals, landlords, the local authority and local suppliers. For example, local insulation or solar PV suppliers need access to individuals or communities requiring installation, while landlords need access to suppliers and funding. The website is designed to route these different user groups to the information and resources they need.

Local Security and Crime

Security and crime in city settings are difficult issues to tackle that can benefit from insights that are generated by combining open and other data sources. For example, the use of hotspot mapping, in which predictions about future crime are based on patterns of historic incidents, has been popular with the police and security agencies (Chaineya et al. 2008). Advances in data ability and analytics are now leading to more sophisticated approaches that are less reliant on human judgement than methods used in the past. The curation of local crime statistics, detailing the type, frequency and severity of incidents, geo-demographic data, insights from social media and individual-level smartphone data, can provide a rich overview of security issues in a particular area. Applications have been developed that use social media to share information about safety concerns and unreported crimes (Furtado et al. 2010) and web based tools that are able to pinpoint unsafe areas (The Guardian 2011). One application, *iSafe*, uses a participatory sensing approach in which smartphone users report their impressions of safety in their current location to build a picture of safety level in their local area (Ballesteros et al. 2012). An algorithm combines and aggregates 'real-time snapshots' from co-located users with historic crime data relating to their current locations. Individuals might use this information to decide whether or not to go to a particular city location and the best route for travelling there safely.

Fig. 5 Intervening in the smart city setting

problems and improving well-being. In these settings, open data, social media analytics, sensor data and citizen data can be brought together through a common technological platform (d'Aquin et al. 2015). Different kinds of sensors can be linked into the data infrastructure, gathering real-time data on issues including travel behaviour and congestion, patterns of energy usage, use of local services, local security issues, and patterns of healthcare. Thus it has become possible to build city data ecosystems which use personal and household technologies to gather data from citizens and communities and then bring that data together with other data sources. These data assemblages have the potential to support behaviour change research, interventions and evaluations that apply the full spectrum of individual social-psychological and societal-level behaviour change approaches.

Behavioural data gathered via a range of technologies (including in-home panels, mobile phones and apps) can be used to examine how a strategic approach to behaviour change to tackle urban problems and improve well-being can be developed as part of an integrated city system. Although the ability to capture and manipulate data within this context makes it possible to deliver programs tailored at the individual level, as Fig. 5 shows, simple forms of segmentation can also work well. The first describes an interactive website that helps citizens to set up sustainable community energy projects. The data infrastructure underpinning the website uses advanced analytics to integrate a variety of open and other data sources. Those using the website gain access to the insights and services provided through tabs that are designed for broadly defined segments: individual citizens, community groups, suppliers and landlords. The website uses complex analytics that are tailored to a particular situation in conjunction with a simple segmentation scheme. The second example, which focuses on reducing crime and increasing security, adopts a "segment of one" approach by providing users with information that is specifically tailored to a particular location at a particular time. They can use this information to inform their decisions about whether to travel to a certain area and how to travel there.

Conclusion

There are rich opportunities for social marketing to develop its segmentation practices. Taking the chapter as whole, several implications emerge for social marketing practitioners:

- Social marketing practitioners need a mindset in which they take greater responsibility for their own segmentation practices. This mindset requires a combination of greater learning and borrowing from commercial marketing and taking the lead in developing new methods and practices.
- Simple segmentation schemes, which group individuals using only a few dimensions, have a role to play alongside those geared towards the "segment of one". While technology is making it easier to understand individual needs and behaviours, simple segmentation can readily be used alongside more tailored approaches.
- Interactive technologies have the potential to bring together formative social marketing research and interventions, so that the gathering of behavioural data is quickly followed by fast intervention responses. Social marketing practitioners

should explore creative ways to build this capability into their behaviour change programs.

- The capacity to curate different data sets within the smart city setting supports a more holistic view of the fit of behaviours within people's lifestyles. Rather than focusing on a single behaviour, such as increasing the amount of exercise taken, cutting down sugar intake, or reducing alcohol consumption, it is feasible to intervene across several behaviours at once.
- Social marketers implementing segmentation schemes face similar implementation barriers to commercial marketers. These include shortfalls in resources such as data, financial resources, and suitably skilled personnel, poor use of methods or badly designed segmentation processes, and poor fit between segment needs and developed program skills. Anticipating the likely barriers at the outset of a segmentation project dramatically increases the likelihood that they can be addressed.

References

Ajzen, I. (1991). The theory of planned behavior. *Organizational Behavior and Human Decision Processes, 50*(2), 179–211.

Andreasen, A. R. (2002). Marketing social marketing in the social change marketplace. *Journal of Public Policy & Marketing, 21*(1), 3–13.

Andreasen, A. R. (2012). Rethinking the relationship between social/non-profit marketing and commercial marketing. *Journal of Public Policy & Marketing, 31*(1), 36–41.

Arora, N., Dreze, X., Ghose, A., Hess, J. D., Iyengar, R., Jing, B., et al. (2008). Putting one-to-one marketing to works: Personalization, customization, and choice. *Marketing Letters, 19*, 305–321.

Ballesteros, J., Rahman, M., Carbunar, B., & Rishe, N. (2012). Safe cities. A participatory sensing approach. In *IEEE 37th Conference Local Computer Networks (LCN)* (pp. 626–634).

Bloom, P. N., & Novelli, W. D. (1981). Problems and challenges in social marketing. *Journal of Marketing, 45*(2), 79–88.

Burchell, K., Rettie, R., & Patel, K. (2013). Marketing social norms: Social marketing and the 'social norm approach'. *Journal of Consumer behaviour, 12*, 1–9.

Chaineya, S., Tompson, L., & Uhlig, S. (2008). The utility of hotspot mapping for predicting spatial patterns of crime. *Security Journal, 21*, 4–28.

Cohn, A. M., Hunter-Reel, D., Hagman, B. T., & Mitchell, J. (2011). Promoting behaviour change from alcohol use through mobile technology: The future of ecological momentary assessment. *Alcoholism, Clinical and Experimental Research, 35*(12), 2209–2215.

d'Aquin, M., Davies, J., & Motta, E. (2015). Smart cities' data: Challenges and opportunities for semantic technologies. In *IEEE Internet Computing* (November–December) (pp. 67–70).

Darnton, A. (2008). *Practical guide: An overview of behaviour change models and their uses.* London: HM Treasury, Crown Copyright, Government Social Research Unit.

Dibb, S. (2013). The emergence of new domains for segmentation—The rapid rise of non-commercial applications. In L. Simkin (Ed.), *To boardrooms and sustainability: The changing nature of segmentation* (p. 37). Henley White Paper, Henley Business School.

Dibb, S. (2014). Up, up and away: Social marketing breaks free. *Journal of Marketing Management, 30*(11/12), 1159–1185.

Dibb, S., & Carrigan, M. (2013). Editorial: Social marketing transformed—Kotler, Polonsky and Hastings reflect on social marketing in a period of social change. *European Journal of Marketing, 47*(9), 1376–1398.
Dibb, S., & Simkin, L. (2001). Market segmentation: Diagnosing and overcoming the segmentation barriers. *Industrial Marketing Management, 30*, 609–625.
Dibb, S., & Simkin, L. (2008). *Market segmentation success: Making it happen!*. New York: The Haworth Press/Routledge.
Donovan, R., & Henley, N. (2003). *Social marketing: Principles and practice*. Melbourne: IP Communications.
French, J. (2011). Why nudging is not enough. *Journal of Social Marketing, 1*(2), 154–162.
French, J., & Gordon, R. (2015). *Strategic social marketing*. London: Sage.
Furtado, V., Ayres, L., de Oliveira, M., Vasconcelos, E., Caminha, C., DOrleans, J., et al. (2010). Collective intelligence in law enforcement: The wikicrimes system. *Information Sciences, 180* (1), 4–17.
Gordon, R., & Gurrieri, L. (2014). Towards a reflexive turn: Social marketing assemblages. *Journal of Social Marketing, 4*(3), 261–278.
Gummesson, E. (1991). Marketing-orientation revisited: The crucial role of the part-time marketer. *European Journal of Marketing, 25*(2), 60–75.
Haider, P., Chiarandini, L., & Brefeld, U. (2012). Discriminant clustering for market segmentation: *KDD'12*. https://www.informatik.tu-darmstadt.de/fileadmin/user_upload/Group_KMA/kma_publications/kdd2012.pdf. Accessed August 12–16, 2015.
Hassan, S., & Craft, S. (2012). Examining world market segmentation and brand positioning strategies. *Journal of Consumer Marketing, 29*(5), 344–356.
Hastings, G. (2007). *Social marketing: Why should the devil have all the best tunes*. London: Routledge.
Hastings, G. (2013). Marketing as if people mattered. In S. Dibb & M. Carrigan (Eds.), *Social marketing transformed—Kotler, Polonsky and Hastings reflect on social marketing in a period of social change* (pp. 1388–1393). *European Journal of Marketing, 47*(9).
Henschen, D. (2012). Sentiment analysis: How companies now listen to the web. *Information week: Healthcare*. http://www.informationweek.com/it-leadership/sentiment-analysis-how-companies-now-listen-to-the-web/d/d-id/1104836
Johnson, E. S., Shu, G., Dellaert, C., Fox, D., Goldstein, G., Haubl, R., et al. (2012). Beyond nudges: Tools of a choice architecture. *Marketing Letters, 23*, 487–504.
Kiritchenko, S., Zhu, X., & Mohammad, S. M. (2014). Sentiment analysis of short informal texts. *Journal of Artificial Intelligence Research, 50*, 723–762.
Kubacki, K., Rundle-Thiele, S., Pang, B., & Buyucek, N. (2015). Minimizing alcohol harm: A systematic social marketing review (2000–2014). *Journal of Business Research, 68*(10), 2214–2222.
Lefebvre, R. C. (2012). Transformative social marketing: Co-creating the social marketing discipline and brand. *Journal of Social Marketing, 2*(2), 118–129.
Liu, Y., Kiang, M., & Brusco, M. (2012). A unified framework for market segmentation and its applications. *Expert Systems with Applications: An International Journal Archive, 39*(11), 10292–10302.
Mahadevan, M. (2012). CMO strategy: Big data makes segmentation more complex but not less crucial. http://adage.com/article/cmo-strategy/big-data-makes-segmentation-complex-crucial/234548/
Neiger, B., Thackeray, R., Barnes, M., & McKenzie, J. (2003). Positioning social marketing in a planning process for health education. *American Journal of Health Studies, 18*(2/3), 75–80.
Newton, J. D., Newton, F., Turk, T., & Ewing, M. T. (2013). Ethical evaluation of audience segmentation in social marketing. *European Journal of Marketing, 47*(9), 1421–1438.
Peattie, S., & Peattie, K. (2003). Ready to fly solo? Reducing social marketing's dependence on commercial marketing theory. *Marketing Theory, 3*(3), 365–385.
Peppers, D., & Rogers, M. (1994). *The one to one future*. London: Piakus.
Peppers, D., & Rogers, M. (2011). *Managing customer relationships*. New Jersey: Wiley.

Roderick, L. (2013). Real-time marketing: Eight ways to make real-time marketing work for you. *The marketer*. http://www.themarketer.co.uk/how-to/tips-and-guides/8-ways-to-make-real-time-marketing-work-for-you/

Rothschild, M. L. (2001). Ethical considerations in the use of marketing for the management of public health and social issues. In A. R. Andreasen (Ed.), *Ethics in social marketing* (pp. 17–38). Washington D.C.: Georgetown University Press.

Sambandam, R. (2009). How to improve segmentation with max-diff. *Quirk's marketing research review*. http://www.trchome.com/docs/pdf-files/11-how-to-improve-segmentation-with-maxdiff/file

Sellen, A., & Whittaker, S. (2010). Beyond total capture: A constructive critique of lifelogging. *Communications of the ACM, 53*(5), 70–77.

Simkin, L. (2013). *To boardrooms and sustainability: The changing nature of segmentation* (p. 37). Henley White Paper: Henley Business School.

Tapp, A., & Spotswood, F. (2013). From the 4 Ps to COM-SM: Reconfiguring the social marketing mix. *Journal of Social Marketing, 3*(3), 206–222.

Thaler, R. H., & Sunstein, C. R. (2008). *Nudge: Improving decisions about health, wealth, and happiness*. New Haven: Yale University Press.

The Guardian. (2011). *UK riots: Every verified incident*. http://www.guardian.co.uk/news/datablog/2011/aug/09/uk-riots-incident-listed-mapped

Thomas, C., & Sharp, V. (2013). Understanding the normalisation of recycling behaviour and its implications for other pro-environmental behaviours: A review of social norms and recycling. *Resources, Conservation and Recycling, 79*, 11–20.

Wedel, M., & Kamakura, A. (2000). *Market segmentation: Conceptual and methodological foundations*. Boston, MA: Kluwer Academic.

Wells, V. K., Chang, S. W., Oliveira-Castro, J. M., & Pallister, J. (2010). Market segmentation from a behavioural perspective. *Journal of Organisational Behaviour Management, 30*(2), 145–175.

Wind, Y. (1978). Issues and advances in segmentation research. *Journal of Marketing Research, 15*(August), 317–337.

Zaidi, Q., Govindji, A., & Ali, H. A. (2008). Social cooking project. Report commissioned by Food Standards Agency. London: Food Standards Agency.

How and Why Segmentation Improves ROI

Nancy R. Lee

Abstract The advantages to selecting and appealing to a priority target audience segment are similar to the advantages of knowing what kind of fish you want to catch when you head out on a fishing trip. (1) First, you'll know what *bait* to use. Knowledge about the segment's unique demographics, psychographics, geographics, related behaviours, stage of change, barriers to overcome, and benefits to promise will inspire a unique offer, one where p*roduct, price* and p*lace* strategies are "custom" designed to appeal to the segment you want to attract. (2) Second, you'll know what kind of *hook* will help "seal the deal". Knowledge about what appeals most to your target audience about your offer will help craft persuasive *messages*, choose credible *messengers*, and develop engaging *creative elements*. (3) Third, you'll know *where* to go to find them. Knowledge about the unique *media* channels that the target audience uses will help you select those channels most likely to reach the greatest numbers, with the least amount of expenditures. (4) Fourth, you'll know *when* they are typically looking for food. Knowledge about unique openings for the segment will inspire the frequency and timing of media placement and selection of the most effective decision points, or situations, when the target audience is most likely to be tempted by your offer and persuaded by *promotional* messages. In the end, by tailoring the 4Ps for an attractive market segment, not only will you "catch more of the fish you want most", you will accomplish this with less time and money, therefore increasing your return on investment (ROI). This chapter will describe each of the four unique advantages in more detail and will then outline the steps involved in calculating a ROI for your efforts. A hypothetical example using diabetes prevention will be used to illustrate the application of the 4Ps. In addition, a brief case story for each of the 4Ps will illustrate how strategies can (and should) be targeted to the unique profile of a target audience. It should be acknowledged that the 4P model used in this chapter is based on the traditional commercial marketing "labels" for the major tools in the marketer's toolbox—ones available to the marketer to influence a target audience to buy their product. Labels, descriptions and the number of tools that social marketers

N.R. Lee (✉)
Social Marketing Services Inc., University of Washington, Seattle, USA

T. Dietrich et al. (eds.), *Segmentation in Social Marketing*
DOI 10.1007/978-981-10-1835-0_5

use to influence target audience behaviours can vary (Peattie and Peattie 2003; Tapp and Spotswood 2013).

How Segmentation Inspires the Offer: Product, Price, and Place Strategies

Based on the distinct profile of a target audience (e.g. sedentary seniors diagnosed with prediabetes), and a specific desired behaviour selected for this audience (e.g. walking 30 min a day), we develop a customised offer that will decrease this audience's unique barriers (e.g. feelings of isolation, sedentary habits, and access to safe and convenient walking trails), and provide them with their priority desired benefit (e.g. diabetes prevention), one they want in exchange for adopting the behaviour. The offer is created using three major tools described in the following sections, including a brief case story on how an offer was inspired by the unique characteristics of a target audience.

Product In social marketing, the product consists of goods and/or services that "help" the target audience perform the desired behaviour. We have three decisions to make regarding the product platform. The first is to identify the "core product", the major benefit this audience wants in exchange for performing the behaviour (e.g. diabetes prevention). Next we select or develop the "actual product", a tangible good or service that we want the target audience to acquire and/or utilise (e.g. a Fitbit to track minutes exercising each day). Third, we explore opportunities for "augmented products", additional elements that might be needed to provide encouragement (e.g. an organised group of walking buddies), and/or remove barriers (e.g. a map of walking trails in a community).

Product Case Story (Lee and Kotler 2015, pp. 280–282)

In 2011, Christopher Charles, a Ph.D. grad student at the University of Guelph in Canada, did a "deep dive" in Cambodia, one with an intention to discover what would influence a unique target audience (women who prepared meals for their families with anaemia) to put a chunk of iron in their food pots. He learned they had not responded positively to the two product ideas tested to date, one a small circle of iron, and the other, one shaped like a lotus flower. His ethnographic research efforts focused on cultural values and beliefs, revealing that the local river fish were believed to be lucky. A new iron piece in the shape of a fish about 3–4 in. long was then designed, large enough to provide about 75 % of the daily iron requirement, yet small enough to be stirred easily. It turned out the women were happy to place the lucky iron-shaped fish in the pots and in the months that followed, iron levels in the village began to climb.

How, then, does designing a product or service to appeal to a priority target segment increase ROI? It's very similar to commercial marketing. A product that meets the unique wants and needs of a target audience will increase the uptake (sales) within that segment, often with less promotional expenditures to achieve adequate reach and frequency. And if the features of the product or service increases perceived value of the exchange, other variables (e.g. monetary incentives) might even be reduced, lowering the cost per sale, therefore increasing the ROI (Farris et al. 2010).

Price The price tool is used to provide monetary and/or non-monetary incentives to decrease unique barriers and increase the desired benefits the target audience associates with performing the behaviour. Monetary incentives may be in the form of cash rewards, discounts or rebates. Non-monetary incentives are most often in the form of recognition, praise and commitments. Back to the diabetes example, a price strategy for this target audience could include a coupon for the Fitbit (monetary incentive), a Fitbit "Yippee" message of congratulations when daily goals are met (non-monetary incentive), and a pledge to a healthcare provider to walk 30 min a day (non-monetary incentive).

Price Case Story (Lee and Kotler 2015, pp. 286–289)

In the Philippines in 2009, a partnership between Innovations for Poverty Action and the Green Bank of Caraga tested several pricing strategies to reduce tobacco use in the country. One particular strategy was inspired by their unique target audience, smokers wanting to quit in order to save money. Those interested signed a contract and opened a savings account with an initial deposit of about US$1. They were encouraged to deposit the money normally spent on cigarettes into this account each week for six months. If, at the six-month milestone, a nicotine test proved that the client was "tobacco free", the entire savings would be given back to the smoker. If not, it would be donated to charity. Authors of the study concluded that this commitment strategy was an effective treatment, when compared with other strategies such as nicotine replacement therapy. They further concluded that the program would pass a return on investment test, taking into consideration a cost per quit in comparison to alternative strategies, employer costs, health improvements, and increases in quality-adjusted years of life.

How, then, does selecting a pricing strategy that has unique appeal for a target audience segment increase ROI? It's the exchange principle. If the target audience sees benefits that outweigh the cost, they are more likely to "buy" the behaviour, again reducing promotional expenditures, perhaps even requiring less resources required for alternative product-related and place-related strategies.

Place The place tool is used to increase convenience of access, as well as the ambiance of the location where the target audience will perform the desired behaviour, acquire any goods, and/or receive any related services. As would be expected, perceptions of convenience and ambiance will be "in the eye of the beholder" with varying preferences based especially on audience demographics, geographics and psychographics. Back to our diabetes prevention example, the chosen target audience was identified as seniors concerned about the ease of access to convenient and safe walking trails, with an implication that those trails featured in the walking map should be ones meeting these expectations; the suggested commitment to the healthcare provider would likely be most convenient at the time of a health exam; and the access to the walking buddy group would most likely be over the phone, internet, or at the desk at a partnering community centre.

Place Case Story (Lee and Kotler 2015, pp. 325–326)

In 2004, the headline of an article in the *Chicago Tribune* read "*Rapid HIV Tests Offered Where Those At Risk Gather: Seattle Health Officials Get Aggressive in AIDS Battle by Heading Into Gay Clubs, Taking a Drop Of Blood and Providing Answers in 20 min.*" This strategy for a unique target audience (men who were at risk of HIV who frequented gay clubs) relied heavily on the place tool: bringing the tests to the gay clubs versus needing to make a special visit to a clinic, and providing results and counselling within 20 min at the same location, versus historic procedures requiring an appointment and a visit to a community clinic a week later. New positive case findings were at a rate of 2.1 %, double the 1 % rate considered cost effective.

How then does convenience of access increase ROI? As noted in this example, different segments have different "definitions" of convenience. By appealing to the unique situation and access preferences of your priority audience, more of them will be likely to adopt the desired behaviour, therefore the "cost per sale".

How Segmentation Inspires Promotional Messages, Messengers, Media Channels

Promotion Promotions are persuasive communications, and the promotional tool is the one we count on to inspire the target audience to action. It is used to highlight product features; shout out about any incentives; ensure the target audience knows where and when to access any goods and services; and to schedule communications at a place and time when this audience is open to considering a behaviour change. There are five major decisions to be made regarding promotions: messages, messengers, creative elements, media channels and their timing and frequency. Each of these are inspired by the unique profile of the target audience.

Messages Messages are informed by a clear understanding of what you want your audience to Do, Know and Believe. These, of course, will vary by target audience segment and based on answers to several questions. First and foremost, what specific, desired behaviour will be the call to action message (e.g. walk 30 min a day)? What does this audience need to know about the offer (e.g. where to buy a Fitbit, get a map of walking trails, and how to join a walking group)? What beliefs unique to this audience segment need to be addressed to ensure adoption (e.g. what evidence exists that by doing walking 30 min a day I will decrease the chances I will get diabetes)?

Message Case Story (Lee and Kotler 2015, pp. 260–264)

In 2004, the American Society for the Prevention of Cruelty to Animals (ASPCA) launched a new program to increase adoption of animals in shelters. They chose a clear audience segment, those wanting to find a dog or cat that met their unique wants and needs—a benefit sought segmentation variable. This focus inspired the development of an innovative strategy, one that involved a scientific match of a shelter dog's personality, traits, and behaviour characteristic with the traits and characteristics of a potential adopter. The program was branded Meet Your Match® and involved an assessment by shelter personnel of the shelter animals that placed them into one of nine "personality" types. Potential adopters answered an 18 question survey that then revealed which of the animal personality types would be their best match. In the end, participating shelters achieved increased gains in adoption, often reaching 15–40 % greater.

Messengers The messenger is who your target audiences perceives to be delivering your messages, with major options including the sponsor of the effort, partners, spokespersons, endorsements, midstream audiences, and/or a mascot. Three criteria often cited for selecting the most credible messenger are perceived *trustworthiness, expertise* and *likability* (Lee and Kotler 2015). Most importantly, perceptions on each of these criteria will vary by target audience. The seniors with prediabetes in our ongoing example might be most inspired to action by the American Medical Association, perceiving their expertise to be more objective and scientific-based than a fitness instructor, entertainer, or a close friend.

Messenger Case Story

The Teen Aware Project in Washington State has allocated grants to public high schools for development of efforts to promote sexual abstinence. One of the criteria for the grants is that the campaigns be youth-driven, helping to ensure messages and messengers will be credible with target audiences. One high school group, for example, interviewed middle school students to explore what they perceived to be the major benefits of postponing having sex. Their findings clearly reflected the uniqueness of the target audience. The middle school students were more concerned about "crabs" than HIV/AIDS, and more turned off by thoughts of the pain of childbirth than getting pregnant. Students were clear that the best, most credible messengers would be "fellow teens" and not the Office of Superintendent of Public Instruction, the funding sponsor of the effort.

Creative elements Creative elements include everything from logos, typeface, taglines, headlines, copy, visuals, and colours in printed materials, to script, actors, scenes, and sounds in broadcast mediums (Lee and Kotler 2015). Decisions regarding each of these elements are clearly driven by the unique preferences of the target audience, or at least they should be. Visuals and slogans that will resonate with the prediabetic, sedentary seniors and motivate them to walk 30 min a day will certainly be different than ones to motivate a young mom recently diagnosed with prediabetes. One classic principle relative to creative elements suggests that your target audience should be able to "see themselves" in your communication, signalling it is something "meant for them". The following case story illustrates this well.

Creative Elements Case Story

In 2012, an estimated 15 % of 10th graders in Pierce County in Washington State used alternative tobacco products, including Hookah, cigars, candy flavoured tobacco, cigarillos, e-cigarettes and chew (Tacoma-Pierce County Health Department 2015). Research indicates that these alternative tobacco products were perceived by youth to be much less harmful than cigarettes. To knock down these "myth barriers" Tacoma-Pierce County Health Department created a campaign to increase awareness about the risks of these substitute products. They branded it *Suck On This* with messages giving users '*something to think about*'

"One hour of hookah is equivalent to 150 cigarettes."

"One cigar may contain as much tobacco as an entire pack of cigarettes and has the same toxic cancer compounds found in cigarettes."

(*see* Fig. 1).

Media channels Media channels are where your communications appear. Broad categories include: advertising, public relations, printed materials, special promotional items, signage and displays, personal selling, social media, websites, and popular/entertainment media. Given this component of a campaign budget often represents the greatest proportion of expenses, selecting channels utilised most frequently by your target audience will give you the "biggest bang for your bucks". Not only do the broad categories vary in usage by target audience, specific channels within these categories will vary as well (e.g. with prediabetic seniors more likely to read newspapers and magazines, and the younger mothers more likely to turn to websites and social media to learn more).

Fig. 1 "Suck on This" (reproduced from Tacoma-Pierce County Health Department 2015)

Media Channel Case Story

Consider an effort to protect water quality, with a focus on influencing households with dogs as pets to not only "scoop the poop" in their yards, but to then bag it and place it in the garbage versus a compost pile or burying it in the backyard. One media strategy would be to select a channel (a free one, by the way) that would be easily seen by next door neighbours—i.e. the tops of garbage cans. A sticker with the words "*We scoop, bag it and place it in the trash*" could be given to households currently doing the desired behaviour to place on the lids of their curb-side garbage containers. This social norming strategy would not only increase perceptions that others are engaged in the behaviour and spread the idea to other pet owners around the neighbourhood, it would have an additional benefit of forewarning the garbage collectors as they dump the container (see Fig. 2).

Fig. 2 Using a garbage container as a media channel for the puget sound starts here campaign

How Segmentation Inspires Timing and Frequency of Communications

Media timing and frequency Media timing and frequency refers to when and how often your communications appear in selected media channels, with decisions based on unique characteristics of your target audience. When your target audience will be most open to communications regarding your desired behaviour will understandably vary by segments. The seniors diagnosed with prediabetes, for example, might be most interested in joining a walking group right after attending a community event announcing the new program. How often this audience will need to be exposed to the communication in order to be persuaded is influenced by such factors as stage of change and competing behaviours, ones that vary by audience segment.

Timing Case Story (Lee and Kotler 2015, pp. 379–381)

The timing of communication efforts of The Australian Red Cross Blood Service in 2011–2013 to increase blood donations varied by three distinct target audiences:

(1) The "Recharge Your Karma" campaign targeting university students focused on persuading potential donors to book an appointment for when Donor mobiles would arrive on campus. Teaser events *prior to the*

arrival of the mobile were supported with a social media campaign encouraging students to talk about their blood donation opportunities on Facebook and take photos and forward them to their friends via their mobile device.

(2) Soup, an agency in Australia specialising in word of mouth communications, developed a campaign for the Australian Red Cross Blood Service that targeted 30–54 year old engaged influencers, described as those who were well connected, and had not donated in the past five years. Over a period of a month they were encouraged to *make a donation and to then "immediately" reach out* on social media to friends and family to encourage them to do the same.

(3) A third effort branded "Battle of the Burbs" challenged residents and city councils in suburbs in Brisbane to compete to see which had the biggest heart. Promotional messages using traditional media were aired over a *six week period* of time, with the winner being the Victorian town with the highest percentage of residents donating during the six-week timeframe.

Frequency Case Story (CDC 2015)

In 2010, the National Healthy Mothers, Healthy Babies Coalition in the US, in partnership with the Centres for Disease Control and Prevention, launched Text4baby, a free cell phone text messaging service designed for pregnant women and the first year of their baby's life. Content of the messages are timed to the pregnant woman's due date and/or the baby's date of birth, and are available in English and Spanish. Messages are sent *three times a week* with information on how to have a healthy pregnancy and a healthy baby, with messages providing tips on topics including: breastfeeding, car seat safety, developmental milestones, emotional well-being, exercise and fitness, immunisations, labour and delivery, nutrition, prenatal care and safe sleep. In the first two years, over 281,000 enrolled in the program, with 96 % of enrollees reporting they would recommend the service to a friend.

How then does developing promotional strategies (messages, messengers, creative elements, media channels and timing) that appeal to your target audience increase ROI? It's simple. Promotional expenditures are often evaluated based on the cost per acquisition. Promotional budgets are divided by the number of sales, providing a metric that can be compared to historic as well as targeted goals. Campaigns that base their promotional strategy on the unique desired benefits and lifestyle preferences of their target audience segment are likely to have lower costs per acquisition.

How Segmentation Increases Return on Investment (ROI)

ROI defined. In the "business world" ROI is often described as the quantifiable benefit the investor receives as a result of an investment of some resource, with a simplistic formula being one that divides net profit or net income by total costs or expenses. Determining and reporting on ROI has several benefits for a social marketer. First, it can provide a solid rationale for continued funding for successful programs. Second, it can help administrators allocate resources, providing a "disproportionate" share to programs with the highest ROI based on an objective, "apples to apples" comparison. Third, it helps funders respond to questions (or criticisms) regarding use of taxpayers or donor contributions, providing a credible evaluation metric many are familiar with in their business or personal lives. And finally, if more and more programs calculate this, we can build and share a database of ROIs that will assist in evaluating programs' efficacy as well as replicating the most cost effective ones.

Despite these benefits, unfortunately this calculation is not often provided for social marketing efforts. More often, campaign evaluations most commonly highlight major program activities and expenses, and levels of increased awareness, attitudes and behaviours changed. Evaluation components used to calculate an ROI appear in Table 1, a modified logic model.

How ROI Is Calculated

Source: Lee (2011), 73 and 75. Reprinted permission of Emerald Publishing.
Most ROIs can be determined with five simple (but not necessarily easy) steps:

(1) Dollars spent: determine total costs of the campaign/program. Ideally this should include staff time as well as direct expenses associated with research, development, implementation and evaluation.
(2) Behaviours influenced: as may seem obvious, if the campaign is a true social marketing effort there will be a clear behaviour objective. Reliable evaluation research will need to determine the number of people who were influenced to adopt the targeted behaviour as a result of the campaign/intervention.
(3) Cost per behaviour influenced: this is the simple step, completed by dividing the dollars spent by the numbers of changed behaviours.
(4) Benefit per behaviour: what is the economic value of this changed behaviour? This can be the most challenging step. It is most often stated in terms of costs avoided as a result of the behaviour adoption (e.g. healthcare costs, emergency response to injuries, landfills developed, and environmental clean-up efforts). In some cases, it may be revenue generated by behaviour adoption (e.g. from home energy audits conducted by a utility).

Table 1 A modified logic model

	Definition	Examples
Inputs	Resources allocated to the campaign or program effort	• Dollars • Incremental staff time • Existing materials • Existing distribution channels • Existing partners
Outputs	Program activities conducted to influence a desired behaviour. These measures do not indicate whether the audience "noticed" or responded to these activities. They only represent what was "put out there"	• Number of materials disseminated • Number of calls made • Numbers and types of distribution channels for any products or services • Number of events held • Web sites created/utilised • Social media tactics • Reach and frequency of communications • Free media coverage • Paid media impressions • Implementation of program elements (e.g. whether on time, on budget)
Outcomes	Audience response to outputs	• Changes in behaviour • Changes in numbers of related products or services "sold" (e.g. children's life vests) • Changes in behaviour intent • Changes in knowledge • Changes in beliefs • Responses to campaign elements (e.g. hits to a Website hits) • Campaign awareness • Customer satisfaction levels • Policy changes • Partnerships and contributions created
Impact	Indicators that show levels of impact on the social issue that was the focus for the effort	• Improvements in health • Lives saved • Injuries prevented • Water quality improved • Water supply increased • Air quality improved • Landfill reduced • Wildlife and habitats protected • Animal cruelty reduced • Crimes prevented • Increases in financial well being
ROI	Economic value of changes in behaviour and the calculated rate of return on the spending associated with the effort	• For every dollar spent, dollars saved or generated • After subtracting expenses, what is the rate of return on the investment

Source Lee (2011), 74. Reprinted permission of Emerald Publishing

(5) ROI: this takes three calculations:

- Number of behaviours influenced (#2) *times* economic benefit per behaviour (#4) *equals* the Gross Economic Benefit (#2 × #4 = Gross Economic Benefit)
- Gross Economic Benefit *minus* the amount spent (#1) *equals* Net Benefit
- Net Benefit divided by the investment costs (#1) × 100 *equals* Rate of Return on the Investment

(End reprint)
The following case story will illustrate this process of calculating a ROI, as well as accentuate the power that selecting an appealing offer for a unique and attractive audience can have on the bottom line.

Return on Investment Case Story (Lee and Kotler 2015, pp. 247–248)
In the spring of 2000, Mike Rothschild, professor emeritus at the University of Wisconsin, accepted an "assignment" from the Wisconsin Department of Transportation. He was to provide a social marketing perspective and approach to an effort with a purpose of reducing alcohol-related crashes in rural Wisconsin. The target audience was 21–34 year old single men who frequented bars after leaving work, and then drove home—often drunk. Audience research included 17 focus groups, 11 with the target audience and 6 with those who observed the target audience (e.g. bar owners, law enforcement). Meetings with the target audience were held in the back of local taverns so that respondents would feel comfortable discussing the issues. Barriers to taking a taxi ride home were made clear: they didn't want the hassle (or cost) of coming back in the morning to get their vehicle; they saw it as a norm among their peers; and at 1:00 a.m., they were fearless, perceiving few other cars on the road and a low risk of getting caught. When asked to help design a ride program that they would use, they made their wishes known. They wanted vehicles that were at least as nice as their own, a ride from home to the bar, between bars, and then home again, and the right to smoke or drink in the vehicle; all at a reasonable price.

The "offer" was certainly inspired by this target audience's barriers and desires (motivators). The resulting service, branded *Road Crew*, offers limousines and other luxury vehicles to pick people up at their home, business, or hotel; it takes them, with their buddies, to the bar of their choice; it takes them between bars; takes them home at the end of the evening; and, as allowed by local ordinances, they may smoke and drink in the vehicles. The cost to the passenger is reasonable, as well, at \$15–\$20 for the evening.

By 2008, the program was operating in 32 small communities in rural Wisconsin and had provided over 97,000 rides and prevented an estimated 140 alcohol-related crashes and six alcohol-related fatalities. Let's do the calculations on the ROI:

(1) Dollars Spent: $870,000 (2000–2007)
(2) Behaviours Influenced: 97,000 rides, preventing 140 alcohol-related crashes
(3) Cost Per Behaviour Influence: $6,214 ($870,000/140 crashes avoided)
(4) Benefit per Behaviour: $231,000 savings per crash
(5) ROI: 3717 % ($23,100/$6214 = $37.17 × 100).

Barriers to Determining and Reporting on ROI for Social Marketers

There are several major factors that have make calculating and reporting on ROI uncommon for social marketing efforts. First, the economic benefit of one changed behaviour is not always known or readily available. My suggestion is to use reasonable estimates and be up front with audiences and continue to work to determine this metric. Second, there is often insufficient funding to conduct rigorous outcome/behaviour change research. A suggestion is to at least do this once, or share examples of another program that benefited from this exercise, like the Road Crew example in this chapter.

Summary

As you review the list of target audience segments mentioned in this chapter, note how interventions were inspired by the unique profile of the target audience segment, and how the audience was, as a result, inspired to action.

- Mothers in Cambodia who prepared meals for their families with anaemia were delighted with the "lucky iron fish".
- Smokers in the Philippines who wanted to quit in order to save money were motivated by depositing their cigarette money in a savings account, and having it be refunded only if they were tobacco-free after six months.
- Men in Seattle who were at risk of HIV who frequented gay clubs found testing at the clubs and receiving results in 20 min more convenient and "pleasant" than going to a community clinic and waiting a week for results.
- Potential shelter pet adopters in the US who wanted to find a dog or cat that met their unique wants and needs felt confident they had found their match based on a rigorous assessment of the personality traits of the pets in the shelters, as well as the potential owners.

- Middle school students in Washington State considering having unprotected sex were most motivated to be abstinent by messages regarding crabs and the pain of childbirth.
- Households in Seattle with dogs as pets not disposing of pet waste by putting in it the trash found out their neighbours were scooping it, bagging it and putting it in the trash.
- In Australia, a unique approach to blood donation was developed for each of the three targeted audiences: University students, 30–54 year old engaged influencers, residents and city councils in suburbs.
- Women in the US who find out they are pregnant and want to be reminded of steps to take for a healthy baby found an easy way to receive helpful and timely tips three times a week on their mobile phone.
- Men 21–34 in rural Wisconsin who frequented bars after leaving work, "got what they wanted" to ensure they did not drive home drunk.

Through segmentation, we divide large heterogeneous markets into smaller more homogeneous ones, ones that inspire our development of intervention strategies that will attract more potential buyers, with less resource expenditures. As the analogy with fishing described, by using the bait (Product, Price, Place and Promotion) the fish you want to catch like, you not only will "catch more of the fish you want most", you will accomplish this will less time and money, therefore increasing your ROI.

References

CDC. (2015). Become a Text4baby partner. http://www.cdc.gov/women/text4baby/. Accessed 18 December 2015.

Farris, P., Bendle, N., Pfeifer, P., & Reibstein, D. (2010). *Marketing metrics: The definitive guide to measuring marketing performance*. Upper Saddle River, NJ: Pearson Education.

Lee, N. (2011). Where's the beef? Social marketing in tough times. *Journal of Social Marketing, 1*, 1–2.

Lee, N., & Kotler, P. (2015). *Social marketing—Changing behaviors for good*. Thousand Oaks, CA: Sage Publications.

Peattie, S., & Peattie, K. (2003). Ready to fly solo? Reducing social marketing's dependence on commercial marketing theory. *Marketing Theory, 3*(3), 365–385.

Tacoma-Pierce County Health Department. (2015). Suck on this. http://www.tpchd.org/health-wellness-1/tobacco-prevention-control/youth-tobacco-prevention-campaign-suck/. Accessed December 21, 2015.

Tapp, A., & Spotswood, F. (2013). Beyond persuasion: A cultural perspective of behaviour. *Journal of Social Marketing, 3*(3), 275–294.

Part II
Segmentation Process, Methods, and Application

Segmentation in Social Marketing: Five Steps to Success

Timo Dietrich

Introduction

Market segmentation dates back to when the German publisher Kliemann (1928) introduced theoretical literature on segmentation that was later developed further by Smith (1956). Wind (1980) stated that segmentation has been intuitively applied by marketers for a long time, but today's practice requires more than intuition to cope with greatly enhanced technological and data mining capabilities (Dibb 2014). Fullerton (2016, p. 6) suggests that 'modern marketing abounds in segmentation', and Weinstein (1987, p. 3) referred to segmentation as 'the key to marketing success'. However, Cahill (2006), an advocate for segmentation, suggested that many segmentation practices are too pragmatic and driven by 'surface validity', meaning that segmentation is not attended to in a systematic manner. Only limited work has been undertaken to advance segmentation theory (Cahill 2006) and the majority of research is dominated by conceptual research, with less attention directed towards empirical studies (Boejgaard and Ellegaard 2010). In practice, segmentation is, as a result, frequently misunderstood, and its implementation and execution is not attended to in a systematic manner (Boejgaard and Ellegaard 2010). In fact, Cahill (2006) pointed out that segmentation remains a confusing mystery to many, and if segmentation is not undertaken correctly or sufficiently then it can be a costly and misleading exercise (Schlegelmilch 2016). The complexities of segmentation result in difficulties for practitioners, many of who struggle to implement complex mathematical models for later conversion of these findings into implementation strategies (Boejgaard and Ellegaard 2010).

This chapter introduces a five-step segmentation process targeted specifically at social marketing program design. Following the introduction to the five-step process, this chapter will present a case study application of the segmentation process

T. Dietrich (✉)
Griffith University, Queensland, Australia
e-mail: t.dietrich@griffith.edu.au

T. Dietrich et al. (eds.), *Segmentation in Social Marketing*,
DOI 10.1007/978-981-10-1835-0_6

that was conducted during the formative research stages of the Blurred Minds social marketing program (www.blurredminds.com.au).

Segmentation and Its Application in Social Marketing

A fundamental assumption of marketing is that the market is not homogenous. Donald A. Norman stated succinctly that '*Market segmentation is a natural result of the vast differences among people*', meaning that markets are comprised of individuals with differences in belief systems, values, thoughts, opinions, habits, behaviours, communication styles, and many other aspects of lifestyle. Ironically, with all their passion for individual differences, most humans are herd animals who like to be accepted and belong to a particular social group (Godin 2008). With this understanding, commercial marketers seek to group individuals who are similar into segments to increase their effectiveness and efficiency through better resource allocation (Cahill 2006; Lefebvre 2013; McDonald and Dunbar 2012). Segmentation aims to identify homogenous segments within a larger heterogeneous marketplace (Donovan et al. 1999; McDonald and Dunbar 2012). Segmentation can help social marketers to decide which groups are worthwhile targets and may result in better-tailored program design. Unlike their counterparts in a commercial setting, social marketers are frequently faced with constrained resources such as much smaller budgets, overreliance on external funding sources, and limited time, to name a few. According to Dibb (2014) and Neiger et al. (2003), the most common barrier to actual segmentation implementation is a lack of expertise among those charged with developing and delivering social marketing programs. In fact, many of those using social marketing to design more engaging and effective behaviour change programs lack the marketing training to do this properly (Tapp and Spotswood 2013).

A number of recent systematic reviews highlight the fact that segmentation has been rarely applied in social marketing across a range of behavioural contexts such as healthy eating (Carins and Rundle-Thiele 2014), alcohol (Dietrich et al. 2016b; Kubacki et al. 2015), physical activity (Fujihira et al. 2015), and interventions with children (Kubacki et al. 2015). For example, Kubacki et al. (2015) identified 23 social marketing interventions of which only two applied segmentation, while Fujihira et al. (2015) reviewed seven social marketing interventions and identified the application of segmentation in three studies. Dietrich et al. (2016b) also found that segmentation had not been used in alcohol programs delivered in school settings.

The Five-Step Segmentation Process

This chapter will now introduce a segmentation process to cater for the unique contexts that social marketers face when applying segmentation. The aim of the five-step segmentation process is to provide social marketing researchers and practitioners with a sequential process to enable them to apply segmentation in social marketing and other behaviour change programs irrespective of their context (health, social, environmental or economic) and budget. The five steps are (P) Priority identification, (A) Analyse, (D) Describe, (A) Assess and (T) Target (see Fig. 1).

Step 1: Priority market identification

The first step requires that a decision be made on who the priority group is, providing that it has not been established by the funding body. Depending on the social issue and the context, the funding body and key stakeholders may have a very clear idea and position on who the priority group is (e.g. adolescents attending high school, senior citizens, or other target audiences) and as such the priority group is defined ahead of the project. Other projects have a broader remit, and the first task may be to understand the extent of market coverage and to establish clear priorities for the social marketing program. In most instances the priority group is broad, and it is important to investigate whether homogenous subgroups can be identified following the steps in the social marketing segmentation process.

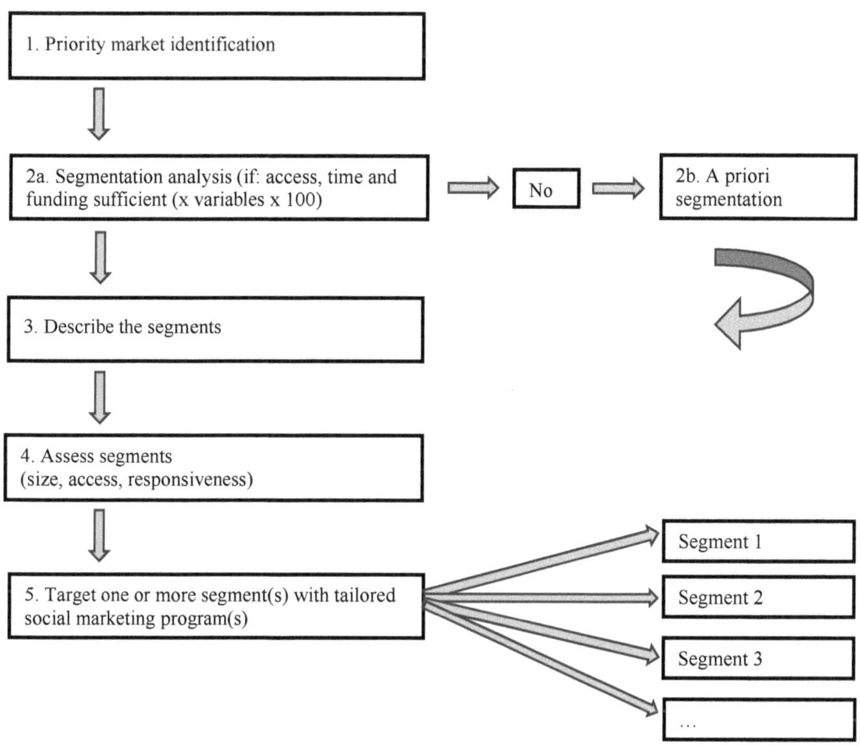

Fig. 1 The five-step segmentation process

Step 2(A): Segmentation analysis

There is no formal mechanism to select appropriate segmentation variables and it is important to note that segmentation results are likely to vary depending on the variables used. Therefore, it is necessary to understand the behaviour change context and the priority group before selecting a range of variables that are to be used to identify meaningful and distinguishable segments. Demographic, psychographic, geographic, and behavioural segmentation are the four key bases that were introduced by Kotler (1980) and these four bases remain easily distinguishable and more commonly used. Demographic segmentation includes quantifiable social characteristics such as age, ethnicity, income, and gender. Geographic variables may range from defined areas such as cities, states and regions to urban, rural, and suburban classifications (Kotler & Armstrong 2001). The oldest segmentation bases (demographic and geographic) are the most frequently used in segmentation studies in social marketing (Dibb 2014), and only over recent decades has a more dominant focus on psychographic and behavioural variables emerged (Dietrich et al. 2015a, b; Gordon et al. 2015; Mathijssen et al. 2012; Rundle-Thiele et al. 2015). Psychographic segmentation moves beyond demographic and geographic segmentation variables by describing individuals' attitudes, values, and other lifestyle characteristics (Kotler 1980). Psychographic segmentation uses a broad range of variables that are likely to differ across the diversity of social, health, environmental and economic issues (Cahil 2006; Kotler 1980). Behavioural segmentation comprises variables such as frequency and quantity of behaviour. Table 1 lists a series of exemplary variables for each of the segmentation bases.

Researchers have argued that one-dimensional variables, such as socio-demographic variables, are unlikely to identify 'true' market segments or subgroups that enable a deeper understanding (Dibb and Simkin 2009). However, multi-base segmentation models (using more than one segmentation base) have yet to be compared with the effectiveness of single segmentation base efforts. Merits of the use of single segmentation bases do exist in social marketing research. For example, when a social marketing program is limited by funding and time or has a very specific priority group, then more sophisticated segmentation models may be neither feasible nor realistic. In fact, many social marketing studies focus on segmenting the market utilising a single segmentation base and have produced promising results (see for example Gordon et al. 2015). A single-base segmentation study used a value-driven criterion to identify value perceptions of consumers regarding energy efficiency (Gordon et al. 2015) whereby a latent class analysis produced seven segments, providing insights into value-based efficiency behaviours that informed social marketing program development. Segmentation helped to develop clearer program insights with regards to the appropriateness of message and overall program design. However, longitudinal research is required to assess the effects of such segmentation strategies on behavioural outcomes. Once the bases and measures to be used are determined, data analysis can commence.

Multivariate analysis techniques are used to identify homogeneous segments. There are a range of techniques available, such as TwoStep cluster analysis (read

Table 1 Segmentation bases

Demographic	Geo (socio)graphic	Psychographic	Behaviour
Age Gender Nationality Race/ethnicity Religion Income Education Height Weight Number in household Number of children Language spoken Country of birth	Postal (zip) code Size and climate Neighbourhoods Communities Towns Counties Cities Regions Countries Rural, suburban and urban areas	Motivators Emotions (e.g. fear) Benefits Beliefs Values Attitudes Social + cultural norms Intentions Opinions Knowledge Awareness Activities (cultural) interests Language nuances Hobbies Peers Role models/idols Resources Skills	What is the behaviour? Where does the target audience do the behaviour? What other behaviours/habits are relevant (i.e. coffee and smoking) Willingness to pay Media consumption patterns TV shows Social media channels Mobile phone use Imagery preferences

more in Chap. 8 of this book about this method and its application), Latent Gold analysis (Kent et al. 2014), K-means (Chiu et al. 2009), hierarchical clustering (Punj and Stewart 1983), *p*-median clustering (Klastorin 1985), and bi-clustering-based market segmentation methods (Wang et al. 2016). A recent study by Kent et al. (2014) compared advanced clustering techniques, namely TwoStep, Latent Gold, and Snob using five unique data sets and concluded that all three clustering methods performed well in predicting subgroups and allocating individuals correctly to those subgroups. This suggests there is not one necessarily superior method, and that the more important consideration is which technique a social marketer is most comfortable using, often driven by the types of measures used. Another important understanding stems from the selected segmentation bases and their respective variables. The above techniques require a large number of respondents per variable used. According to Dolnicar et al. (2016), increasing the sample size to '100 times the number of variables is the most effective', which has significant cost implications for social marketers. A word of caution comes from management research (Lemmens et al. 2012) which reminds us that segments, just like markets, are intrinsically dynamic and never remain the same. Dynamic segmentation models with growth mixture models provide evidence of this phenomenon (Bassi 2016; Müller and Hamm 2014) and may be helpful to better understand dynamic changes (Cahill 2006).

Step 2(B): A priori *segmentation*

Should time and resources be limited, social marketers may need to move directly to step 2(B), a priori segmentation (read more about a priori segmentation in Chap. 7 of this book). This may also apply to situations where social marketers have detailed knowledge of the market, when the priority is predefined, or the behavioural issue affects only a small, defined population. Equipped with this understanding, the key characteristics that describe the segments as well as their motivations and abilities will need to be defined. Ideally (even if on a smaller scale), data should be collected to validate any assumptions. However, it is not necessary to produce statistical analysis to validate any segment solutions, and the data is used merely to gain further insights to engage better with the respective segments. Whether you are targeting just one, a few or all segments, a different program is likely to emerge.

Step 3: Describing your segments

In order to design more tailored program solutions, a clear understanding of segment similarities and segment differences need to be established, although Cahil (2006) suggests that one should think about the similarities of homogenous sub-groups rather than their differences. A helpful tool post segment identification is to employ the use of personas (Lefebvre 2013) to deliver visual cues that can help decision makers to better distinguish between segments. Personas are fictitious characters that represent a customer segment and are given names, faces, clothes, and families to match the true representation of the customer segment as closely as possible (Lefebvre 2013). Each segment will require a meaningful and interpretive name possibly accompanied by a short, vivid description to guide managerial decision making. Asking important questions such as 'What are the concerns, worries, and interests of the segment?' or 'Where does the segment spend most of their time and how do they receive information?' can be helpful. However, it is important to note that there is not a single way to create personas (Chang et al. 2008). A picture can say more than a thousand words and finding a persona that represents a segment may provide program staff and other involved stakeholders with a better understanding of the priority group (Chang et al. 2008; Lefebvre 2013). The following example provides a high level of process-driven work that can go into the formation and creation of these segments and personas, and showcases what is possible for social marketers seeking to design more tailored programs that resonate with their target audiences.

Rescue, a San Diego based behaviour change agency uses pictures to develop underlying associations between behaviours and teen subcultures. Participants take part in ID-Projection Groups™ (ID-PGs) which are identified using a screening survey. ID-PGs investigate young people's motivations to perform or avoid risk behaviours, and groups are structured to contrast those who engage in risk behaviours from those who do not. Probing methods, such as presenting images of unknown teens to project one's identity, are used to explore the often subconscious motivations that drive risk behaviours, and individual and group activities are conducted to avoid group bias and capture as many perspectives as possible. These ID-PGs are also designed to reveal which youth ‘peer crowds’ exist in the local area and which of those peer crowds are most associated with risk behaviours. Informed by the data collected during the ID-PGs, Rescue researchers then explore the local cultural environment through social events and participant observation. These observations and interviews are used to design programs that are relevant to the respective segments. You can see more of Rescue’s work at www.rescueagency.com.

Step 4: Assessing your segments

Segments need to be assessed before deciding which identified segments should be targeted. The selection of target segments does not come without ethical controversy. Thus, it is important to acknowledge the potential ethical issues involved when targeting only some, but not all members of the population (Donovan and Henley 2010). However, while a one-size-fits-all (‘universal’) approach may avoid stigmatisation, these programs do not reach ‘everyone’ and alternative programs are not offered (Newton et al. 2013). The arguments for the merits of applying one program solution for all fails since there are important differences between people that impact the effectiveness of social marketing programs. Segmentation can produce, or enhance, stigma in a social marketing setting if executed carelessly; done correctly it is a powerful process tool that can help to create better and more scalable behaviour change programs. More specifically, identifying segments and directing available resources to particular subgroups is helpful for targeting either those most vulnerable, or those for whom the program can achieve most change. The latter may create an ethical issue of prioritising effectiveness over needs. Most importantly, acknowledging subgroups within a larger heterogeneous market ensures that social marketers reach more of the market more often. A smaller audience with a larger impact represents a much better return-on-investment (ROI), and is more likely to attract follow-up funding, than a program that aims wide and misses most. Four key criteria are proposed for segment evaluation:

- *Size*—Is the segment big enough to develop a full program around?
- *Access*—Can we get to the audience?
- *Responsiveness*—Is the segment ready & willing to change? Want can we offer in exchange?
- *Level of need*—As social marketers it is our obligation to consider targeting those segments that are in most need.

Step 5: Target your segment

The final phase of the segmentation process requires that the needs and wants of each chosen segment are understood and catered to where possible. Each homogeneous segment is likely to require a unique social marketing program tailored to their specific needs and wants (Jenkins and McDonald 1997). For example, segmented audiences can be further assessed using formative investigation methods such as co-design workshops (see for example Dietrich et al. 2016a) to identify what drives and motivates a particular segment. This segment-level understanding can then be used to develop programs meeting the requirements of each identified segment. By meeting respective needs and wants, more efficacious and cost-efficient programs can be expected (Albrecht and Bryant 1996; Beane and Ennis 1987). Finally, it is recommended, throughout all five stages of the segmentation process, that social marketers consult with the main stakeholder groups (e.g. program partners, sponsors, funding bodies) to ensure that segmentation and targeting decisions are supported.

Following this introduction of the five-step social marketing segmentation process, the next section of this chapter will demonstrate how to apply the five-step process to a social marketing program using a program currently in development and planned to be delivered as part of a larger cluster stratified randomized controlled trial design.

The Blurred Minds Social Marketing Program—Gamifying Alcohol Education

The Blurred Minds social marketing program (www.blurredminds.com.au) is currently in development and aims to gamify alcohol education. Blurred Minds is dedicated to delivering relevant and engaging information surrounding alcohol in an engaging and interactive manner. The cluster stratified randomized controlled trial is being conducted in partnership with the Queensland Catholic Education Commission (QCEC), who commissioned Social Marketing @ Griffith and The University of Queensland's Centre for Youth Substance Abuse Research to tackle alcohol education using a social marketing approach.

Step 1: Identify priority group

Along with the aim of tackling adolescent drinking through a prevention program, QCEC also provided the research team with a specific priority group in the form of high school students. The average initiation age for alcohol drinking in Australia was identified as 15 years (AIHW 2014). Therefore, in consultation with QCEC, the decision was to target Year 10 students (14–16 years old) attending Catholic secondary schools in Queensland, Australia. This represents a market size of 12,277 adolescents. Extensive formative research was conducted throughout the initial project years to develop better consumer insights. For example, the formative research process involved an extensive general literature review of alcohol education and a systematic literature review of programs that targeted high school students (Dietrich et al. 2016b); focus groups and co-design workshops with adolescents (Dietrich et al. 2016a); pilot program testing (Rundle-Thiele et al. 2013); and finally, segmentation analysis (Dietrich et al. 2015a, 2016b).

Step 2a (Yes): Segmentation analysis

Given the market size was large enough and funding was available, multivariate segmentation analysis was conducted. Using secondary data collected through a baseline survey from a previous trial elaborated in Game On: Know Alcohol (Dietrich et al. 2015a, 2016b), segmentation analysis was performed, using TwoStep cluster analysis (see Chap. 8 of this book for more details on this segmentation cluster analysis technique). Twenty-two items were sourced from three different segmentation bases (demographic, psychographic, behavioural) to identify homogeneous subgroups within the 14–16 year-old target market (Fig. 2). Baseline data of more than 2000 respondents formed the basis for the segmentation analysis. Dietrich et al. (2016b) provides a full description of the method applied.

The three key segments that emerged were labelled *Bingers*, *Moderate Drinkers*, and *Abstainers*. Although all three segments share very similar, narrow geo- and demographic profiles, these three groups are in fact very different to each other. As the priority group was demographically homogenous, behavioural and psychographic variables drove the segment formation (Dietrich et al. 2015b). More specifically, four items had the highest predictor score of 1 (ranging from 0 least important to 1 most important), including two intention items (*How likely is it that you will binge drink over the next two weeks/Do you intend to binge drink over the next two weeks*) and two drinking behaviour items (*How often do you have a drink containing alcohol/Have you had a full alcoholic drink before?*). Further important

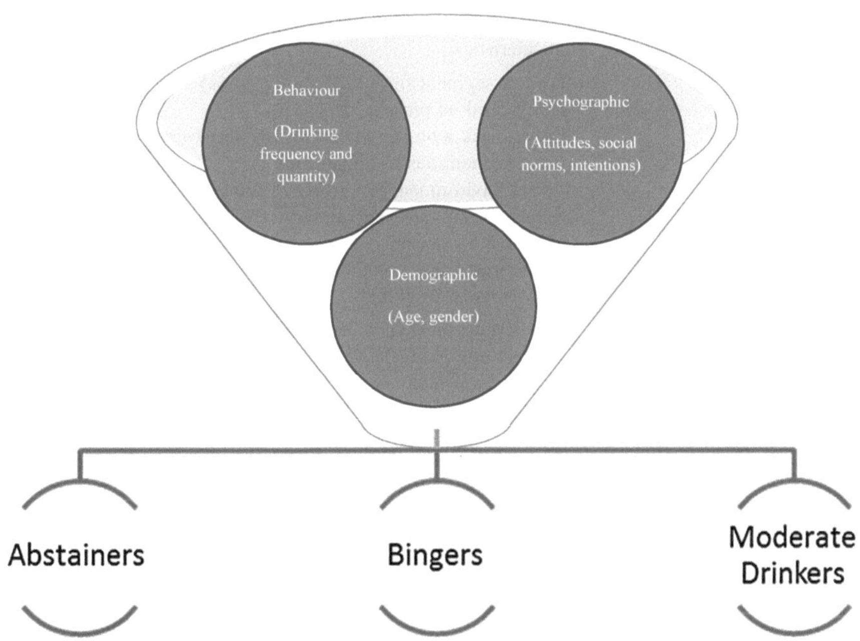

Fig. 2 Segment formation

predictor variables were all six social norm items (ranging from 0.69 to 0.87) and all five attitudinal items (0.41–0.66). The least important predictor variables were knowledge (0.15), time spent doing homework (0.12), father's drinking behaviour (0.05), gender (0.02), and age (0.02). In summary, psychographic and behavioural measures were the strongest and most important variables and drove the segment formation, while demographic factors were less important (which appears logical since they were very similar across the data sample).

Step 3: Describing the segments

After identifying the segments, each can now be described in depth. Each of the three segments identified are featured next and deliver a richer description (see Table 2).

Segment 1 (Abstainers) was the largest adolescent segment (n = 1223; boys: 54 %) with only 5 % having ever consumed a full alcoholic drink. All of the adolescents in this segment were not currently engaging in drinking activities. They possessed the lowest risk attitudes towards binge drinking, reported the lowest intentions to binge drink, and were surrounded by a social environment that neither engages in nor supports binge drinking. Abstainers recorded the highest knowledge score of all three segments at baseline. Furthermore, this segment was characterised by spending more time doing homework and having less parental drinking influence (e.g. the father) compared to the other segments. Differences for age were not observed between the segments.

Table 2 Segment characteristics

Segment	Characteristics
Abstainers (58 %)	– Largest segment (n = 1223; boys: 54 %) – Don't drink at present – Lowest risk attitudes towards binge drinking – Lowest intentions to binge drink – Social environment less likely to drink excessively – Social environment not supportive of binge drinking – Most knowledgeable – More time doing homework – Less parental drinking
Bingers (17 %)	– Smallest segment (n = 363; boys: 69 %) – Highest ratio of male adolescents – Lowest knowledge – Positive attitudes towards binge drinking – Highest intentions to binge drink – Drank alcohol more regularly and every third binged monthly – 1 in 10 reported binge drinking weekly – Social environment encourages drinking – More parental drinking
Moderate drinkers (25 %)	– Second biggest segment (n = 528; boys: 49 %) – Everyone has tried a full alcoholic drink – 70 % reported drinking alcohol at least once a month – Majority drank lower volumes of alcohol than the Bingers – 66 % did not engage in binge drinking

Segment 2 (Bingers) was the smallest segment (n = 363; boys: 69 %) with the highest ratio of male adolescents compared to the other two segments. They featured the lowest knowledge score together with the most positive attitudes towards alcohol drinking and they reported the highest intentions to binge drink. About two-thirds of this segment drank alcohol regularly and every third adolescent binged monthly. Every tenth adolescent in this sample reported binge drinking at least once a week. The high mean score of subjective norms suggested that Bingers are surrounded by a social environment where drinking is more normative than in the other segments.

Segment 3 (Moderate Drinkers) had an even gender split and was the second largest segment (n = 528; boys: 49 %). Everyone in this group had tried a full alcohol drink in their lifetime and 70 % of adolescents reported drinking alcohol on a monthly or less frequent basis. This segment's knowledge score fell between the Bingers and Abstainer's score at baseline, with the majority in this group (91 %) reporting drinking lower volumes of alcohol (less than five standard drinks) than the Bingers. Sixty-six percent of adolescents in the Moderate Drinkers segment did not engage in binge drinking sessions, but Moderate Drinkers had more positive attitudes towards binge drinking than the Abstainers segment.

Step 4: Assessing identified segments

The three key segments were then evaluated according to size, access, responsiveness and level of need.

Size

The three segments differ in size, with Abstainers (n = 1223) remaining the largest by far, followed by the Moderate Drinker (n = 528) and the Binger (n = 363) segments. Each segment is large enough to warrant consideration in program design and planning. Interestingly, one segment requires behaviour maintenance while two segments require behaviour change, indicating that a different focus is required in program offerings to meet this dual need. Based on these findings, we see merit in creating different program components for each of the segments.

Access

Schools are under pressure to deliver a range of health and physical education programs to complement their academic curricula. High schools still represent one of the most cost-efficient ways of targeting large numbers of adolescents, although not without difficulty. A one-size-fits-all approach remains the most popular means of delivering programs in school settings, with an earlier review indicating that segmentation had yet to be applied (Dietrich et al. 2016b). Creating tailored social marketing programs for different audience segments introduces practical limitations such as the screening and allocation of students to program variations prior to program commencement to ensure each student receives the most relevant program. Utilising technology for a more economical and larger-scale distribution has the potential to meet the needs and wants of the young technology savvy generation, allowing for more effective data collection methods and larger-scale implementation (Dietrich et al. 2015a). Furthermore, tailored content in the form of games or quizzes dramatically increases program costs; in this case, costs could increase threefold given the identification of three segments. Following segment identification, a customised program could be delivered through a range of different types of online modules (e.g. games, quizzes, and other tailored content). Students would need to take a baseline survey to then classify them into one of three segments to receive tailored program content.

Responsiveness

The audience of 14–16 year-olds is targeted by commercial organisations as a most sought after audience. For this reason it is particularly difficult to design and build content likely to engage this audience in alcohol education programs that are mostly a mandatory school-based activity of which students are not particularly fond (Tupper 2008). Adolescents have different risk-taking propensities (Steinberg 2007), attitudes towards alcohol, and their drinking behaviours range from abstinence to extreme use (Fry 2011). Adolescents around this particular age group are at their final cognitive developmental (formal operational) stage (Piaget 1952) and during this stage (11–16 years) they experience the development of hypothetic-deductive reasoning and the possibility to assess propositional logic (Piaget 1952). In short, this is probably one of the most difficult audiences to engage and work with. However, previous research indicates that programs can engage student segments differentially. Strongest positive change effects post participation were observed for the Bingers segment, while mixed effects were evident for Moderate Drinkers and Abstainers (Rundle-Thiele et al. 2015). For example, while the program had the desired effect on attitudes towards binge drinking across all segments, a substantial reduction in intentions to binge drink was observed only for the Bingers segment. Similarly, strongest significant positive change effects (reduced social norms) were observed for the Bingers segment, while no significant segment effects were observed between Abstainers and Moderate Drinkers and both social norms measures remained unchanged. Both the Abstainers' and Moderate Drinkers' behavioural intentions to binge drink increased slightly. For further details of this study, see Dietrich et al. (2015b).

Level of need

The identification of three segments along with differential program effects pose the important future consideration of whether the Blurred Minds Program should target all three segments with a tailored program or select segments to be targeted, or whether a one-size fits all approach remains the most feasible in a school context. Equipped with the insight from the segmentation analysis it can be argued that the Bingers, as the group most likely to be suffering from current and future alcohol-related problems, is the segment most at need. Although positive initial program effects were observed for this group, it was evident that the program was able only to maintain this segment's behavioural intentions towards excessive drinking. The Abstainer segment appears to be a generally more protected segment, yet it remains important to encourage this segment to refrain from drinking for as long as possible, while Moderate Drinkers need encouragement to either not drink or consume as little as possible.

Step 5: Target segment(s)

The results of the case study showcase three main findings. First, even in a target audience as narrow as the high school student population, homogenous subgroups (segments) exist. Second, it demonstrates potential for improvement in tailoring the new Blurred Minds program for different audiences to further increase relevance and efficacy in achieving desired behavioural change. The segmentation process helped uncover these insights which may not have been produced otherwise. Further formative research with each segment in co-design workshops revealed that segment-level preferences for particular activities and games existed (Dietrich et al. 2016a). Several important changes to program design (i.e. not all games and activities were liked by the segments) must be considered to effectively tailor program content to the three segments. Further details can be viewed in Dietrich et al. (2016a). Owing to the challenges of implementing a tailored program version for each of the three segments in a Year 10 cohort, it is suggested that in creating three programs, differential activities should be provided online where possible.

Conclusion

Segment formation depends on the collected data and the variables used in the segmentation analysis. Given that most social marketing programs do not apply the benchmark criterion of segmentation, this chapter aimed to provide a guiding process to assist the uptake of segmentation in social marketing practice. A five-step process was introduced for the application of segmentation unique to social marketing research and practice that can be applied irrespective of budgets and social contexts. The five steps, (P) Priority identification, (A) Analyse, (D) Describe, (A) Assess, and (T) Target (PADAT), are delineated to assist the design of better tailored social marketing programs. This process was explicated using a social marketing program currently in development. Social marketers and other behaviour change agents are encouraged to apply the five-step segmentation process and social marketing researchers are invited to test the process with empirical research to further its conceptual development.

References

AIHW. (2014). National Drug Strategy Household Survey detailed report 2013 (Vol. Drug statistics series no. 28. Cat. no. PHE 183, pp. 1–151). Canberra, Australia.

Albrecht, T., & Bryant, C. (1996). Advances in segmentation modeling for health communication and social marketing campaigns. *Journal of Health Communication, 1*(1), 65–80.

Bassi, F. (2016). Dynamic segmentation with growth mixture models. *Advances in Data Analysis and Classification*, 1–17. doi:10.1007/s11634-015-0230-x

Beane, T., & Ennis, D. (1987). Market segmentation: A review. *European Journal of Marketing, 21*(5), 20–42.

Boejgaard, J., & Ellegaard, C. (2010). Unfolding implementation in industrial market segmentation. *Industrial Marketing Management, 39*(8), 1291–1299. doi:10.1016/j.indmarman.2010.06.004

Cahill, D. (2006). *Lifestyle market segmentation*. Philadelphia: Haworth Press.

Carins, J., & Rundle-Thiele, S. (2014). Eating for the better: A social marketing review (2000–2012). *Public Health Nutrition, 17*(7), 1628–1639.

Chang, Y.-N., Lim, Y.-K., & Stolterman, E. (2008). *Personas: From theory to practices*. Paper presented at the Proceedings of the 5th Nordic conference on Human-computer interaction: Building bridges, Lund, Sweden.

Chiu, C.-Y., Chen, Y.-F., Kuo, I., & Ku, H. (2009). An intelligent market segmentation system using k-means and particle swarm optimization. *Expert Systems with Applications, 36*(3, Part 1), 4558–4565. doi:http://dx.doi.org/10.1016/j.eswa.2008.05.029

Dibb, S. (2014). Up, up and away: Social marketing breaks free. *Journal of Marketing Management, 30*(11–12), 1159–1185.

Dibb, S., & Simkin, L. (2009). Implementation rules to bridge the theory/practice divide in market segmentation. *Journal of Marketing Management, 25*(3–4), 375–396. doi:10.1362/026725709X429809

Dietrich, T., Rundle-Thiele, S., Leo, C., & Connor, J. (2015a). One size (never) fits all: Segment differences observed following a school-based alcohol social marketing program. *Journal of School Health, 85*(4), 251–259.

Dietrich, T., Rundle-Thiele, S., Schuster, L., & Connor, J. (2016a). Co-designing social marketing programs. *Journal of Social Marketing, 6*(1), 41–61.

Dietrich, T., Rundle-Thiele, S., Schuster, L., & Connor, J. (2016b). A systematic literature review of alcohol education programmes in middle and high school settings (2000–2014). *Health Education, 116*(1), 50–68.

Dietrich, T., Rundle-Thiele, S., Schuster, L., Drennan, J., Russell-Bennett, R., Leo, C., … Connor, J. (2015b). Differential segmentation responses to an alcohol social marketing program. *Addictive Behaviors, 49*, 68–77.

Dolnicar, S., Grün, B., & Leisch, F. (2016). Increasing sample size compensates for data problems in segmentation studies. *Journal of Business Research, 69*(2), 992–999. doi:10.1016/j.jbusres.2015.09.004

Donovan, R., Egger, G., & Francas, M. (1999). TARPARE: A method for selecting target audiences for public health interventions. *Australian and New Zealand Journal of Public Health, 23*(3), 280–284.

Donovan, R., & Henley, N. (2010). *Principles and practice of social marketing: An international perspective*. Cambridge, UK: Cambridge University Press.

Fry, M. (2011). Discourses of consumer's alcohol resistant identities. *Journal of Nonprofit & Public Sector Marketing, 23*(4), 348–366. doi:10.1080/10495142.2011.623506

Fujihira, H., Kubacki, K., Ronto, R., Pang, B., & Rundle-Thiele, S. (2015). Social marketing physical activity interventions among adults 60 years and older: A systematic review. *Social Marketing Quarterly, 21*(4), 214–229. doi:10.1177/1524500415606671

Fullerton, R. (2016). Segmentation in practice—An historical overview of the eighteenth and nineteenth centuries. In D. Jones & M. Tadajewski (Eds.), *The Routledge companion to marketing history*. New York: Routledge.

Godin, S. (2008). *Tribes: We need you to lead us*. London: Penguin Group.

Gordon, R., Butler, K., Magee, C., Waitt, G., & Cooper, P. (2015). *Using value theory for segmentation in social marketing*. Paper presented at the World Social Marketing Conference Proceedings Book, Sydney, Australia.

Jenkins, M., & McDonald, M. (1997). Market segmentation: Organizational archetypes and research agendas. *European Journal of Marketing, 31*, 17.

Kent, P., Jensen, R., & Kongsted, A. (2014). A comparison of three clustering methods for finding subgroups in MRI, SMS or clinical data: SPSS TwoStep cluster analysis, latent gold and SNOB. *BMC Medical Research Methodology, 14*(1), 113.

Klastorin, T. (1985). The p-median problem for cluster analysis: A comparative test using the mixture model approach. *Management Science, 31*, 84–95.

Kliemann, H. (1928). *Wo erfasse ich Käuferschichten Stuttgart*. Germany: Poeschel.

Kotler, P. (1980). *Principles of marketing*. Englewood Cliffs, NJ: Prentice Hall.

Kotler, P., & Armstrong, G. (2001). *Principles of marketing* (9th ed.). Upper Saddle River, N.J: Prentice Hall.

Kubacki, K., Rundle-Thiele, S., Pang, B., & Buyucek, N. (2015a). Minimising alcohol harm: A systematic social marketing review (2000–2014). *Journal of Business Research, 68*(10), 2214–2222.

Kubacki, K., Rundle-Thiele, S., Parkinson, J., & Lahtinen, V. (2015b). Systematic review of social marketing interventions targeting children (2000–2014). *Young Consumers, 16*(2), 141–158.

Lefebvre, C. (2013). *Social marketing and social change: Strategies and tools for health, well-being, and the environment*. CA, San Francisco: Jossey-Bass.

Lemmens, A., Croux, C., & Stremersch, S. (2012). Dynamics in international market segmentation of new product growth. *International Journal of Research in Marketing, 29*(1), 81–92.

Mathijssen, J., Janssen, M., van Bon-Martens, M., & van de Goor, I. (2012). Adolescents and alcohol: An explorative audience segmentation analysis. *BMC Public Health, 12*(742), 1–10.

McDonald, M., & Dunbar, I. (2012). *Market Segmentation: How to do it and how to profit from it* (Vol. 4). United Kingdom: Wiley.

Müller, H., & Hamm, U. (2014). Stability of market segmentation with cluster analysis—A methodological approach. *Food Quality and Preference, 34*, 70–78. doi:10.1016/j.foodqual.2013.12.004

Neiger, B., Thackeray, R., Barnes, M., & McKenzie, J. (2003). Positioning social marketing in a planning process for health education. *American Journal of Health Studies, 18*(2/3), 75–80.

Newton, J., Newton, F., Turk, T., & Ewing, M. (2013). Ethical evaluation of audience segmentation in social marketing. *European Journal of Marketing, 47*(9), 1421–1438.

Piaget, J. (1952). *The origins of intelligence in children*. New York: International University Press.

Punj, G., & Stewart, D. (1983). Cluster analysis in marketing research: Review and suggestions for application. *Journal of Marketing Research, 20*(2), 134–148.

Rundle-Thiele, S., Kubacki, K., Tkaczynski, A., & Parkinson, J. (2015). Using two-step cluster analysis to identify homogeneous physical activity groups. *Marketing Intelligence & Planning, 33*(4), 522–537.

Rundle-Thiele, S., Russell-Bennett, R., Leo, C., & Dietrich, T. (2013). Moderating teen drinking: Combining social marketing and education. *Health Education, 113*(5), 392–406. doi:10.1108/HE-07-2012-0041

Schlegelmilch, B. (2016). *Segmenting targeting and positioning in global markets global marketing strategy: An executive digest* (pp. 63–82). Cham: Springer.

Smith, W. (1956). Product differentiation and market segmentation as alternative marketing strategies. *Journal of Marketing, 21*(1), 3–8.

Steinberg, L. (2007). Risk taking in adolescence: New perspectives from brain and behavioral science. *Current Directions in Psychological Science, 16*(2), 55–59.

Tapp, A., & Spotswood, F. (2013). From the 4Ps to COM-SM: Reconfiguring the social marketing mix. *Journal of Social Marketing, 3*(3), 206–222.

Tupper, K. (2008). Teaching teachers to just say "know": Reflections on drug education. *Teaching and Teacher Education, 24*(2), 356–367.

Wang, B., Miao, Y., Zhao, H., Jin, J., & Chen, Y. (2016). A biclustering-based method for market segmentation using customer pain points. *Engineering Applications of Artificial Intelligence, 47*, 101–109. doi:10.1016/j.engappai.2015.06.005

Weinstein, A. (1987). *Market segmentation: Using niche marketing to exploit new markets.* Chicago, IL: Probus Publishing Inc.

Wind, Y. (1980). Going to market: New twists for some old tricks. *The Wharton Magazine, Spring Edition,* 34–39.

Methods in Segmentation

Sara Dolnicar and Bettina Grün

Abstract Irrespective of the method used, market segmentation analysis is exploratory in nature. This means that any analysis, with any kind of data, will lead to a result, and different competing solutions might emerge where no clear best solution is discernible. It is critical, therefore, to be aware of all potential methodological pitfalls. This chapter discusses all steps required for successful application of both common sense and data-driven market segmentation. Critical decisions are highlighted. In particular, in data-driven market segmentation: (1) data should be collected carefully and in view of the intended segmentation analysis; (2) the sample size should be sufficient to accommodate the number of variables in the segmentation base; (3) data structure should be explored to learn about the most appropriate segmentation concept and to select the most suitable number of segments; (4) a suitable algorithm should be chosen; and (5) segments should be profiled in detail to meaningfully inform target segment selection and, ultimately, the development of an effective marketing mix.

Introduction

There is no universally best market segmentation method. Which method is the most appropriate in any given situation depends on at least two factors: (1) the strategic aims of marketing managers who wish to use segmentation as the basis of their marketing action; and (2) the characteristics of the data set that serves as the basis for the segmentation study.

In situations where marketing managers have intimate knowledge of the market and are aware of the key characteristics that describe their segments, it may be sufficient to collect data from these known segments and describe them in detail in order to optimise marketing messages. For example, if a foster care organisation

S. Dolnicar (✉)
University of Queensland, Brisbane, Australia
e-mail: s.dolnicar@uq.edu.au

B. Grün
Johannes Kepler University Linz, Linz, Austria

T. Dietrich et al. (eds.), *Segmentation in Social Marketing*,
DOI 10.1007/978-981-10-1835-0_7

knows that couples who are facing difficulties having children of their own consider becoming foster carers, marketing managers already know the key characteristics of a possible target segment: couples without children who would like to have a family. In order to best communicate with them, it is only necessary to collect data from this very group and learn about their feelings about foster care, their fears, and their information sources and so on.

The kind of segmentation analysis that is conducted in such a situation is referred to as a priori (Mazanec 2000) or *common sense segmentation* (Dolnicar 2004) because the segment is actually known in advance; it only requires common sense, not statistical techniques to identify it. Nevertheless, market data about this segment are critical to the ability to profile people in this group in detail and, based on such market insights, develop the most promising marketing mix to target them. The steps required in a common sense segmentation study are illustrated in Fig. 1.

Alternatively, there might be situations where marketing managers are not convinced that they know which target segments are most attractive. Marketing managers may also want to explore whether there are any attractive segments that are currently not catered for, but may represent promising target segments. For example, a charitable organisation providing essential medical care to children in developing countries may wish to determine which segments of the market are most likely to donate money to support their cause. In this case, the answer is not obvious. It could be highly educated high income earners because they are aware of the problem and have the means to donate. In contrast, it could also be people with very modest means who themselves have experienced suffering and are therefore willing to help others.

The approach that can help in such circumstances is referred to as a posteriori (Mazanec 2000), *post hoc* (Myers and Tauber 1977) or *data-driven segmentation* (Dolnicar 2004). As all those terms indicate, the segments are not known in advance. Rather, market data needs to be collected and on the basis of this data segments are revealed or created for the purpose of assessing whether potentially attractive target segments can be identified.

The data-driven nature of such a market segmentation study means that several additional steps need to be undertaken, as opposed to that which occur with common sense segmentation (see Fig. 2). First, data suitable for data-driven segmentation analysis needs to be collected. Second, the structure of this data needs to be well understood, and an appropriate method for extracting segments (heuristic clustering methods, finite mixture models and so on) needs to be selected. This step is critical

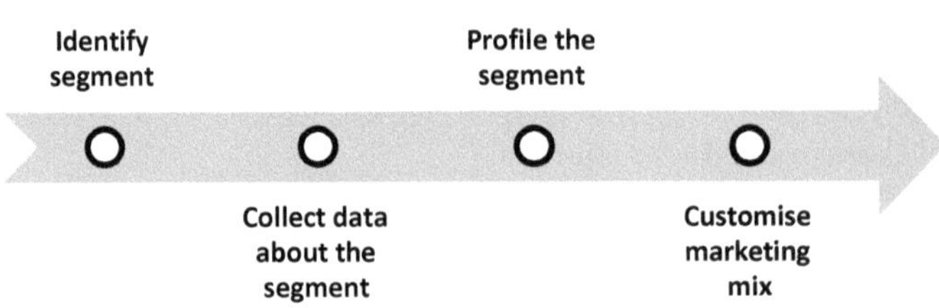

Fig. 1 Steps in common sense market segmentation

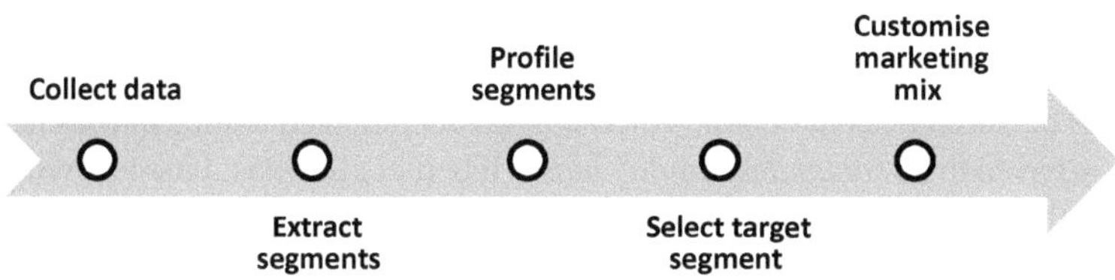

Fig. 2 Steps in data-driven market segmentation

because all techniques available to extract segments will return a solution. Furthermore, a wide range of algorithms can be used. Determining the best option depends primarily on data characteristics but also on the segmentation purpose. After having extracted segments, they need to be profiled to enable marketing managers and data analysts—in a next step—to determine which segment(s) to target. Finally, if an attractive target segment is identified, the market insights available from the data allow the design of an optimal, customised marketing mix for the segment.

In the following sections all steps required for data-driven segmentation are explained in more detail. Note that the sections on collecting data, profiling segments and customising the marketing mix are also relevant to common sense segmentation studies.

Collecting Suitable Data

Market segmentation studies can only ever be as good as the data they are based on. Data are used for two purposes in market segmentation. In data-driven segmentation studies data form the basis of the actual segmentation solution (see 'Extract segments' in Fig. 2). The information used to identify or create market segments is referred to as the segmentation base (Wedel and Kamakura 2000) and typically includes a number of variables. The second point at which empirical data are required is segment profiling, which is done in both the data-driven and the common sense segmentation approaches.

Data requirements for extracting segments in data-driven segmentation have a major impact on the validity of the segmentation solution. The data requirements for the profiling step are not as critical as the requirements for the extraction of segments. It is important, however, that all the information required to gain detailed insight into the segment and develop an optimal marketing mix is available.

Most data-driven segmentation studies in social marketing are based on survey data. Survey data are not the most valid and reliable data source because they can be biased in several ways. For instance, people can have tendencies to use certain answer options, irrespective of question content. This is referred to as a *response style* (Paulhus 1991) and is well documented in the context of cross-cultural research (e.g. Hui and Triandis 1989; Marin et al. 1992; Dolnicar and Grün 2009).

This stream of research indicates that respondents from different cultures vary systematically in the use of response options. Such variation can easily be misinterpreted as differences in beliefs. Another well documented source of bias in survey data is referred to as *social desirability bias* (Hebert et al. 1995). It occurs when there are societal expectations in relation to the topic of the survey, and respondents wish to be seen as being in compliance with those societal expectations. The gap between what people say in surveys when asked about the impact of environmental sustainability on their tour booking behaviour and the actual impact has been recently illustrated by Karlsson and Dolnicar (2016) in the context of booking a boat tour; 60 % of tourists indicated that they considered the environment in travel-related decisions, but only 14 % booked the eco-certified boat and knew that they had.

If survey data are used as the basis of a segmentation study, the following aspects should be considered:

- Preferably, the data should be binary or metric in nature. Binary data are generated by offering response options such as *yes-no* or *agree-disagree*. Metric data results if respondents are asked to indicate something in units that can actually be counted, for example: how many kWh of electricity and litres of water were used. The reason that binary or metric variables are preferable is that all heuristic segmentation methods are based on dissimilarity or distance computations. Distance is clearly defined for binary and metric variables. It is not clearly defined, however, for ordinal variables. Responses to the popular Likert scale, for example, generate ordinal data: the options are ordered (*strongly agree* is more than *agree*), but the distance between the options is unknown. When model-based methods are used, specific models that take the ordinal nature into account need to be used. These models are more complicated; they require the estimation of more parameters and are harder to interpret.
- Preferably, raw data should be used, as opposed to aggregations of variables such as factors emerging from an exploratory factor analysis conducted to reduce the number of variables in the segmentation base. Segmentation solutions based on so-called *factor-cluster analysis* have been shown to not necessarily provide superior segmentation solutions, even if the data-generating process follows a factor analytic model (Dolnicar and Grün 2008). Furthermore, the purpose of most market segmentation analyses is to generate segments that can be interpreted in a meaningful way. This can be done if each segment is described by the original survey questions. If, however, segments have been generated in a transformed factor analytic space where the composition of factors is not clear, and where a substantial amount of information contained in the original variables has been lost, an interpretation is difficult. Ideally, if data is collected specifically for a market segmentation study, the variables should represent distinctly different pieces of information which are suitable for direct use as a segmentation base.
- Preferably, variables in the segmentation base should not be correlated. The wide adoption of Churchill's scale development paradigm (Churchill 1979) in business and market research studies led to much redundancy in survey

questions to achieve high coefficient alpha values within constructs. This is problematic not only because of the reduction of data quality as a consequence of survey fatigue caused by a large number of additional questions (Johnson et al. 1990), but also because many segmentation algorithms struggle with additional variables that do not contain distinctly different information. Heuristic methods often implicitly assume that items are uncorrelated when determining the dissimilarity between observations. In the model-based context, simpler models can be employed if the assumption that the items are uncorrelated holds.

In addition to responses to survey questions, objective measures can also serve as a segmentation base. As opposed to survey measures, which typically represent a subjective self-assessment by the respondent, objective measures are not affected by personal bias; rather, they represent facts. If a measure is truly objective, two independent raters should on average obtain the same value. In the context of social marketing, objective measures can include energy use, water use, number of times sunscreen is applied, number of cigarettes smoked, dollars donated to charity among others. These can be obtained by observation or by the analysis of secondary data, such as energy and utility bills. Objective measures are usually more difficult to collect (which may explain why they are not commonly used in segmentation studies), but represent a more valid and reliable basis for segmenting the market.

Independent of the nature of the variables used as the basis for market segmentation, it is important to be aware of minimum sample size requirements. Segmentation bases in data-driven segmentation studies typically include a large number of variables. Each additional variable increases the complexity of the segmentation task. For the segmentation algorithm to be able to handle this complexity, it requires a sufficiently large sample. If the sample is not large enough, it is not possible for any algorithm to detect naturally occurring segments, even if the data is well structured. A rule of thumb for this relationship has recently been proposed by Dolnicar et al. (2016), who simulated sample size requirements under a range of typical survey data circumstances and recommend the use of at least 100 data points (respondents, observations) for each variable in the segmentation base. For example, if the aim is to segment the Australian population using 15 motives for donating money to a charity, responses from a minimum of 1500 respondents would be required.

Extracting Segments

Clustering aims at finding or constructing groups in data such that observations within groups are "similar" and observations from different groups are "dissimilar" to one another. Clustering methods can be classified into heuristic and model-based methods. Heuristic methods rely on dissimilarity measures between observations which need to be suitably chosen and use an algorithm for constructing the groups. For an overview and introduction to heuristic clustering methods, see Kaufman and

Rousseeuw (1990) or Everitt et al. (2010). Model-based methods assume a (simple) probabilistic model for each cluster, and each cluster has its own data-generating process differentiating it from other clusters, with the similarity of observations measured by the likelihood that they are generated from the same probabilistic model. The complete model is then the combination of these simple cluster-specific models weighted by their cluster sizes. This is referred to as a finite mixture model. An introduction to finite mixture models is given in McLachlan and Peel (2000) and Frühwirth-Schnatter (2006).

Heuristic methods Heuristic methods require the specific choice of how to measure similarity or dissimilarity between observations and groups of observations. The choice depends on two factors: (1) whether variables are on the same scale level. For example, survey respondents can be asked about their frequency of volunteering (which is a metric variable) and whether or not a list of volunteering motives apply (which is a series of binary *yes-no* variables), and (2) whether each variable has the same impact or is measured in comparable units. This is not the case for the previous example where the frequency of volunteering and the agreement with a volunteering motive are collected on different scales. In addition, it needs to be decided if the importance of the agreement to a single volunteering motive should be comparable to the frequency of volunteering, or if this should hold for the complete set of all volunteering motives.

The left column in Table 1 provides an overview of available dissimilarity measures which can be used for different scale levels of the variables. Table 1 can therefore be used to select suitable measures. The formulae given for the dissimilarity measures assume that p variables are observed on the same scale level and that the dissimilarity between two observations x and y are determined, where each consists of a vector with p values.

Suitable dissimilarity measures for metric variables are the Euclidean distance or Manhattan distance, but a range of other measures has been proposed for metric data. Examples of metric data in the context of non-profit organisations include the age of volunteers, the number of hours they volunteer per week, and the number of non-profit organisations they volunteer for. The specific choice of the measure depends, among other things, on the extent to which extreme observations are present and how they should influence the analysis. The impact of such outliers is much larger for the Euclidean than for the Manhattan distance.

Binary variables take only two different values: 0 or 1. Binary variables occur frequently in market research data. Examples relevant to non-profit organisations include yes-no responses to a range of motives that drive people to donate their time to a range of volunteering tasks they engage in, or to a range of non-profit organisations they volunteer for. Binary variables can be symmetric or asymmetric. For symmetric variables, both values are equally valuable and contain the same amount of information, and for asymmetric variables, the outcomes are not equally important and the absence of the less important outcome is disregarded for calculating dissimilarities. The simple matching coefficient can be used as a dissimilarity

Table 1 Overview of methods in dependence of scale level of variables for heuristic and model-based clustering

Scale level	Heuristic methods: dissimilarity measure $d(x, y)$	Finite mixture models: component model $f(x)$
Metric	Euclidean distance: $\sqrt{\sum_{j=1}^{p}(x_j - y_j)^2}$ Manhattan distance: $\sum_{j=1}^{p}\lvert x_j - y_j\rvert$ Other metric distance measure	Continuous data: multivariate normal distribution (arbitrary variance-covariance matrices, restricted variance-covariance matrices) Discrete data: product of Poisson distributions assuming conditional independence for count data
Binary	Simple matching coefficient: $\frac{1}{p}\sum_{j=1}^{p}\lvert x_j - y_j\rvert$ Jaccard distance: $\left(\sum_{j=1}^{p}\lvert x_j - y_j\rvert\right)/\left(\sum_{j=1}^{p}\max(x_j, y_j)\right)$	Product of Bernoulli distributions with success probabilities $\pi_j, j = 1, \ldots, p$ assuming conditional independence: $\prod_{j=1}^{p}\pi_j^{x_j}(1 - \pi_j)^{1-x_j}$ Latent multivariate normal distribution with mean μ and variance-covariance matrix Σ and thresholds $\tau_j, j = 1, \ldots, p$
Nominal	Dummy coding of different values to use a binary dissimilarity measure for each of the dummy variables	Product of multinomial distributions with success probability vectors $\pi_j, j = 1, \ldots, p$ assuming conditional independence: $\prod_{j=1}^{p}\pi_{jx_j}$
Ordinal	Score assignment and use of a dissimilarity measure based on ranks Score assignment and use of a metric dissimilarity measure Dummy coding of different values to use a binary dissimilarity measure (i.e., treating the variable as nominal)	Score assignment and use of metric component model Latent multivariate normal distribution with mean μ and variance-covariance matrix Σ and threshold vectors τ_j, $j = 1, \ldots, p$
Mixed	Weighted combination of dissimilarity measures of variables on the same scale level (Gower 1971)	Product of different distributions for each of the scale levels, assuming conditional independence Latent multivariate normal distribution with mean μ and variance-covariance matrix Σ and threshold vectors τ_j, $j = 1, \ldots, p$, for binary, nominal or ordinal variables

measure for symmetric binary variables, and the Jaccard distance for asymmetric binary variables. For example, potential foster carers can be asked to indicate reasons for considering becoming foster carers. They could do so by ticking only the reasons that apply to them. Such *pick-any* answer formats are known to generate a smaller number of agreements than forced choice binary answer formats do (Dolnicar et al. 2012). The resulting data contains asymmetric binary information, because ticking a reason is much stronger than not ticking a reason. If, on the other hand, a foster carer is asked to indicate, for a set of support services offered by the foster care agency, which ones they have used and which ones they have not used, each of these responses is equally informative. In such a case, dissimilarity can be measured in a symmetric way, implying that two foster carers *not using* a certain service actually makes them similar to each other.

Nominal variables (for example, profession and cultural background) can be transformed into binary variables by creating dummy variables for each possible value. For ordinal variables (for example, age provided by indication of belonging to a certain age group), scores can be assigned, distances can be calculated based on ranks, or answer options can be treated as nominal.

The selection of the scale of the variables depends on what is being measured. It is not possible to make a general recommendation. The social sciences are heavy users of the so-called Likert scales, which ask study participants to indicate their agreement with a statement on a five- or seven-point scale. Likert scales do not represent a good starting point for segmentation studies because they lead to ordinal variables where the distance between scale points is not defined. For example, it is not clear that the distance between 'strongly agree' and 'somewhat agree' is the same as the distance between 'somewhat agree' and 'slightly agree'. If possible, Likert scales should therefore be avoided if data are being collected for segmentation studies.

After having selected a suitable dissimilarity measure, a decision needs to be made about how these dissimilarity values will be combined over different variables to produce an overall value. The combination scheme needs to account for the importance of the different variables in measuring similarity between objects. This requires specifying a weighting of the variables. One possibility is to standardise metric variables before calculating dissimilarities in order to ensure that each of the variables contributes equally to the cluster solution.

Algorithms for extracting clusters in heuristic methods are grouped into hierarchical and partitioning approaches. Hierarchical clustering results in a hierarchy of nested partitions into 1 to n clusters (for n observations) given the dissimilarity between observations and a measure for determining dissimilarities between groups of observations. This so-called *linkage method* has a strong impact on the clusters formed: *single linkage* adopts a 'friends-of-friends' strategy and *complete linkage* results in compact clusters. Partitioning methods aim at finding an optimal partition into k groups, with k given and fixed according to some optimality criterion. The k-means algorithm (MacQueen 1967), for example, minimises the sum of squared Euclidean distances of observations to their cluster centre. An extension of the k-means algorithm to general dissimilarity measures is given in Leisch (2006).

Hierarchical methods rely on deterministic algorithms to obtain solutions. However, the algorithm is not computationally feasible for large data sets, and because a greedy search is employed, the optimal solution for a given number of clusters is not obtained. Partitioning methods aim to find this optimal solution, but because this is an NP-hard problem, any algorithm usually only returns a locally optimal solution. This implies that the result from using a partitioning algorithm is random because the final solution depends on the (randomly chosen) starting points. The algorithm uses an iterative scheme to improve the solution from those starting points. Thus, the selection of starting points can be crucial to ensure that good solutions are identified. One way to manage this challenge is to randomly choose a number of starting points (say, 100), start the algorithm from all these starting points, and select the solution returning the best result.

Both clustering methods, hierarchical or partitioning, result in a partition of the data if the number of clusters k is selected. Given these partitions, segments can be profiled using variables in the segmentation base and additional background variables.

Model-based methods If finite mixture models are used for market segmentation, each market segment is assumed to follow its own underlying statistical model. The model for the complete market is the result of summing over the segment models weighted with the segment sizes. As pointed out by Fraley and Raftery (2002), model-based methods have the advantage that they allow for a principled statistical approach to determine the number of clusters or which model fits the data better.

Again, depending on the scale level of variables, different models need to be considered for the segments. Finite mixtures of multivariate Gaussian distributions are the standard approach for metric continuous data. Finite mixtures of independent Bernoulli distributions are typically employed for binary data. For metric discrete data corresponding to count data, finite mixtures of independent Poisson distributions can be used. Extensions of these basic models have been proposed to allow for special data structures. For example, the case of ordinal variables is considered in Vermunt (2001). An overview on possible segment-specific models available for different scale levels of the variables is given in the right column in Table 1. Again, the p variables in the formulae are assumed to be observed on the same scale level, and the segment model is specified for this p-dimensional vector. The finite mixture models considered in market segmentation often use the same parametric model for each segment, such that the segment-specific models only differ in the parameter values, and these parameter values can be used to characterise and profile the segments.

Finite mixture models can be fitted within a frequentist approach using maximum likelihood estimation or within a Bayesian setting, leading to estimates of the posterior distribution. The estimation is complicated by the fact that the likelihood of a finite mixture model is multimodal, including spurious modes, or is even unbounded. Furthermore, the number of parameters increases linearly with the number of segments. Maximum likelihood estimation of the finite mixture model with the number of segments fixed at k is typically performed using the expectation-maximisation (EM) algorithm (Dempster et al. 1977). This algorithm employs an iterative scheme similar to the k-means algorithm. In each step, the likelihood is increased, ensuring that the algorithm usually converges. Failure of convergence might occur due to unbounded likelihoods, and spurious solutions might also be returned. As the final solution depends on the initialisation, the detection of a suitable solution relies on the initialisation scheme to be employed.

Bayesian methods can be used to alleviate the problem of unbounded likelihoods and spurious solutions. They also allow the inclusion of prior information about the cluster solution aimed at, for example, segments of similar size. However, Bayesian estimation relies heavily on computational methods such as Markov chain Monte Carlo sampling and is also prone to getting stuck in local optima. Additional complications, if not addressed, include the label-switching problem, which prevents segment-specific analysis of the sampled posterior distributions.

Estimation of the finite mixture model results (under both frequentist and Bayesian frameworks) in estimates for the segment sizes and the segment parameters. Cases (typically representing survey respondents) are assigned to segments on the basis of each case's a posteriori probability of being generated from each of the segments. This assignment can be made either: (1) by assigning each observation to the segment where the a posteriori probability is maximum; or (2) by drawing the cluster membership from a multinomial distribution with success probability equal to the a posteriori probabilities.

Selecting Suitable Segmentation Solutions

The application of any clustering algorithm, heuristic or model, will always return a solution. However, the results need to be critically assessed to check if a suitable clustering solution from a statistical point of view has been obtained, and if the segmentation solution is useful with respect to the application in social marketing. From the statistical point of view, solutions might be considered problematic for two different reasons. First, they could represent only a suboptimal solution because the estimation algorithm got stuck in a local optimum, and second, they could reflect a spurious solution. Spurious solutions are often characterised by including clusters that are of very small size and are obtained only for the specific data set.

Furthermore, even a solution which is statistically optimal may not be the most suitable solution from a managerial perspective. It is advisable, therefore, to inspect several cluster solutions before committing to proceed with a specific one. This recommendation reflects the fact that cluster analysis is an exploratory method for data analysis that provides insight into the data by forming groups.

To assess the quality of a cluster solution from a statistical point of view, and to determine a suitable number of clusters, a range of different criteria has been suggested (for an overview, see Milligan and Cooper 1985). No recommendation of a single best criterion has emerged. In addition, these criteria generally assume that a cluster structure is present in the data, which is revealed by the cluster procedure. However, often in market segmentation the aim is not to find natural segments in the market, because they do not exist, but rather to construct a segmentation of the market that allows for suitable positioning and the development of successful marketing strategies.

Dolnicar and Leisch (2010) thus propose to assess the stability and reproducibility of cluster results. They suggest that solutions which can be obtained repeatedly across independent calculations (with slight changes in the algorithm or the data) are preferable. The idea behind this approach is that spurious solutions obtained by clustering algorithms can be eliminated from the consideration set of solutions. An additional benefit of this approach is that it provides insight into the structure of the data. For example, it points to the existence of naturally occurring market segments in the data, which in general might be considered a rare situation in social marketing. If such natural clusters are not present, the procedure shows whether or not certain segmentation solutions can at least be replicated across computations or not. If they cannot be, the data analyst needs to work even more closely with the manager, because each resulting segmentation solution is different, and it is up to the user to decide which of the statistically equally valid solutions should be used. This suggests that the criteria proposed by Dolnicar and Leisch (2010) can be used in combination with other criteria available for heuristic clustering methods and finite mixture models to decide on a suitable number of clusters and a suitable model or classification of the observations.

Profiling Segments

Once segments have been extracted, they need to be profiled using variables in the segmentation base and additional variables of interest, such as sociodemographic variables (including gender and age) and behavioural variables such as volunteering behaviour for different non-profit organisations. The variables need to provide all the information required to select a suitable target segment based on the criteria assessed to be important. In this analysis, segments need to be cautiously compared with respect to variables in the segmentation base because the algorithm used for extracting segments often aims at maximising the differences between segments with respect to these variables precluding the use of standard tests and their *p*-values.

The selection of a suitable segmentation solution and the extraction of segments cannot be performed by relying solely on statistical methods and strategies. Rather, the input of the user, typically the marketing manager, is required to assess the value of a segmentation solution obtained based on segment characteristics. It is also critical to understand that often organisations only want to cater for one market segment—not all segments contained in any specific segmentation solution. The quality of the overall segmentation solution, therefore, is not really of particular interest. Rather, it is the presence of a single attractive market segment which matters.

The results of market segmentation analyses in social marketing are typically presented to managers who select target segments. Consequently, it is critical that information about market segments is well presented. High quality presentations are characterised by providing as much information as possible in an easily digestible way. Typical executive summaries that only present a very small subset of information are dangerous because they do not provide the full picture. Simultaneously, a lot of information presented badly (in large tables for example), is not helpful because it overwhelms managers. Not much research has been dedicated to high quality presentations of market segmentation solutions. An example of how graphical statistics techniques can be used to visualise substantial amounts of information about segments in a simple way is provided by Dolnicar and Leisch (2013).

Selecting the Target Segment

The process of selecting target segments has received surprisingly little attention in the literature, despite the fact that it is arguably the most critical step because it determines the long-term focus of an organisation. Although most authors who have published on the topic of market segmentation propose a list of criteria that should be considered when selecting market segments (see Table 2 for a few alternative lists of segment assessment criteria), not much attention has been paid to

Table 2 Segment assessment criteria (modified from Karlsson 2015)

Authors	Criteria for the assessment of market segments
Croft (1994)	Segment size, segment growth, level of competition, segment profitability, likely technological changes, price sensitivity, barriers to entry, buyer or supplier bargaining power, socio-political considerations, cyclicality and seasonality, life-cycle position
Day (1984)	Measurable, substantial, accessible, sufficiently different, life-cycle stage if durable
Dibb and Simkin (2008)	Homogeneous, attractive in size and profit potential, stable, accessible, compatible, actionable
Kotler and Keller (2012)	Measurable, substantial, accessible, differentiable, actionable, segment rivalry (competition), potential entrants, substitutes, power of buyers, power of suppliers, fit with company objectives, competence, resources
Perreault and McCarthy (2002)	Substantial, operational, heterogeneous between, homogeneous within
Sharp (2013)	Measurable, targetable, size, profitable
Solomon et al. (2011)	Differentiable, measurable, substantial, accessible, actionable
Wedel and Kamakura (2000)	Identifiable, substantial, accessible, responsive, stable, actionable
West et al. (2010)	Size, income and purchasing power, characteristics of the segment, reachability, able to serve segment, large enough to be profitable, truly distinct from other segments, capacity to develop marketing programs to efficiently identify, attract, and serve the segment
Winer and Dhar (2011)	Parsimonious, sufficient in size, sufficient in growth rate, potential competitive position

how these criteria are best operationalised, and who in the organisation assesses the segments with respect to those criteria, to ultimately arrive at a final selection of the target segment.

Based on a survey of 167 responses from marketing managers, Dolnicar and Lazarevski (2009) conclude that approximately one third of managers have difficulties interpreting segmentation solutions. This is a concerning starting point for selecting and committing to a target segment for the longer term. Karlsson (2015) conducted an experiment with business students and found that an unstructured approach to selecting target segments leads to significantly worse choices than a structured one. He also showed that setting a team of experts from the organisation the specific task of selecting the best target segments, and instructing them which criteria to consider (a more structured approach implemented in form of a checklist), led to significantly better decisions.

Ultimately, selecting the target segment is something the organisation needs to do. The organisation needs to determine which of the (many possible) selection criteria are the most important to them and how they wish to weight them. Consequently, it is impossible to give general recommendations beyond suggesting that organisations take a structured, systematic approach to target segment selection to ensure all possible criteria are considered, and that there is agreement about which should be included and how heavily they should be weighted.

Conclusion

The problem with market segmentation studies is that, no matter how badly they are executed, they always lead to a result. How meaningful this result is, however, depends on the quality of the data, the extent to which the structure of the data set was understood before segments were extracted and the methods chosen to extract segments, as well as the presentation of results to inform the choice of the most promising target segment. It is critical, therefore, that marketing managers in organisations with a social mission either have a good understanding of the key decisions that need to be made when segmentation analyses are conducted, or have access to an expert who can advise objectively on possible methodological problems with the analysis. The unit or external firm commissioned with the segmentation study is unlikely to be able to serve as such an objective assessor if not provided with background information such as insights on suitable characteristics of the target segment.

Market segmentation is an extremely powerful tool to improve the achievement of an organisation's mission and to reduce marketing expenditures by avoiding mass marketing and instead, investing resources into those target markets which are most promising. Great segmentation studies rely on great segmentation analysis. Good methods matter.

Acknowledgments We thank the Australian Research Council (ARC) for funding support under Project DP110101347.

References

Churchill, G. A. (1979). A paradigm for developing better measures of marketing constructs. *Journal of Marketing Research, 19*(1), 64–73.

Croft, M. J. (1994). *Market segmentation: a step-by-step guide to profitable new business*. New York: Routledge.

Day, G. S. (1984). *Strategic market planning*. Minnesota: West Publishing Company.

Dempster, A. P., Laird, N. N., & Rubin, D. B. (1977). Maximum likelihood from incomplete data via the EM-algorithm. *Journal of the Royal Statistical Society B, 39*(1), 1–38.

Dibb, S., & Simkin, L. (2008). *Market segmentation success: Making it happen!* New York: The Haworth Press.

Dolnicar, S. (2004). Beyond "commonsense segmentation"—A systematics of segmentation approaches in tourism. *Journal of Travel Research, 42*(3), 244–250.

Dolnicar, S., & Grün, B. (2008). Challenging "factor cluster segmentation". *Journal of Travel Research, 47*(1), 63–71.

Dolnicar, S., & Grün, B. (2009). Response style contamination of student evaluation data. *Journal of Marketing Education, 31*(2), 160–172.

Dolnicar, S., Grün, B., & Leisch, F. (2016). Increasing sample size compensates for data problems in segmentation studies. *Journal of Business Research, 69*, 992–999.

Dolnicar, S., & Lazarevski, K. (2009). Methodological reasons for the theory/practice divide in market segmentation. *Journal of Marketing Management, 25*(3/4), 357–374.

Dolnicar, S., & Leisch, F. (2010). Evaluation of structure and reproducibility of cluster solutions using the bootstrap. *Marketing Letters, 21*(1), 83–101.

Dolnicar, S., & Leisch, F. (2013). Using graphical statistics to better understand market segmentation solutions. *International Journal of Market Research, 56*(2), 97–120.

Dolnicar, S., Rossiter, J. R., & Grün, B. (2012). "Pick-any" measures contaminate brand image studies. *International Journal of Market Research, 54*(6), 821–834.

Everitt, B., Landau, S., Leese, M., & Stahl, D. (2010). *Cluster analysis* (5th ed.). New York: Wiley.

Fraley, C., & Raftery, A. E. (2002). Model-based clustering discriminant analysis and density estimation. *Journal of the American Statistical Association, 97*(458), 611–631.

Frühwirth-Schnatter, S. (2006). *Finite mixture and Markov switching models*. Berlin: Springer.

Gower, J. C. (1971). A general coefficient of similarity and some of its properties. *Biometrics, 27*(4), 857–871.

Hebert, J. R., Clemow, L., Pbert, L., Ockene, I. S., & Ockene, J. K. (1995). Social desirability bias in dietary self-report may compromise the validity of dietary intake measures. *International Journal of Epidemiology, 24*(2), 389–398.

Hui, C. H., & Triandis, H. C. (1989). Effects of culture and response format on extreme response style. *Journal of Cross-Cultural Psychology, 20*(3), 296–309.

Johnson, M. D., Lehmann, D. R., & Horne, D. R. (1990). The effects of fatigue on judgments of interproduct similarity. *International Journal of Research in Marketing, 7*(1), 35–43.

Karlsson, L. (2015). *The impact of checklists on organizational target segment selection*. PhD Thesis, University of Wollongong.

Karlsson, L., & Dolnicar, S. (2016). Does eco certification sell tourism services? Evidence from a quasi-experimental observation study in Iceland. *Journal of Sustainable Tourism, 24*(5), 694–714.

Kaufman, L., & Rousseeuw, P. J. (1990). *Finding groups in data: An introduction to cluster analysis*. New York: Wiley.

Kotler, P., & Keller, K. L. (2012). *Marketing management* (14th ed.). Essex: Pearson Education.
Leisch, F. (2006). A toolbox for K-centroids cluster analysis. *Computational Statistics & Data Analysis, 51*(2), 526–544.
MacQueen, J. B. (1967). Some methods for classification and analysis of multivariate observations. In *Proceedings of 5th Berkeley Symposium on Mathematical Statistics and Probability*, (pp. 281–297). California: University of California Press.
Marin, G., Gamba, R. J., & Marin, B. V. (1992). Extreme response style and acquiescence among Hispanics—The role of acculturation and education. *Journal of Cross-Cultural Psychology, 23*(4), 498–509.
Mazanec, J. A. (2000). Market segmentation. In J. Jafari (Ed.), *Encyclopaedia of tourism*. London: Routledge.
McLachlan, G., & Peel, D. (2000). *Finite mixture models*. New York: Wiley.
Milligan, G. W., & Cooper, M. C. (1985). An examination of procedures for determining the number of clusters in a data set. *Psychometrika, 50*(2), 159–179.
Myers, J. H., & Tauber, E. (1977). *Market structure analysis*. Chicago, IL: American Marketing Association.
Paulhus, D. L. (1991). Measurement and control of response bias. In J. P. Robinson, P. R. Shaver, & L. S. Wrightsman (Eds.), *Measures of personality and social psychological attitudes* (pp. 17–59). San Diego: Academic Press.
Perreault, W. D., & McCarthy, J. (2002). *Basic marketing: A global-management approach* (14th ed.). New York: McGraw-Hill Irwin.
Sharp, B. (2013). *Marketing: Theory, evidence, practice*. South Melbourne: Oxford University Press.
Solomon, M. R., Hughes, A., Chitty, B., Fripp, G., Marshall, G. W., & Stuart, E. W. (2011). *Marketing 2: Real people, real choices*. Frenchs Forest: Pearson Education Australia.
Vermunt, J. K. (2001). The use of restricted latent class models for defining and testing nonparametric and parametric item response theory models. *Applied Psychological Measurement, 25*(3), 283–294.
Wedel, M., & Kamakura, W. A. (2000). *Market segmentation: Conceptual and methodological foundations*. Boston: Kluwer Academic Publishers.
West, D., Ford, J., & Ibrahim, E. (2010). *Strategic marketing: Creating competitive advantage* (2nd ed.). Oxford: Oxford University Press.
Winer, R., & Dhar, R. (2011). *Marketing management* (4th ed.). London: Pearson.

Segmentation Using Two-Step Cluster Analysis

Aaron Tkaczynski

Abstract The purpose of this chapter is to explain the rationale for employing TwoStep cluster analysis as a market segmentation method within social marketing. Here, the key stages to be performed and the validation techniques required for effective application of this clustering technique are outlined. To further support the application of this cluster analysis technique as a profiling tool, a review of 25 recent market segmentation studies that have utilised this method is provided. Finally, a case study is provided to demonstrate how TwoStep cluster analysis is employed to segment respondents for an active school travel social marketing campaign that was being developed in Queensland at time of writing. Based on a sample of 537 respondents, three segments were identified and validated, each of which differed significantly based on psychographic, behaviour, geographic and demographic variables. Limitations of the TwoStep Cluster Analysis method are also provided, and opportunities for future research employing TwoStep cluster analysis within a social marketing context conclude this chapter.

Introduction

TwoStep Cluster Analysis is a cluster analysis algorithm that is available in Predictive Analytics SoftWare (PASW). TwoStep Cluster Analysis is a statistical procedure that is employed by a user to identify similar groups or "clusters" of people or objects within data sets (Norusis 2011). This segmentation method allows users to retain full information, providing rich explanation for managerial decision-making purposes. TwoStep cluster analysis is also considered more reliable and accurate when compared to traditional clustering methods such as the k-means clustering algorithm (Norusis 2007). Since being introduced in Version 11.5 of the Statistical Packages for the Social Sciences (SPSS), TwoStep cluster analysis has been increasingly utilised in a variety of fields such as tourism (Hsu

A. Tkaczynski (✉)
University of Queensland, Brisbane, Australia
e-mail: a.tkaczynski@uq.edu.au

T. Dietrich et al. (eds.), *Segmentation in Social Marketing*,
DOI 10.1007/978-981-10-1835-0_8

et al. 2006; Tkaczynski et al. 2015), health (Griffin et al. 2014; McLernon et al. 2012), transport (Cerin et al. 2007; Chang and Yeh 2007) and psychology (Fillman et al. 2013; Ulstein et al. 2007).

TwoStep Clustering Procedure

The TwoStep clustering procedure, as the name suggests, involves two distinct stages. As a first phase, original cases are grouped into preclusters (Okazaki 2007). The goal of this step, classed as *preclustering*, is to reduce the size of the matrix that contains distances between all possible pairs of cases (Norusis 2011). This clustering method assumes that all variables are independent, that continuous variables have a normal distribution, and categorical variables have a multinominal distribution (Norusis 2007). The categorical and ordinal variables are treated as nominal. The cluster parameter employs a hierarchical method and the scale parameter for each continuous variable is the standard deviation of each continuous variable. If this is unavailable, the default is one (IBM 2011). If categorical and continuous variables are employed, the log-likelihood algorithm is required. Alternatively, if only continuous items are to be analysed, the Euclidian algorithm can be chosen. Based on this procedure, it is assumed that the variances are identical over variables and clusters. The cases represent the objects to be clustered, whereas the variables represent attributes on which clustering is based (Norusis 2007). The algorithm randomly chooses to assign an observed case to a cluster. As each case is read, the algorithm decides if the current case should be merged with a previously formed precluster. Alternatively, the algorithm can choose to start a new precluster. When preclustering is complete, all cases in the same precluster are treated as a single entity (Norusis 2007).

In the second step, the preclusters are clustered using the hierarchical clustering algorithm. This stage is classed as *clustering*. Forming clusters hierarchically lets the researcher explore a range of solutions with different numbers of clusters (Norusis 2007). This stage produces a range of solutions which is then reduced to the best number of clusters based on the Schwarz's Bayesian information criterion (BIC) (Norusis 2011). In addition, outliers can be identified and screened out in the algorithm (Chiu et al. 2001). Once the cluster solution is formed, chi-square tests are conducted for categorical variables and student t-tests for continuous variables to examine the importance of individual variables in a cluster and to identify if the item is valid in the total solution (Norusis 2007). If an item has an insignificant value ($p > 0.05$) it is invalid and should be removed from the analysis. The TwoStep cluster analysis is then rerun until only valid items remain.

Whilst TwoStep cluster analysis can be completed within two stages, an additional phase that is available for market segmentation researchers is running chi-square tests for binary or dichotomous variables once the clusters have been formed. TwoStep cluster analysis creates a cluster membership variable that allows variables that may have been combined into one to be tested for their significance at the individual level. This helps to overcome the limitation of one type of variable (e.g. motivations, interests) biasing a cluster solution to a specific type of variable/s. TwoStep cluster analysis treats all individual variables with equal importance. If 20 motivational items, four demographic items and a geographic variable were analysed simultaneously, this would bias the cluster solution to a motivation focus due to 80 % of the items relating to this type of variable. Therefore, for variables that contain multiple items (Rundle-Thiele et al. 2015; Tkaczynski and Prebensen 2012) which were relevant in forming clusters in the TwoStep cluster analysis, can be individually tested (e.g. number of activities). This determines whether each segment is significantly different from the other items based on the individual items.

TwoStep Cluster Validation

Four final validation techniques need to be employed for a TwoStep cluster analysis solution to be accepted. First, when using the BIC for statistical inference, the silhouette measure of cohesion and separation is required to be at or above the required level of 0.0 (highest being 1.0). This stage measures the relationship of the variables within and between clusters. A score above 0.0 would ensure that the within-cluster distance and the between-cluster distance was valid among the different variables as there is some variation between variables (Norusis 2011). It is more beneficial if the silhouette measure of cohesion and separation is above 0.2 as this showcases that there is a *fair* separation distance between clusters.

Second, all variables within a solution need to be statistically significant ($p < 0.05$). Thus, insignificant variables should be removed from the analysis. Consequently, variables that might be particularly relevant to the study (e.g. gender, club membership) might need to be removed if there is no difference between the clusters based on this variable. Recall, that for market segmentation to be purposeful, clusters need to be distinguished on different classifying variables. The removed variables might still be important for social marketing strategies, but they are irrelevant for differentiating respondents.

Third, when considering the input (predictor) importance to determine the importance of variables in a cluster solution, variables with a low rating (0.02 or below) must be carefully considered for their usage in the final solution. Items with a negative value should be removed from the analysis due to being insignificant (Tkaczynski et al. 2015). Usually, these variables will be the same variables that are outlined in the second validation stage—i.e. those that are statistically insignificant. Variables that have a predictive importance of 0.00 or 0.01 can be included, but it should be noted that the responses to these variables will likely be similar across the different clusters.

The fourth and final validation technique that is recommended by multivariate analysis experts (e.g. Hair et al. 2006) is to randomly split the sample in two and compare the results with the final solution. If the same number of clusters is found in both the final and split solutions, and the characteristics and significance variables of the solutions are similar, then validation is confirmed. Note, for a cluster solution to have a higher chance of being validated, it is recommended that the user collects a large sample size. As segmentation authors such as Dolnicar et al. (2014) argue, for valid results, at least 70 cases should be employed for each variable in data driven segmentation research; therefore, a small sample size (e.g. <300) would be very difficult to validate with only 150 cases in each split solution, particularly if many variables are being cluster analysed simultaneously.

TwoStep Cluster Analysis: An Alternative Solution

While a variety of statistical techniques such as exploratory factor analysis, Pearson's chi-square test, bootstrap analysis and k-means clustering deliver beneficial findings to market segmentation researchers, TwoStep cluster analysis enables an alternative approach to market segmentation which provides distinct advantages, as outlined below.

Application of both categorical and continuous data The first and arguably the greatest advantage of TwoStep cluster analysis is its ability to segment data based on any form of data measurement (e.g. binary, Likert or categorical) simultaneously. Thus, while certain forms of analysis such as k-means clustering require numeric measurement to work effectively, the TwoStep cluster analysis algorithm standardises all of the variables unless the option is specifically overridden by the user (Norusis 2011). As distance measures can be quite sensitive to differing scales or magnitudes among the variables, and variables with larger dispersion (e.g. larger standard deviations) have more impact on the final similarity value (Hair et al. 2006), it has been argued that clustering variables should be standardised whenever possible (Baeza-Yates 1992). TwoStep cluster analysis not only ensures that through standardisation, one variable does not dominate the cluster solution, but also that these variables can be overridden if required (Norusis 2011).

Works well with large data sets The second benefit of TwoStep cluster analysis is that it works extremely well on large data sets. While this clustering method has been employed in social marketing contexts (e.g. Stranak et al. 2014; Ulstein et al. 2007) with small data sets ($n < 500$), it is more advantageous when applied to large data sets (Norusis 2011). Large data sets available, such as census data from major industries such as health, finance, religion or education, can be utilised by researchers with great success (e.g. Rundle-Thiele et al. 2015; Griffin et al. 2014).

Automatically determines the number of clusters A third advantage of TwoStep cluster analysis is that unless specifically overridden by the user, the cluster algorithm automatically determines the number of clusters within a cluster solution (Tkaczynski et al. 2010). Therefore, if the research is exploratory and the characteristics of groups are not known a priori, TwoStep cluster analysis provides a viable solution to a user for determining how many clusters (groups) might be within the data. As a consequence, the user's judgment is not the determining factor when identifying the number of clusters, which can be very beneficial when trying to identify constructs of clusters and the most significant and relevant segmentation variables.

Determines the predictor importance of variables in a cluster solution The fourth advantage of TwoStep cluster analysis is that it enables the user to identify the importance of each item in the cluster solution and how it might be statistically significantly different amongst clusters post analysis. This can be very important when seeking to determine how relevant a specific variable is to the total solution (Tkaczynski et al. 2015). For example, while social marketing studies will traditionally use psychographic (e.g. motivations, perceptions, interests) or behavioural (e.g. physical activity participation, media usage, club membership) variables as a first phase of classifying segments (i.e. people) into groups, the importance of these variables in differentiating the cluster solutions might be minimal, or even insignificant. Rather, it is descriptive variables (e.g. age and gender) that are often used to distinguish psychographic or behavioural items as a post analysis validity measure (e.g. Atlantis et al. 2009; Dietrich et al. 2015a) which might provide the most differentiation in a cluster solution. Identifying which variables are most important in a cluster solution can help market segmentation researchers to plan for differences by focusing on these key variable differences when applying strategic marketing plans or market communication strategies.

Social Marketing and TwoStep Cluster Analysis: A Review

To further examine TwoStep Cluster Analysis's potential for social marketing, a review (see Table 1) is undertaken. These 25 studies were conducted in a variety of countries, such as Australia (Atlantis et al. 2009; Dietrich et al. 2015a), US (e.g. Hu et al. 2009; Stranak et al. 2014) and Norway (Glasø et al. 2007; Ulstein et al. 2007). The focus of the studies varies immensely but a common emphasis on health practices for social good, such as healthy food consumption (Honkanen 2010; Hu et al. 2009), alleviating stress and anxiety (Nielsen & Knardahl 2014; Ulstein et al. 2007), and moderating substance usage (Fleury et al. 2015; Mason and Korpela 2009) was identified. There is a major focus on differentiating patients currently struggling with identified social issues (Bamvita et al. 2014; Créton et al. 2009) based on predefined variables such as demographics and geographic region lived.

In examining the applicability of TwoStep cluster analysis to social marketing, it is noted that a high percentage (68 %) of studies have a sample size smaller than 500. Therefore, one of the most pronounced and promoted strengths of TwoStep cluster analysis—working well with large data sets (Norusis 2011)—is not being fully utilised within these market segmentation studies. Almost two-thirds (64 %) of the studies develop three or four valid clusters (segments), and have a main focus of aiming to differentiate respondents on a pre-conceived classification variable such as behaviour (Chan et al. 2005; Rompré et al. 2007). Despite TwoStep cluster analysis's ability to develop significant and valid clusters as a sole segmentation method, nearly all of the studies employ additional methods pre or post cluster

Table 1 Social marketing studies

Author	Country	Study focus	Respondents	Sample size	Number of clusters	Other methods
Atlantis et al. (2009)	Australia	Metabolism	Male patients	1195	2	II, IV
Bamvinia et al. (2014)	Canada	Hepatitis C virus	Patients	60	4	II
Chan et al. (2005)	Hong Kong	Computerisation skills	Practitioners	954	3	II, VIII, IX
Chan et al. (2006)	Hong Kong	Spiritual care	Part-time nurses	193	3	I, II, V
Créton et al. (2009)	Netherlands	Hypodontia characteristics	Patients	189	4	IV
Dietrich et al. (2015b)	Australia	Alcohol consumption	High school students	2114	3	I, II, IV, IX
Dietrich et al. (2015a)	Australia	Alcohol consumption	High school students	371	3	VII
Fairburn et al. (2007)	England	Eating disorders	Patients	170	4	IV, VIII
Ferreira et al. (2008)	Brazil	Quality of life	Cancer patients	113	2	I, III, IV, VIII
Fleury et al. (2015)	Canada	Substance dependence	Participants	121	4	III
Glasø et al. (2007)	Norway	Workplace bullying	Victims, Non victims	144	2	I, IV, VI, VII
Griffin et al. (2014)	Australia	Health behaviour	Older Australians	96276	6	I, III, VII, IX
Helm and Eis (2007)	Germany	Chemical susceptibility	Outpatients	196	3	II, VIII
Honkanen (2010)	Russia	Food preferences	Consumers	1081	5	I, II, VII
Hu et al. (2009)	America	Blueberry jam attributes	Customers	202	2	I, IX
Lopez-Alonzo et al. (2014)	Spain	Motor evoked potentials	Respondents	56	2	I, II, IV, VII
McLernon et al. (2012)	Scotland	Lifestyle choices	Older women	3218	3	II, IX
Mason and Korpella (2009)	America	Substance use and health	Adolescents	68	2	I
Murphy and Marelich (2008)	America	Young children resiliency	Children	111	2	I, IX
Nielsen and Knardahl (2014)	Norway	Coping strategies	Employees	3738	3	I, IV, VI, VII

(continued)

Table 1 (continued)

Author	Country	Study focus	Respondents	Sample size	Number of clusters	Other methods
Polymeros et al. (2015)	Greece	Consumer preferences	Consumers	149	2	II
Rompré et al. (2007)	Canada	Sleep bruxism	Participants	143	3	I, VII
Rundle-Thiele et al. (2015)	Australia	Physical activity	Residents	1459	4	
Stranak et al. (2014)	America	Hypotension strategies	Physicians	216	4	I, II
Ulstein et al. (2007)	Norway	Relative stress scale	Carers	194	3	I, VII

Note I = Descriptive statistics, II = chi-square test, III = regression, IV = t-test, V = factor analysis, VI = correlation, VII = ANOVA, VIII = Mann Whitney, IX = Other

analysis to further explain respondents. Not surprisingly, descriptive statistics (56 %) is the most popular method, followed by chi-square (36 %) and analysis of variance (32 %).

Social Marketing Case Study

To further showcase the strength and applicability of TwoStep cluster analysis, this clustering technique was employed within a larger social marketing formative study involving carers of primary school-age children in Queensland, Australia. This study aimed to explore the behaviours, behavioural intentions, attitudes, social norms and perceived risks in the context of active school travel for primary school-aged children.

An online questionnaire containing 32 items was designed for this project to cover four bases of segmentation (Kotler and Armstrong 2008). The questionnaire included a series of demographic (i.e. age [of child], carer's age, gender, gender [of child], carer's relationship [with child], education level, weekly income, number of cars, responsibility for getting the child/children to/from school, employment status, geographic (place of residence, distance from school), psychographic (three intention items, three perceived risk items, three social norm items, two perceived behavioural control items, eight attitude items) and behavioural (transport mode) questions. The questionnaire was completed by parents (carers) of primary school-aged children across a variety of regions throughout Queensland including Brisbane, the Gold Coast and the Wide Bay-Burnett region. To increase participation, incentives of winning one of ten AUD$30 gift vouchers were offered.

In total, 537 respondents completed the survey and these responses were analysed using TwoStep Cluster Analysis (Version 22.0). This method was specifically chosen for the analysis since (1) both continuous (e.g. attitudes, risk perceptions) and categorical (e.g. child gender, distance from school) measures were used in the study, (2) an available large sample size (n > 500) would allow TwoStep Cluster Analysis to produce potentially reliable and valid segments based on several key classification variables, and (3) this was an exploratory study in which the number of clusters could not be determined in advance and the user allowed TwoStep Cluster Analysis to automatically determine the number of clusters.

TwoStep Cluster Validation

Recall that variables within solutions need to be identified as a requirement for cluster validation. While the inceptive cluster analysis initially produced three clusters, the solution could not be validated. Most noticeably, *your relationship to the child* and *your gender* items were not significant and generated limited predictor importance in the cluster solution—most respondents were *mothers* (over 90 %). Respondents were also largely aged between *30 and 40, employed* and had a family weekly income in excess of *AUS$2000 per week*. Furthermore, the majority of children in the study were aged *under 6* and respondents were not differentiated by the region [in Queensland] in which they lived. As these items were all insignificant ($p > 0.05$) they were removed from further analysis.

The cluster analysis was rerun and a three cluster solution was again formed. All 25 items were identified as significant ($p < 0.05$) and contributed to predictive importance in cluster formation. When the file was split in two for validation purposes, it was also confirmed that the same number of clusters could be identified in both the split solutions and the respondent characteristics and predictive importance of the variables for the three clusters was similar to the final solution. Consequently, the TwoStep cluster analysis solution was confirmed for this study.

Examining the Segments Generated by TwoStep Cluster Analysis

The average silhouette measure of cohesion and separation was 0.3 for the cluster solution. This indicates that the distance measured between clusters was *fair* and therefore acceptable for further analysis. Tables 2 and 3 describe the clusters. Table 2 consists of the continuous variables which were all measured on a bi-polar (−3 strongly disagree to +3 strongly agree) scale. Table 3 outlines the categorical variables. The predictive importance of all variables in the TwoStep cluster analysis is listed in brackets next to each variable. As mentioned previously, if an item has a rating of between 0.8 and 1.0, it is extremely important in predicting cluster formation. Conversely, items with a score of 0.0–0.2, while significant, are less important in forming the three clusters.

Table 2 Cluster Solution (continuous variables)

Variable	Non-walking oriented parents—n = 62 (13.0 %)	Long distance safety concerned parents—n = 283 (59.5 %)	Walking-focused health conscious parents—n = 131 (27.5 %)
Attitude			
Walking to/from school is good/bad (1.00)	−2.47	1.82	2.61
Walking to/from school is valuable/worthless (0.92)	−2.42	1.69	2.47
Walking to/from school is beneficial/harmful (0.82)	−2.33	1.84	2.62
Walking to/from school is enjoyable/unenjoyable (0.63)	−2.13	1.35	1.95
Walking to/from school is healthy/unhealthy (0.60)	−0.47	2.73	2.98
Walking to/from school is pleasant/unpleasant (0.55)	−2.06	1.24	1.82
Walking to/from school is exciting/boring (0.43)	−1.79	1.01	1.56
Walking to/from school is important/unimportant (0.35)	−1.10	1.17	2.27
Intentions			
I plan to increase the number of times the child walks to/from school this week (0.48)	−2.31	−2.88	−0.53
I will increase the number of times the child walks to school this week (0.48)	−2.32	−2.88	−0.53
I intent to increase the number of times the child walks to/from school this week (0.43)	−2.23	−2.33	−0.5
Perceived Behavioural Control			
The distance between the school and the child's home is too far to walk (0.69)	0.48	2.11	−2.17
How much do you feel that the child walking to/from school next week is beyond your control? (0.03)	0.65	0.37	1.37
Perceived risk			
The traffic along the route to/from school makes the walk unsafe (0.24)	0.74	1.89	−0.27
Streets are dangerous to cross along the route to/from school (0.18)	0.89	1.93	0.08

(continued)

Table 2 (continued)

Variable	Non-walking oriented parents—n = 62 (13.0 %)	Long distance safety concerned parents—n = 283 (59.5 %)	Walking-focused health conscious parents—n = 131 (27.5 %)
The dangers of crime along the route to/from school makes the walk unsafe (0.14)	−0.48	0.22	−1.66
Social norms			
People who are important to me walk their children to/from school (0.36)	−1.23	−1.51	0.98
People who are important to me think the child should/should not walk to/from school (0.29)	−1.06	−1.24	1.02
People who are important to me would disapprove/approve of me walking my child to school (0.20)	−1.05	−0.96	1.08

Note the number in brackets after the variable represents the importance of the variable in cluster formation. This is between 1.0 and 0.0. The closer to 1.0, the more important it is

From viewing Tables 2 and 3 in Chap. 7, it can be noted that the attitude variables, *walking to school is good/bad* (1.00), *valuable/worthless* (0.92) and *beneficial/harmful* (0.82), have the highest predictive importance amongst all variables and are the most relevant in defining differences amongst the three clusters. Furthermore, *distance between the school and the child's home is too far to walk* (0.69), *transport mode* (0.52) and *distance from child's home to school* (0. 47) also have relatively high predictive importance. Variables of less importance to cluster formation include *gender of child* (0.02), *child responsibility* (0.02), and *education level* (0.01).

Non-walking Oriented Parents

In seeking to understand the three clusters, the following exploratory notes are provided. The first cluster is the smallest (13.0 %) and has a negative attitude towards their child/children walking to school. Responses such as *walking is bad* (−2.47), *worthless* (−2.42) and *harmful* (−2.33) are identified. Despite a high percentage of respondents (32.3 %) living close to the school (<2 km), these guardians largely drive their children to school in a *family vehicle* (48.4 %), and appear to care less how they are perceived by friends and family when considering the form of transport that their children used when going to and from school. This cluster is the least educated (45.7 % did not have a university degree) and is the

Table 3 Cluster solution (categorical variables)

Variable	Non-walking oriented parents—n = 62 (13.0 %)	Long distance safety concerned parents—n = 283 (59.5 %)	Walking-focused health conscious parents—n = 131 (27.5 %)
Transport mode (0.52)			
Walk	4.8	0.0	23.7
Bicycle	8.1	0.7	3.1
Family vehicle	48.4	78.4	8.4
Carpool	1.6	1.1	0.8
Bus	6.5	3.5	10.7
Walk + Bicycle + Family vehicle	1.6	0.0	9.2
Walk + Family vehicle	11.3	0.4	35.1
Family vehicle + Carpool	6.5	1.8	1.5
Family vehicle + Bus	3.2	6.4	0.0
Two or more (not already chosen)	4.8	3.5	8.4
Three or more (not already chosen)	3.2	1.8	9.9
Other	0.0	2.5	0.0
What is the approximate distance from the child's home to school? (0.47)			
<1 km	7.8	2.1	40.5
1–2 km	32.3	6.4	44.3
2–3 km	9.7	15.2	10.7
3–4 km	8.1	13.4	2.3
4–5 km	14.5	8.8	0.8
5 km+	27.4	54.1	1.5
Number of cars (0.03)			
None	0.0	14.1	2.3
1 car	24.2	21.9	41.9
2 cars	61.3	66.4	44.3
>2 cars	14.5	10.2	11.5
Are you responsible for getting the child/children to/from school? (0.02)			
Yes	71.0	86.6	76.3
Sometimes	27.4	11.3	22.9
No	1.6	2.1	0.8
Gender of child (0.02)			
Male	56.5	45.9	59.5
Female	43.5	54.1	40.6
Education level of respondent (0.01)			
School	12.9	15.9	10.7
Diploma	41.9	28.6	26.7

(continued)

Table 3 (continued)

Variable	Non-walking oriented parents—n = 62 (13.0 %)	Long distance safety concerned parents—n = 283 (59.5 %)	Walking-focused health conscious parents—n = 131 (27.5 %)
Bachelor degree	27.4	40.3	35.9
Postgraduate degree	17.7	15.2	26.7

Note the number in brackets after the variable represents the importance of the variable in cluster formation. This is between 1.0 and 0.0. The closer to 1.0, the more important it is

least responsible (71.0 %) for how their children arrive and depart school. Based on these key defining characteristics, this cluster is defined as *non-walking orientated parents*.

Long Distance Safety Concerned Parents

Cluster two, which is the largest cluster (59.5 %), has a positive attitude towards their children walking to school. They rate *walking to school is healthy/unhealthy* particularly high (2.73). Despite its positive attitude towards this form of physical exercise, this cluster is extremely negative (e.g. −2.88 for two items) in the likelihood of their child/children walking more to or from school in the next week. Over half (54.1 %) of these respondents live *over 5kms from their child/children's school* and the child/children under their supervision were *girls* (most likely under the age of 6). This cluster rates the risk items of walking to school most highly amongst clusters and also *drive* their child/children to school most frequently in a family vehicle (78.4 %). Of interest is that a very small percentage of this segment allows their children to also arrive/depart school via *bicycle* (0.7 %), *carpool* (1.1 %) or a *bus* (3.5 %). These respondents are also most responsible (86.6 %) for how their child/children get to and from school, and do not appear to care how they are perceived by their friends or family for not allowing their children to walk to school, with negative ratings for all of the perception items. Based on the key defining cluster characteristics, this segment is defined as *long distance safety concerned parents*.

Walking-Focused Health Conscious Parents

The third cluster represents approximately a quarter (27.5 %) of respondents. These respondents have the most positive attitude towards their children walking to/from school out of the clusters. For example, cluster three respondents provide almost a perfect score (2.98) for considering walking to school as *healthy*. This cluster is distinguishable based on the majority of respondents (84.8 %) living within a proximal distance (< 2 km) to their child's school. Despite cluster three respondents having *two cars*, these respondents have a high percentage of their children walking to school (23.7 %) and noticeably, rated the risks of their child/children walking to school as the lowest amongst clusters. This is likely due to parents knowing the paths the child/children might take based on the proximity of the school to their house. This cluster agrees that impressing people with allowing their children to walk to and from school is important (e.g. people who are important to me would approve of me walking my child to school =1.08), and had the highest control (1.37) of whether their child/children walked to school. This cluster was also the most educated (62.6 % had finished a university degree) and also had the highest percentage of children being male (59.5 %). Due to the focus on their children walking to school and the positive perceptions and attitudes that this activity exhibits to these respondents, this cluster is labelled as *walking-focused health conscious parents.*

Discussion and Conclusion

It is argued by Lefebvre (2013, p. 125) that the *"core of social marketing is the people we intend to serve"* and that "*segmentation reinforces and builds on the core tenet of marketing that we should be customer or people focused.*" By segmenting people based on key social marketing criteria, such as their attitude towards physical activity and substance consumption, marketers can design messages, products and services to potentially enable people to engage in positive behavioural changes which will improve their lifestyle and, potentially, their psychological, emotional and physical well-being. This chapter provides (1) an outline of the TwoStep cluster analysis procedure, (2) a review of TwoStep cluster analysis studies conducted in a social marketing context, and (3) a case study to demonstrate use of TwoStep cluster analysis in social marketing. Future considerations based on the active school travel case study are discussed below.

For market segmentation to be relevant, it needs to purposeful. In other words, segments need to be accessible, actionable, sustainable and measurable (Kotler and Armstrong 2008). Many social marketing practitioners work for not-for-profit institutions and segmentation can be a viable tool to target the most fruitful segments (i.e. readiness to change). Examining the walking to school segmentation results, it can be argued that the *long distance safety concerned parents* (cluster 2) need to be a priority segment for Queensland schools and health practitioners. This segment represents over half of the sample, so investment within this group of people could potentially provide positive manifested outcomes if targeted appropriately. Notwithstanding their positive attitude towards walking, parents within this cluster live a long distance from their children's schools (over 5 km), which presents a geographical barrier that cannot be easily overcome. It is suggested that providing infrastructure tools to help realise this cluster's walking to school intention is the key. Another recommended option is to include designated drop-off zones and walking school buses in combination as a solution to deliver safe active travel options for this segment.

The third cluster, *walking-focused health conscious parents*, is a prime segment that should be targeted. These respondents live within a close radius of their child's school across the different regions of Queensland, and have their children actively walking to and from school. However, as less than a quarter (23.7 %) choose this as the only method, additional marketing of the benefits of this activity could be an option. However that external factors such as rain or time restrictions (e.g. running late) might imply (but is not confirmed in this study) that a family vehicle is sometimes required, further promoting the health, emotional and physical benefits of walking could increase the numbers of children walking as their principal transport mode. Furthermore, parents could act as group leaders for walking groups of students or organise activities such as "ride your bike to school day" to encourage more active to and from school travel.

The *non-walking orientated parents* cluster has a negative attitude towards walking and is thus a challenging segment. However, given this segment is small and is likely hard to please, it should not be targeted specifically. Recall that for segmentation to be purposeful, segments need to be accessible, actionable, sustainable and measurable. Since this segment is the least responsible for their child getting to and from school, it is hoped that when their children are older (perhaps 9 or 10) they may, based on the promoted benefits of daily walking, choose to do so for themselves.

Limitations and Opportunities for Future Research

TwoStep cluster analysis provides many benefits for social marketers. A major limitation of the method has been that in previous versions (before 20.0) of TwoStep cluster solution, the user had the choice to consider a solution with or without missing data. However, the option with missing data will usually present a higher BIC and will consequently be preferred. Ultimately, TwoStep cluster analysis now removes all cases with missing data. Although this study had limited missing data, other studies with items that are known to have a high number of non-responses (such as age or annual income) could have a high percentage of their sample removed. A recommendation here is to design questionnaires in such a way that options for non-response are limited, for example, compulsory online survey options or providing a financial motivation to complete paper surveys. A second major limitation is that TwoStep cluster analysis is extremely sensitive to changes in entry, and the final solution may depend on the order of the cases in the file. Therefore, in splitting the file in two, it is recommended that every odd and even case be considered, since time differences or regional differences could produce quite divergent results when cases are split. A third limitation of TwoStep cluster analysis is that while certain academic papers have successfully employed this method to profile customers, more research is required to compare and contrast the different clustering methods (e.g. TwoStep, k-means, R). Consequently, the strength of TwoStep cluster analysis in comparison to other methods is relatively unknown. There is an opportunity for future statistical research to improve this useful method by comparing its strengths and weaknesses with other clustering methods.

References

Atlantis, E., Martin, S. A., Haren, M. T., Taylor, A. W., & Witter, T. G. A. (2009). Inverse associations between muscle mass, strength, and the metabolic syndrome. *Metabolism, Clinical and Experimental, 58*, 1013–1022.

Baeza-Yates, R. A. (1992). Introduction to data structures and algorithms related to information retrieval. In W. B. Frakes & R. Baeza-Yates (Eds.), *Information retrieval: data structures and algorithms*. Upper Saddle River, NJ: Prentice Hall.

Bamvita, J. M., Roy, E., Zang, G., Jutras-Aswad, D., Artenie, A. A., Levesque, A., et al. (2014). Portraying persons who inject drugs recently infected with hepatitis C accessing antiviral treatment: A cluster analysis. *Hepatitis Research and Treatment*, 1–7.

Cerin, E., Leslie, E., Du Toit, L., Owen, N., & Frank, L. D. (2007). Destinations that matter: Associations with walking for transport. *Health & Place, 13*, 713–724.

Chan, M. F., Chung, L., Y. F., Lee, A. S. C., Wong, W. K., Lee, G. S. C., Lau, C. Y., et al. (2006). Investigating spiritual care perceptions and practice patterns in Hong Kong nurses: Results of a cluster analysis. *Nurse Education Today, 26*, 139–150.

Chan, M. F., Day, M. C., Suen, L. K. P., Tse, S. H. M., & Tong, T. F. (2005). Attitudes and skills of Hong Kong Chinese medicine practitioners towards computerization in practice: A cluster analysis. *Medical Informatics and the Internet in Medicine, 30*, 55–68.

Chang, H. L., & Yeh, T. H. (2007). Motorcyclist accident involvement by age, gender, and risky behaviors in Taipei, Taiwan. *Transportation Research Part F: Traffic Psychology and Behaviour, 10*, 109–122.

Chiu, T., Fang, D. P., Chen, J., & Wang, Y. J. C. (2001). A robust and scalable clustering algorithm for mixed type attributes in large database environment. In *7th ACM SIGKDDD International Conference on Knowledge Discovery and Data Mining*. San Francisco: ACM SIGKDDD.

Creton, M., Cune, M. S., De Putter, C., Ruijter, M., & Kuijpers-Jagtam, A. M. (2009). Dentofacial characteristics of patients with hypodontia. *Clinical Oral Investigations, 14*, 467–477.

Dietrich, T., Rundle-Thiele, S., Leo, C., & Connor, J. P. (2015a). One size (Never) fits all: Segment differences observed following a school-based alcohol social marketing program. *Journal of School Health, 85*, 251–259.

Dietrich, T., Rundle-Thiele, S., Schuster, L., Drennan, J., Russell-Bennett, R., Leo, C., et al. (2015b). Differential segmentation responses to an alcohol social marketing program. *Addictive Behaviors, 49*, 68–77.

Dolnicar, S., Grun, B., Leisch, F., & Schmidt, K. (2014). Required sample sizes for data-driven market segmentation analyses in tourism. *Journal of Travel Research, 53*, 296–306.

Fairburn, C. G., Cooper, Z., Bohn, K., O'Connor, M. E., Doll, H. A., & Palmer, R. L. (2007). The severity and status of eating disorder NOS: Implications for DSM-V. *Behaviour Research and Therapy, 45*, 1705–1715.

Ferreira, K. A. S. L., Kimura, M., Teixeira, M. J., Mendoza, T. R., Da NóBrega, J. C. M., Graziani, S. R., et al. (2008). Impact of cancer-related symptom synergisms on health-related quality of life and performance status. *Journal of Pain and Symptom Management, 35*, 604–616.

Fillman, S. G., Cloonan, N., Catts, V. S., Miller, L. C., Wong, J., McCrossin, T., et al. (2013). Increased inflammatory markers identified in the dorsolateral prefrontal cortex of individuals with schizophrenia. *Molecular Psychiatry, 18*, 206–214.

Fleury, M. J., Grenier, G., Bamvita, J. M., Perreault, M., & Caron, J. (2015). Typology of individuals with substance dependence based on a montreal longitudinal catchment area study. *Administration and Policy in Mental Health and Mental Health Services Research, 42*, 405–419.

Glaso, L., Matthiesen, S. B., Nielsen, M. B., & Einarsen, S. (2007). Do targets of workplace bullying portray a general victim personality profile? *Scandinavian Journal of Psychology, 48*, 313–319.

Griffin, B., Sherman, K. A., Jones, M., & Bayl-Smith, P. (2014). The clustering of health behaviours in older Australians and its association with physical and psychological status, and sociodemographic indicators. *Annals of Behavioral Science, 42*, 205–214.

Hair, J. F., Black, W. C., Babin, B. J., Anderson, R. E., & Tatham, R. L. (2006). *Multivariate data analysis*. Upper Saddle River, NJ: Prentice Hall.

Helm, D., & Eis, D. (2007). Subgrouping outpatients of an environmental medicine unit using SCL-90-R and cluster analysis. *International Journal of Hygiene and Environmental Health, 210*, 701–713.

Honkanen, P. (2010). Food preference based segments in Russia. *Food Quality and Preference, 21*, 65–74.

Hsu, C. H. C., Kang, S. K., & LAM, T. (2006). Reference group influences among Chinese travelers. *Journal of Travel Research, 44*, 474–484.

Hu, W., Woods, T., & Bastin, S. (2009). Consumer Cluster analysis and demand for blueberry jam attributes. *Journal of Food Products Marketing, 15*, 420–435.

IBM. (2011). *Two step Cluster analysis* [Online]. IBM SPSS Statistics Information Center. http://pic.dhe.ibm.com/infocenter/spssstat/v21r0m0/index.jsp?topic=%2Fcom.ibm.spss.statistics.help%2Fclusterviewer_clusters_panel.htm

Kotler, P., & Armstrong, G. M. (2008). *Principles of marketing*. California, USA: Prentice-Hall.

Lefebvre, R. C. (2013). *Social marketing and social change*. USA: Jossey-Bass.

Lopez-Alonzo, V., Cheeran, B., Rio-Rodriguez, D., & Fernandez-Del-Olmo, M. (2014). Inter-individual variability in response to non-invasive brain stimulation paradigms. *Brain Stimulation, 7*, 372–380.

Mason, M. J., & Korpela, K. (2009). Activity spaces and urban adolescent substance use and emotional health. *Journal of Adolescence, 32*, 925–939.

Mclernon, D. J., Powell, J. J., Jugdaohsingh, R., & Macdonald, H. M. (2012). Do lifestyle choices explain the effect of alcohol on bone mineral density in women around menopause? *The American Journal of Clinical Nutrition, 95*, 1261–1269.

Murphy, D. A., & Marelich, W. D. (2008). Resiliency in young children whose mothers are living with HIV/AIDS. *AIDS Care, 20*, 284–291.

Nielsen, M. B., & Knardahl, S. (2014). Coping strategies: A prospective study of patterns, stability, and relationships with psychological distress. *Scandinavian Journal of Psychology, 55*, 142–150.

Norusis, M. J. (2007). *SPSS 15.0 advanced statistical procedures companion.* Chicago, IL: Prentice Hall.

Norusis, M. J. (2011). *IBM SPSS statistics 19 procedures companion.* Reading, MA, Addison-Wesley.

Okazaki, S. (2007). Lessons learned from i-mode: What makes consumers click wireless banner ads? *Computers in Human Behavior, 23*, 1692–1719.

Polymeros, K., Kaimakoudi, E., Schinaraki, M., & Batzios, C. (2015). Analysing consumers' perceived differences in wild and farmed fish. *British Food Journals, 117*, 1007–1016.

Rompre, P. H., Daigle-Landry, D., Guitard, F., Montplaisir, J. Y., & Lavigne, G. J. (2007). Identification of a sleep bruxism subgroup with a higher risk of pain. *Journal of Dental Research, 86*, 837–842.

Rundle-Thiele, S., Kubacki, K., Tkaczynski, A., & Parkison, J. (2015). Using two-step cluster analysis to identify homogeneous physical activity groups. *Marketing Intelligence & Planning, 33*, 522–537.

Stranak, Z., Semberova, J., Barrington, K., O'Donnell, C., Marlow, N., Naulaers, G., et al. (2014). International survey on diagnosis and management of hypotension in extremely preterm babies. *European Journal of Pediatrics, 173,* 793–798.

Tkaczynski, A., & Prebensen, N. K. (2012). French nature-based tourist potentials to Norway: Who are they? *Tourism Analysis, 18*, 181–193.

Tkaczynski, A., Rundle-Thiele, S., & Beaumont, N. (2010). Destination segmentation: A recommended two-step approach. *Journal of Travel Research, 49*, 139–152.

Tkaczynski, A., Rundle-Thiele, S. R., & Prebensen, N. K. (2015). Segmenting potential nature-based tourists based on temporal factors: The case of Norway. *Journal of Travel Research, 54*, 251–265.

Ulstein, I., Wyller, T. B., & Engedal, K. (2007). High score on the relative stress scale, a marker of possible psychiatric disorder in family carers of patients with dementia. *International Journal of Geriatric Psychiatry, 22*, 195–202.

Part III
Segmentation in Practice

Increasing Civic Engagement Through Market Segmentation

Melanie Randle and Sara Dolnicar

Abstract Most societies depend on the willingness of community members to donate their time for the provision of essential services, such as delivering meals to homes of people with mobility issues, distributing food to the homeless, and protecting people's homes and lives in cases of natural disasters. However, somewhat alarmingly, recent figures indicate that after 15 years of consistent increases in the number of adults demonstrating civic participation through volunteering, rates fell from a high of 36 % in 2010 down five percentage points to 31 % in 2014. As a consequence, many organisations that rely on volunteers for the provision of a range of services are under substantial pressure to retain current, and recruit more, volunteers. This chapter discusses the potential benefits of marketing techniques for organisations that depend on individuals donating their time to help a social cause; elaborates on why market segmentation is a suitable approach to encourage civic participation and why it is likely to outperform mass marketing; and offers practical examples of how market segmentation has been applied to (1) increase the participation of community members from distinctly different cultural backgrounds in environmental volunteering, (2) identify different patterns of volunteering motivations which can be targeted with marketing messages to increase recruitment, and (3) determine which sections of the general population represent promising targets for foster carer recruitment. The key message of this chapter is that organisations with noble missions would benefit from overcoming the perception that marketing is not noble enough for them to engage in. Instead, they should embrace marketing in general, and market segmentation specifically, as effective tools which will help them achieve their goals.

M. Randle (✉)
University of Wollongong, Wollongong, Australia
e-mail: mrandle@uow.edu.au

S. Dolnicar
University of Queensland, Brisbane, Australia
e-mail: s.dolnicar@uq.edu.au

T. Dietrich et al. (eds.), *Segmentation in Social Marketing*,
DOI 10.1007/978-981-10-1835-0_9

Introduction

Civic participation "refers to the ways in which citizens participate in the life of a community in order to improve conditions for others or to help shape the community's future" (Adler and Goggin 2005, p. 236). The term includes a wide range of activities citizens can engage in, including community service, collective action and political involvement. This chapter focuses on one specific aspect of civic participation, that of community service and uses the following definition: "an individual's duty to embrace the responsibilities of citizenship with the obligation to actively participate, alone or in concert with others, in volunteer service activities that strengthen the local community" (Diller 2001, p. 21).

Such civic participation is critical to the functioning of society as we know it. Australia has more than half a million non-profit organisations. Only about 60,000 of these non-profits pay staff to work (Commonwealth of Australia 2011). In addition, many organisations not classified as non-profits, such as schools, local governments and organisations within the arts sector benefit significantly from residents donating their time to help them achieve their mission.

According to recent Australian Government figures, 5.8 million Australian residents aged 15 and over donate about 743 million hours every year (on average 128 h per volunteer) to contribute to the improvement of their communities (Australian Bureau of Statistics 2015). Estimates of the monetary value of these volunteering hours range from $25 billion (Volunteering Australia 2015) to $200 billion (O'Dwyer 2013). The kinds of activities such volunteers engage in include high profile roles such as saving people's lives and property in the case of natural disasters, but also lending a helping hand in ways rarely visible to society, such as driving elderly people to the shops, meeting a person with a disability for a chat or offering an extra pair of hands to a family in outback Australia.

However, of some concern are recent Australian Bureau of Statistics figures which show that, while the percentage of the adult population volunteering rose consistently between 1995 and 2010, this trend has reversed with the volunteering rate dropping five percentage points from a high of 36 % in 2010 to 31 % in 2014 (Australian Bureau of Statistics 2015). The reasons for this decline are still unclear, however scholars have hypothesised that it could be due to several reasons, including: modern day life simply makes people too busy to volunteer; younger generations may have more negative perceptions of volunteering and are therefore less interested in participating; or the shrinking and ageing population has reduced the supply of volunteers (Oppenheimer et al. 2015). In order to ensure that all of the critical community services provided by volunteers can be maintained, it is therefore essential to either increase the pool of individuals who engage in community service work, increase the number of hours each individual volunteer donates or increase retention rates such that rates of volunteering do not decline even further.

Although the non-profit and community services sectors have traditionally been reluctant to utilise marketing tools to achieve their mission (Dolnicar and Lazarevski 2009), it is marketing tools that are most likely to assist them with this challenge. Market segmentation, one of the key strategic marketing tools, has particular advantages as it encourages organisations to gain insights into the people whose behaviour they wish to modify, and develop customised products and communication messages for similar groups of people (Dolnicar et al. 2005). As will be discussed in detail later, this approach has advantages over the mass marketing approach because it taps into the particular issues or concerns that are particularly important to that specific group within the population.

Organisations relying mostly on community members donating their time, however, face a number of challenges in the implementation of market segmentation. As mentioned above, they can be reluctant to use any marketing at all because of a perception that it does not align with their ideology, viewing marketing simply as an act of manipulation. But in addition to this attitudinal barrier to uptake, volunteer organisations also typically face a number of structural barriers preventing them from effectively harvesting marketing techniques to their benefit. First, they are usually struggling to deliver their core services, leaving little time for additional tasks such a market research and marketing. Second, they often lack the funding to effectively conduct the required research to inform and implement a marketing plan. Third, they do not typically have staff with high levels of experience in marketing because their primary focus is on recruiting people with expertise in the specific operational field of their social service delivery.

An empirical study of marketing in non-profit organisations in the UK, US and Australia (Dolnicar and Lazarevski 2009) concluded that "*non-profit organisations are far from having reached the full potential through marketing*" and offered two key reasons for this: (1) the perception of non-profits that not all of the marketing mix is under their control, as is the case with consumer goods—they typically feel they have limited ability to modify the product, the price or choose a distribution channel, and (2) the perception of marketing as deceitful and evil and therefore contrary to their organisational mission which is honourable and good. A degree of cognitive dissonance can result from using tools perceived to be inherently bad for the purposes of social marketing which aims to achieve social good. Yet, if the barriers to embracing marketing generally, and strategic marketing specifically, can be overcome, the reward for non-profits in terms of achievement of the organisation's mission is likely to be substantial.

Why Market Segmentation Is Better Than Mass Marketing

In the social marketing literature questions have been raised regarding the extent to which strategic marketing concepts such as segmentation and targeting are appropriate in the context of social behaviour change (as discussed by Hoek and Jones 2011). This argument, more commonly found in the context of public health, is based on the notion that small behavioural change in large populations often constitutes a greater aggregate shift than large changes in smaller target groups.

This argument reflects a misunderstanding of the concept of market segmentation because it assumes that marketing action is limited to a subsection of the market. This is not necessarily the case. The original definition of market segmentation specifies that it "*consists of viewing a heterogeneous market (one characterised by divergent demand) as a number of smaller homogeneous markets*" (Smith 1956, p. 6). How many of those smaller, homogeneous submarkets are targeted is entirely up to the organisation. An organisation could choose to target only one specific market segment, some of them, or all of them.

Irrespective of the number of market segments targeted, adopting a segmentation approach has a number of benefits (Dolnicar 2008). First, both the offer (in this case engaging in civic participation) and the communication of the offer can be customised to the target group, thus increasing the likelihood of uptake in the short term. For example, communicating the employment benefits of environmental volunteering to people who are currently studying environmental science is likely to immediately increase environmental volunteering by this segment. In the longer term the customisation is likely to lead to a clearer positioning or a distinct image of the organisation, which offers a competitive advantage over alternatives when people choose who to donate their time to. For example, an environmental volunteering organisation may, over time, develop a reputation to be an excellent training ground for students and write reference letters which help people find paid employment. Such a reputation can translate into long-term competitive advantage over other environmental volunteering organisations. Second, if only a subset of possible market segments is targeted an additional benefit is that the cost of marketing initiatives is reduced because communication channels are selected to reach the target market of interest rather than being wasted on the entire population. For example, instead of paying mass media to advertise for environmental volunteers, a small organisation could target the local university instead, at much lower cost and, potentially, with a far greater chance of successfully recruiting new volunteers. The cost is lower because advertising time in mass media is extremely expensive both in absolute terms and in relative terms (per successful recruitment).

There are limited recent examples of sophisticated market segmentation studies conducted with the ultimate aim of increasing levels of civic participation. For the most part, segmentation studies are conducted a priori (Mazanec 2000), a method also known as *common sense* segmentation (Dolnicar 2004), using socio-demographic criteria or volunteering intention/behaviour as the segmentation base. For example, Wymer (2011) segmented volunteers according to their gender to investigate differences in preferences for volunteer organisations, types of roles and supervision arrangements. An online survey of 742 adults (including volunteers and non-volunteers) revealed numerous differences between males and females, including that females prefer volunteering for serving roles in organisations which help the needy, and also roles that involve working closely with children or young people. They also prefer organisations with a community focus and supervisors that seek input and ideas from volunteers. Males, on the other hand, are more likely to prefer roles that involve dangerous situations or risk taking, and also those that come with a degree of authority. They are also more prepared than females to volunteer for roles that might involve confrontation or conflict.

More recently, Randle and Dolnicar (2015) used *common sense* segmentation to examine whether individuals who would consider volunteering for an environmental cause in the future ("potential environmental volunteers") differed from individuals who would not consider it. Using data collected through an online survey of 1318 adults a number of significant differences were found between the groups. These included that 'potential environmental volunteers' had stronger pro-environmental attitudes, different personal values and different motivations for volunteering. Findings can be used by environmental volunteering organisations to design marketing strategies that include messages which are likely to resonate with 'potential environmental volunteers' and prompt action, which then turns them into actual environmental volunteers.

There are also examples of more sophisticated analytical techniques being used to segment the market a posteriori (Mazanec 2000), also known as *data driven* segmentation (Dolnicar 2004), in an effort to increase civic participation. In their Canadian study of MS fundraisers, Wood et al. (2010) performed hierarchical cluster analysis using four identity measures: self-identity fundraising, social identity fundraising, self-identity cycling, and social identity cycling, as the segmentation base. Four segments were identified, labelled event enthusiasts, because fundraisers, road warriors and non-identifiers, which differed in terms of their length of involvement with the event and the quantity of funds raised. The authors use results to recommend target segments (event enthusiasts and cause fundraisers) and also provide practical recommendations for appropriate marketing strategies, for example in relation to event design and promotions.

Another example of *data driven* segmentation was conducted by Randle et al. (2013), who examined whether a strategy of competition or collaboration was more appropriate for volunteering organisations for attracting volunteers. Using data from an online study of 1415 Australian adults they investigated whether brand images of volunteer organisations are perceived by volunteers as being complementary or in competition with each other. Findings reveal that volunteers consider some organisations in isolation, but others are considered in combination with specific other non-profit brands. Findings can be used by non-profit organisations to develop marketing strategies which are most appropriate for their particular brand, and which may or may not include collaborative marketing efforts with other volunteer organisations.

However, despite the growing number of segmentation studies being conducted by academic researchers, community service providers and small non-profits rarely engage in systematic market segmentation. This is despite the fact that (1) national volunteering strategies explicitly point to different approaches being required for different sections of the population. For example, the National Volunteering Strategy (Commonwealth of Australia 2011) points to a number of clear target segments in which growth is desired, including young Australians which can be accessed through schools and universities, older Australians and jobseekers. And (2), non-profits are very clear about the benefits they communicate to the population in advertisements posted on the Volunteering Australia website (for example, "*Do you have good handwriting and enjoy writing Christmas cards?*", "*Get industry experience, learn new skills and meet interesting people…*"). Yet, in order to be exposed to those targeted messages, a potential volunteer must have already been proactive at searching out volunteering opportunities, whereas pursuing a market segmentation strategy would involve identifying people with those skills and needs and directing them to the possibility of volunteering.

Three examples of how market segmentation can be used to encourage civic participation are provided below. All three are the result of many years of research collaboration with small non-profits which have enabled the authors to gain insight into the challenges, but also the rewards of using market segmentation to increase civic participation. The examples have been chosen to illustrate alternative ways segmentation can be used according to the range of different challenges faced by non-profit organisations. These include the challenges associated with operating in communities that are particularly diverse in terms of socio-cultural composition, wanting to attract volunteers with a particular mindset or motivation for becoming involved, and needing to find volunteers for roles that are highly involved and require considerable investment and/or sacrifice on the part of the volunteer. The examples chosen also use different data collection methods and analysis techniques, but all provide market insights that can be used to target specific segments of the population with customised marketing strategies. Of course, while many other examples could have been chosen, the ones included here offer quite varied examples that may prompt practitioners to broaden their thinking in terms of the different ways market segmentation could be used within their organisation to solve the particular challenges they face.

Attracting Environmental Volunteers from a Specific Cultural Group

In modern Western societies many communities, particularly in large cities, are characterised by high levels of multiculturalism. This presents challenges for marketers because different marketing messages can be interpreted and processed differently depending on the background of the individual exposed to it. It is recognised that different cultures can consume the same products or perform the same behaviour for different reasons. Mass marketing strategies are often ineffective because they do not target any group effectively and appeal to no-one in particular. Therefore, in order to appeal effectively to any one cultural group, strategies are required which will overcome the specific barriers faced by that group and provide the particular experience desired.

This example includes a qualitative comparative study of three different cultural groupings: (1) Australian, (2) Anglo-Celtic (English, Irish and Scottish) and (3) Southern European (Greek, Italian, Macedonian, Serbian) (see Randle and

Dolnicar 2009a, for methodological details). The behaviour of interest was volunteering for a local environmental volunteering program, *Bushcare*. This program involves groups of volunteers regularly meeting at the same council-designated location and working together to restore and regenerate the natural environment. The Theory of Planned Behaviour served as the theoretical framework for the research, which focused on understanding differences between cultural groups in terms of (1) their beliefs about volunteering for an environmental program, (2) how others within their social circle feel about their environmental volunteering, and (3) the factors that make it easier or harder for individuals to volunteer.

A number of differences were identified across the three groups. In terms of attitude, the Australian and Anglo-Celtic groups had positive attitudes towards volunteering, while the attitude of the Southern European group was more heterogeneous (i.e. evidence of both positive and negative attitudes). The Southern European group was more likely to consider the views of important others in their decision to volunteer, Australians gave them moderate consideration, and the Anglo-Celtic group gave them the least consideration. In terms of perceived behavioural control, or the ability to volunteer, the Australian group expressed a high level of control, the Anglo-Celtic group moderate control, and the Southern European group the lowest control (for more detail see Randle and Dolnicar 2009a, summary p. 235).

Taking the Southern European group as an example, findings from this segmentation study are helpful in enabling Bushcare to develop customised marketing strategies should it wish to target this group. In terms of motivation, it was important to Southern Europeans that any volunteering efforts benefitted members of their own communities. While this benefit was not immediately obvious in the case of environmental volunteering, the introduction of volunteer groups which include other members of the Southern European community would provide socialisation and support for others within the community. There was some concern expressed about the possibility of volunteer labour being exploited by government. For this reason it may be optimal to avoid the use of the term "volunteering" and instead describe potential involvement in terms of activities and behaviours. It was also evident that, generally speaking, gardening and working outside was considered a role more suitable for males rather than females within this particular segment of potential volunteers. Therefore targeting groups of men from this group and emphasising the socialising and supportive aspects of group volunteering is likely to be an effective marketing strategy for Bushcare.

The study also revealed that Southern Europeans were the group most influenced by important others in their decision to volunteer. The challenge for marketers, therefore, is to not only target promotions at individuals, but also to build a positive brand image within the community as a whole, particularly among community leaders. Importantly, the Southern European group experienced the most barriers to volunteering when compared to the other groups. Barriers include language, transport and family commitments. Changes to Bushcare's offering could possibly overcome some of these barriers. For example, volunteer groups from the same cultural background could be scheduled to help overcome language issues, community transport to Bushcare worksites could be offered to overcome transport issues, and active engagement of children in volunteering groups could help overcome the perceived barrier of family commitments standing in the way of volunteering engagement.

This example demonstrates how a simple *common sense* segmentation study, based on a qualitative research design requiring nothing more than a few thorough interviews with a number of representatives of market segments which are known in advance, can be used to create a successful social marketing strategy to attract volunteers from a particular community. Having similar information to that above for each cultural group enabled Bushcare to determine which group to target, and then make the appropriate changes to its marketing strategy to attract them successfully. The volunteer manager later reported that target volunteer numbers had been achieved and consequently the organisation had been able to refocus resources towards retaining volunteers rather than attracting new ones.

Targeting Volunteers with Particular Motivations

The notion of marketing centres on fully understanding customer needs such that an offering can be provided that meets these needs (Kotler and Armstrong 2010). In the context of volunteering, this involves understanding what people want out of their volunteering experience and, as far as possible, providing this. It also involves communicating the offering in a way that emphasises the specific aspects of the experience that are most valued and are of most benefit to that individual.

Numerous studies have found that for complex behaviours such as volunteering, which usually involves a reasonable commitment of time and effort by the individual, motivations for volunteering are rarely singular and almost always multifaceted (Hibbert et al. 2003; Randle and Dolnicar 2009b). One of the most widely cited classifications of volunteer motivations is the Volunteer Functions Inventory (VFI, Clary et al. 1992) which groups motivations according to the six functions they serve for the individual. The functions are values (the volunteer can act on deeply held beliefs about the importance of helping others), career (the volunteer learns particular skills that will help with their career), understanding (the volunteer gains understanding of the people they are helping, the organisation they volunteer for or themselves), social (volunteering results from the influence of important others in their life), enhancement (the volunteer feels needed and important) and protective (the volunteer can escape from negative feelings about their own life). The proposed measurement tool includes five items for each function, and evidence has been produced for the reliability and validity of the VFI in measuring volunteer motivations (Clary and Snyder 1999; Clary et al. 1992; Marta et al. 2006). However, placing individuals into one of these segments would ignore the fact that their motivations are likely to cut across more than one function. It may be that they are motivated by one or more aspect of multiple functions, although the common combinations of motivations within the population are not observable and require further investigation.

A posteriori (Mazanec 2000), post hoc (Myers and Tauber 1977) *or data-driven* (Dolnicar 2004) segmentation techniques enable just this: to identify groups within the population who are similar to each other in aspects that may not be immediately obvious to others, as is the case with people from different cultural backgrounds. In terms of volunteering motivations, this means groups of people can be identified who share similar combinations of motivations, regardless of the overarching function each motivation might represent.

This example is based on a study of 4267 Australian volunteers who were presented with a list of 12 different volunteering motivations and asked to indicate whether each applied to them (see Dolnicar and Randle 2007 for methodological details). Data was analysed using topology representing networks (Martinetz and Schulten 1994), a technique which looks at individual responses and groups participants together based on the similarity of their answers. The segmentation solution is chosen based on stability measures, and so the number of resulting segments is determined not by the researcher but largely by the analytical procedure.

In this analysis six segments were identified. "*Classic volunteers*" are motivated by doing something worthwhile, helping others and gaining a sense of personal satisfaction. "*Dedicated volunteers*" identify with all motivations more than average which suggests a specific, particularly dedicated and positive, volunteer. "*Personally involved volunteers*" participate for one primary reason: their personal involvement in the cause. "*Personal satisfaction volunteers*" donate their time because they want to gain a sense of personal satisfaction, but are less concerned with altruistic motivations such as helping others. "*Niche volunteers*" state that they are motivated by a range of factors: they are more likely than average to feel obliged to volunteer, want to obtain work experience, volunteer because of their religious beliefs, and are also the segment most likely to have become involved in volunteering by accident. Finally, "*Altruists*" volunteer because they want to help others.

The segments which resulted from the segmentation analysis were then compared to identify significant differences in terms of personal characteristics, specifically their socio-demographic characteristics and their volunteering behaviour. This information is useful for the development of customised marketing strategies. For example, organisations whose volunteers require significant training (e.g. emergency services) may wish to target individuals who, once volunteering, give the highest number of hours and continue volunteering for a long time, and are the "Dedicated volunteers". This group contains a high proportion of members who are not active in the labour force as well as a relatively high proportion of women. As they are motivated by multiple factors, communications which include a range of possible benefits from volunteering are likely to be effective.

Alternatively, organisations requiring volunteers to provide teaching or instruction services may wish to target the "Classic volunteers" who are the segment most likely to have been involved in this activity before. This group is one of the older segments and more than one third of the volunteers in this segment are no longer employed. Communications focusing on helping others by doing something worthwhile, as well as the personally satisfying nature of volunteering are likely to appeal to this group.

This type of a posteriori segmentation enables managers to detect market segments whose identifying characteristics may not be immediately obvious, and design marketing strategies that are more effective in attracting them and offering them a volunteering experience of value to them in order to maximise their retention.

Increasing Foster Carers by Overcoming Barriers to Participation

Children enter foster care when they are identified by public authorities as being exposed to unacceptable levels of risk in their home environments and are removed from their birth families and placed with carers who look after them until it is considered safe for them to return.

In Australia, the number of children in out-of-home care has increased by 20 % in the past decade (Australian Institute of Health and Welfare 2015), but at the same time the number of people volunteering to be foster carers has decreased (McHugh and Pell 2013). The shortage of foster carers has forced foster care agencies to make greater and more sophisticated use of marketing techniques such as market segmentation in an attempt to attract enough foster carers to provide homes for children in need.

This example involves a study of 756 adults aged between 18–65 years who had never considered becoming a carer before (see Randle et al. 2014 for methodological details). Participants were presented with a list of 29 possible reasons for not having considered foster caring and indicated whether each reason applied to them. When considered at the aggregate level, the most common reasons for not having considered the role before were that no-one had ever asked them to; it being too big a commitment; because of their personal circumstances, the opportunity never arose; and they did not know anything about foster caring. However, when a posteriori segmentation was conducted with a reduced set of barriers, four segments emerged which differed significantly in their psychological and sociodemographic characteristics.

The "*Mums and dads*" segment had not considered foster caring because they were too busy with their own children. The "*Not interested*" segment identified with almost all barriers to foster caring, particularly not wanting to give the child back and feeling as if they would not be able to rise to the challenge of welcoming a foster child into their family. The "*Couldn't cope*" segment had little interest in children, was particularly concerned about not being able to cope with a foster child, and felt they were either too young or too old. Finally, the "*Never been asked*" segment indicated that the primary reason they had not previously considered the role was that no-one had ever asked them to.

Clearly, while the *Couldn't cope* and *Not interested* segments state reasons for non-consideration that likely make them unsuitable for the role of foster carer, the *Mums and dads* and *Never been asked* segments offer great potential as targets of customised communication messages. The barrier to foster caring cited by *Mums and dads* (i.e. being busy with their own children) makes them unsuitable at present for the role, but suggests they may be suitable in future when their own children are grown and this barrier is removed. This suggests that a long-term strategic marketing approach, which builds awareness and organisational preference, may be critical in converting these individuals to foster carers in future. The fact that they have lower incomes suggests that communications emphasising the support available for carers, such as financial assistance to help cover the household costs of caring for a foster child, may help to break down some of the perceived barriers to becoming a foster carer. Given they are parents, communication channels such as school newsletters or sporting competitions are likely to be effective in reaching this group.

The group which shows more immediate potential for foster care marketing strategies is the *Never been asked* segment. This market segment does not cite a lack of confidence or disinterest in children as some of the other segments do. Rather, the personal characteristics of this market segment are quite distinct: they tend to be older and have higher incomes, and also display higher levels of hope and problem solving skills. Communications targeting this group should be very informative and include direct appeals for immediate action towards becoming a foster carer. Messages emphasising the difference carers make in the lives of foster children are also likely to appeal to their feelings of hope and optimism. The fact that members of this market segment are older, and more likely to be male, suggests that publications with high readership amongst these groups would be effective, as would media stories that can include richer information about the role and the positive impact carers have on the lives of some of society's most vulnerable children.

This a posteriori segmentation analysis is effective in identifying the barriers that prevent different segments of the market from considering the role of a foster carer and identifying the groups likely to be receptive to different types of marketing messages. It also provides insights that would enable foster care agencies to reach these individuals and prompt them to take action.

Conclusions

The work of non-profit organisations is critical to the functioning of many modern societies around the world. These organisations could not provide their services, which often benefit our most vulnerable citizens, animals and the environment, without the assistance of other community members who are prepared to contribute their time for the good of others, the broader community and future generations.

Yet, non-profits are finding it increasingly challenging to recruit enough volunteers to achieve their goals. With the size of the third sector increasing, and more organisations calling for public assistance, non-profits will need to be more proactive, embrace marketing concepts and harvest them to their benefit. This is particularly the case for strategic marketing—not typically a focus amongst non-profits—which is critically important in terms of the long-term prosperity of the organisation. Market segmentation is a key building block of strategic marketing. Market segmentation, based on thorough market research, allows organisations to gain insight into systematic differences in the individuals whom they wish to attract as volunteers. Once these are understood, the organisation can reassess which segments are most suitable for their organisation and most likely to be interested in volunteering for their cause. Such systematic differences can then be used for the development of customised communication messages, and possibly also for customising the volunteering experience itself. Such customisation leads to a higher likelihood of marketing activities being successful in converting community members into active volunteers.

A number of tangible recommendations can be derived from the three examples described in detail in the present study:

1. Non-profit organisations must charge someone within the organisation with the responsibility for marketing. Of course, optimally, the person responsible has formal qualifications in marketing. If this is not the case, training should be made available. It is important the person responsible for marketing appreciates the positive effects that embracing marketing can have on the mission of the organisation.
2. Non-profit organisations should invest time and other resources focusing on strategic marketing, including market segmentation and product positioning. Decisions on matters of strategic marketing should be based on market research; however, the research does not necessarily have to be expensive or large-scale. It can be as simple as systematically collecting comments from people about why they would or would not donate their time to the non-profit organisation's cause, or from volunteers about what benefits they derive from volunteering for their organisation. Another simple source of market insight could involve conducting interviews with "experts" in the relevant fields (e.g. front line managers of volunteers). Critically, making good strategic marketing decisions involves adopting a bigger picture perspective than limiting attention to the everyday logistics of core service delivery.
3. Only when the non-profit organisation's optimal positioning and segmentation strategy have been identified should any operational or tactical marketing action be planned. The effectiveness of operational and tactical marketing, such as advertising, pricing, distribution and product design, depends on solid strategic marketing decisions. This insight is critical, since many non-profit organisations which try to implement marketing programs are tempted to engage in

advertising *before* clarifying internally what they stand for and, subsequently, who they want to target.

4. Non-profit organisations should put in place monitoring systems that allow them to measure the effect of their marketing efforts. This is the best possible "marketing of marketing" to organisations which often have inherent reservations about embracing marketing.

Acknowledgments We are grateful to the Australian Research Council (ARC) for supporting this research through salary funding under the Discover Scheme, projects DP110101347 and DE120102003.

References

Adler, R. P., & Goggin, J. (2005). What do we mean by "civic engagement"? *Journal of Transformative Education, 3*(3), 236–253.

Australian Bureau of Statistics. (2015). *General social survey: Summary results, Australia 2014*. http://www.abs.gov.au/AUSSTATS/abs@.nsf/Lookup/4159.0Main+Features12014?OpenDocument. Accessed November 4, 2015.

Australian Institute of Health and Welfare. (2015). Child protection Australia 2013–14. *Child Welfare Series Number, 58*. http://www.aihw.gov.au/publication-detail/?id=60129550762

Clary, E. G., & Snyder, M. (1999). The motivations to volunteer: Theoretical and practical considerations. *Current Directions in Psychological Science, 8*(5), 156–159.

Clary, E. G., Snyder, M., & Ridge, R. (1992). Volunteers' motivations: A functional strategy for the recruitment, placement, and retention of volunteers. *Nonprofit Management and Leadership, 2*(4), 333–350.

Commonwealth of Australia. (2011). *National volunteering strategy*. https://www.ag.gov.au/EmergencyManagement/Community/Volunteers/Documents/national-volunteering-strategy.pdf. Accessed November 2, 2015.

Diller, E. C. (2001). *Citizens in service: The challenge of delivering civic engagement training to national service programs*. Washington, DC: Corporation for National and Community Service.

Dolnicar, S. (2004). Beyond "commonsense segmentation"—A systematics of segmentation approaches in tourism. *Journal of Travel Research, 42*(3), 244–250.

Dolnicar, S. (2008). Market segmentation in tourism. In A. Woodside & D. Martin (Eds.), *Tourism management—Analysis, behaviour and strategy* (pp. 129–150). Cambridge: CABI.

Dolnicar, S., Freitag, R., & Randle, M. (2005). To segment or not to segment? An investigation of segmentation strategy success under varying market conditions. *Australasian Marketing Journal, 13*(1), 20–35.

Dolnicar, S., & Lazarevski, K. (2009). Marketing in non-profit organizations—An international perspective. *International Marketing Review, 26*(3), 279–291.

Dolnicar, S., & Randle, M. (2007). What moves which volunteers? Psychographic heterogeneity among volunteers in Australia. *Voluntas: International Journal of Voluntary and Nonprofit Organizations, 18*(2), 135–155.

Hibbert, S., Piacentini, M., & Al Dajani, H. (2003). Understanding volunteer motivation for participation in a community-based food cooperative. *International Journal of Nonprofit and Voluntary Sector Marketing, 8*(1), 30–42.

Hoek, J., & Jones, S. (2011). Regulation, public health and social marketing: A behaviour change trinity. *Journal of Social Marketing, 1*(1), 32–44.

Kotler, P., & Armstrong, G. (2010). *Principles of marketing*. Upper Saddle River, NJ: Prentice Hall.

Marta, E., Guglielmetti, C., & Pozzi, M. (2006). Volunteerism during young adulthood: An Italian investigation into motivational patterns. *Voluntas: International Journal of Voluntary and Nonprofit Organizations, 17*(3), 221–232.

Martinetz, T., & Schulten, K. (1994). Topology representing networks. *Neural Networks, 7*(3), 507–522.

Mazanec, J. A. (2000). Market segmentation. In J. Jafari (Ed.), *Encyclopaedia of tourism*. London: Routledge.

McHugh, M., & Pell, A. (2013). *Reforming the foster care system in Australia: A new model of support, education and payment for foster parents*. http://www.berrystreet.org.au/Assets/2583/1/ProfessionalisedFosterCareSystemfullpaper.pdf. Accessed November 4, 2015.

Myers, J. H., & Tauber, E. (1977). *Market structure analysis*. Chicago, IL: American Marketing Association.

O'Dwyer, L. (2013). *Beyond the value of time: Towards a methodology for quantifying the other impacts of volunteering*. Paper presented at the 2013 National Volunteering Conference, Adelaide.

Oppenheimer, M., Haski-Leventhal, D., Holmes, K., Lockstone-Binney, L., & Meijs, L. (2015). Where have all the volunteers gone? *The Conversation*. https://theconversation.com/where-have-all-the-volunteers-gone-47192

Randle, M., & Dolnicar, S. (2009a). Does cultural background affect volunteering behaviour? *Journal of Non-profit and Public Sector Marketing, 21*(2), 225–247.

Randle, M., & Dolnicar, S. (2009b). Not just any volunteers: Segmenting the market to attract the high contributors. *Journal of Non-profit and Public Sector Marketing, 21*(3), 271–282.

Randle, M., & Dolnicar, S. (2015). The characteristics of potential environmental volunteers: Implications for marketing communications. *Australasian Journal of Environmental Management, 22*(3), 329–339.

Randle, M., Leisch, F., & Dolnicar, S. (2013). Competition or collaboration? The effect of nonprofit brand image on volunteer recruitment strategy. *Journal of Brand Management, 20*(8), 689–704.

Randle, M., Miller, L., Dolnicar, S., & Ciarrochi, J. (2014). The science of attracting foster carers. *Child and Family Social Work, 19*(1), 65–75.

Smith, W. (1956). Product differentiation and market segmentation as alternative marketing strategies. *Journal of Marketing, 21*, 3–8.

Volunteering Australia. (2015). Key facts and statistics about volunteering in australia. http://www.volunteeringaustralia.org/wp-content/uploads/VA-Key-statistics-about-Australian-volunteering-16-April-20151.pdf. Accessed November 2, 2015.

Wood, L., Snelgrove, R., & Danylchuk, K. (2010). Segmenting volunteer fundraisers at a charity sport event. *Journal of Nonprofit & Public Sector Marketing, 22*(1), 38–54.

Wymer, W. (2011). The implications of sex differences on volunteering preferences. *Voluntas: International Journal of Voluntary and Nonprofit Organisations, 22*(4), 831–851.1

Segmenting Caregivers to Gain Insights for Social Marketing Program Design

Francisco Crespo Casado, Sharyn Rundle-Thiele and Timo Dietrich

Abstract Providing a healthy lunchbox is one (of many) means that may assist to combat the childhood obesity epidemic. Segmentation permits homogeneous groups to be identified from a heterogeneous market to inform strategy and assist resource optimisation. The purpose of the present study is to investigate whether segments exist within carers of primary school-aged children using a TwoStep cluster analysis method. A convenience sample of 876 carers/guardians of primary school-aged children formed the basis of this exploratory study. Segments were examined using three commonly used segmentation bases, namely demographic, psychographic and behavioural variables. Three different carer segments emerged: (1) wealthy and less concerned, (2) concerned with low socioeconomic status and (3) concerned, wealthy and educated. Carers in the wealthy and less concerned segment reported the most negative attitudes towards packing lunchboxes and had the lowest intentions to increase the number of healthy lunches provided to their children. Further, they reported packing significantly less servings of vegetables and fruit than the other segments. Different segments require differently tailored social marketing programs. Implications are outlined.

F. Crespo Casado (✉)
Centre for Health and Social Research, Faculty of Health
Sciences, Australian Catholic University, Level 5 / 215 Spring Street,
Melbourne, Victoria 3000, Australia
e-mail: francisco.crespo-casado@acu.edu.au

S. Rundle-Thiele · T. Dietrich
Menzies Health Institute Queensland, Griffith University, Nathan, Australia
e-mail: s.rundle-thiele@griffith.edu.au

T. Dietrich
e-mail: t.dietrich@griffith.edu.au

S. Rundle-Thiele · T. Dietrich
Department of Marketing, Griffith University, 170 Kessels Road,
Nathan, QLD 4111, Australia

T. Dietrich
Centre for Youth Substance Abuse, Faculty of Medicine and Biomedical Sciences,
University of Queensland, Herston, QLD 4029, Australia

T. Dietrich et al. (eds.), *Segmentation in Social Marketing*,
DOI 10.1007/978-981-10-1835-0_10

Introduction

The estimated social and economic costs of obesity for Australia in 2008 were AUD $58.2 billion (Access Economics 2008). If no further action is taken to slow the growth of obesity, it will lead to an additional 2.4 million obese people by 2025 and AUD$87.7 billion in additional costs over the next 10 years (Price Waterhouse Coopers 2015). According to estimations from the World Health Organisation (WHO) (2015) in 2014, over 1.9 billion people (18 years and older) were overweight, and over 600 million people were obese. The situation for children is not any better. The prevalence of childhood overweight and obesity under the age of five has increased from 4.2 % in 1990 to 6.7 % in 2010, and 40 million children within this age range are now overweight (de Onis et al. 2010; WHO 2014). Australia is one of the most overweight developed nations, with overweight and obesity now affecting one in four children (ABS 2013a). The conditions for which obesity predicts higher mortality and/or morbidity include cardiovascular disease, type 2 diabetes, forms of cancer, and osteoarthritis (Kelishadi 2007). In addition, overweight and obesity are also strongly related with a wider range of conditions such as mental health, sleep apnoea, reproductive and back problems (Lobstein et al. 2004). The increased risk that overweight and obese children will become obese adults and suffer from chronic diseases at a much younger age amplifies the gravity of the public health issue (Magarey et al. 2003; Lobstein et al. 2004).

According to Queensland Health (2012), obesity among children 5–12 years old can be explained in significant part due to unhealthy dietary choices. Efforts aimed to improve children's diets have to compete with food advertisements that promote preference for unhealthy foods among children by increasing its perceived tastiness and providing more compelling advertisements (Portsmouth and Donovan 2012). The food industry conveniently takes advantage of children's innate preference for sweet and salty tastes (overcoming natural precaution for bitter poisons), by offering food products high in sodium and added sugars (Birch and Fisher 1998). Parents play a critical component and need to act as role models for improved food eating behaviours (Gortmaker et al. 2011).

Bell and Swinburn (2004) found in the National Nutritional Survey from 1995 to 1996 that over one-third of primary school-aged children's energy intake is consumed at school and the majority of primary school-aged children (86.2 %) bring their lunch from home in lunchboxes. Sanigorski et al. (2005) measured the lunchbox contents of 1,681 children from the South-Western region of Victoria, which were mostly from low socioeconomic status (SES) areas. This was measured by the Socio-Economic Index for Areas – SEIFA. Sanigorski et al. (2005) described the typical school lunch brought from home as "*about one sandwich, two biscuits, a piece of fruit, a snack of either a muesli/fruit bar or some other packaged snack and a drink of fruit juice/cordial or water*" (p. 1312). Studies on lunchbox contents have invariably identified a low presence of vegetables, a high intake of fruit/cordial drinks and an excessive amount of "extras" (Bell and Swinburn 2004; Sanigorski et al. 2005). "Extras" (or "discretionary choices") have been defined as foods with a low nutritional value and/or high in added salt, fat or sugar (Bell and Swinburn 2004). The recommendations are to limit consumption of these foods and keep quantities small. The Australian Guide to Healthy Eating (AGHE) recommends up to 1–2 servings per day of extras for primary school children (NHMRC 2013). Brennan et al. (2010) audited for at least three days the lunchbox contents of 170 children (between 5 and 8 years of age) from metropolitan Melbourne, and they reported that 33.6 % of school lunchboxes had 1–2 servings of extras and 28.8 % had 2 or more. However, in the study from Brennan et al. (2010) sandwiches were not opened and sandwich fillings were not assessed, meaning that the number of "extras" present could have been higher. Even in the unlikely case that children did not eat more "extras" outside the school, many would have already exceeded the healthy standards set by the guidelines. The food brought to school might be a reflection of the child's overall diet consumed at home (St-Onge et al. 2003), and parents appear to be facing barriers when packing a healthier lunchbox, based on the findings of the qualitative study performed by Bathgate and Begley (2011) with parents of low SES from Perth. Taken together, research indicates room for improvement in the contents of Australian primary school children's lunchboxes and the need for other behaviour change approaches, such as social marketing, which co-create programs to motivate the target audience to change rather than inform and educate or impose restrictions.

Literature Review

Social marketing Social marketing adopts commercial marketing techniques to design and implement programs to facilitate behaviour change (iSMA 2013). In line with commercial marketing, social marketing planning and program design requires understanding of the audience, a behavioural focus, segmentation, competition, and theory (Hopwood and Merritt 2011) in order to develop a product and/or service offering (marketing mix) that meets the needs and wants (exchange) of the audience (s) targeted.

There are different behaviour change strategies that social marketing programs targeting obesity may try to achieve and the most common is changing dietary intake (Pettigrew 2015), which may involve offering more healthful eating alternatives. Typically, efforts to improve people's diet have focused on developing healthier eating habits, including increasing fruit and vegetables intake and reducing snacking (Croker et al. 2012). Efforts are needed to design and deliver to market healthful food alternatives that are desired by the target audience.

Market segmentation in nutritional contexts Market segmentation is underpinned by the idea that a heterogeneous market can be divided into smaller homogeneous markets based on differing product preferences (Smith 1956). Wills et al. (2014) suggest that the members of a segment have unique combinations of barriers and motivations around a behaviour that differentiate them from other segments that, in turn, require tailored messages or incentives relevant to them.

Individuals who share similar characteristics can be identified and grouped so that companies can target the group(s), enhancing appeal by delivering tailored offerings (Kalwani and Morrison 1977; Fine 1980; Dibb 1998). At the core of segmentation lies a desire to optimise the efficiency and effectiveness of marketing efforts. Marketing acknowledges differences between consumer groups that affect how they respond (Lotenberg et al. 2011) and empirical evidence is emerging that segments respond uniquely to social marketing programs (Dietrich et al. 2015a, b). There is a strong trend towards a more individualised approach that reflects the audience needs, involving customisation of the product/service offer (Helfert et al. 2002) aided by the exponential growth of the internet and digital capability. Given that social marketing programs have limited resources available (Newton et al. 2013) and funding timeframes are short, resources need to be allocated efficiently to maximise program outcomes. As Pettigrew (2015) posited, there are just a few products that can be promoted to everyone without any modification in response to differences among consumers.

The market segmentation process starts by segmenting the audience, followed by deciding on the target and positioning the offer (Kotler 1997). Marketers can use four segmentation bases to identify potential groups, namely demographic, geographic, psychographic and behaviour (Kotler et al. 2002; McLeay and Oglethorpe 2013). Doyle (2011) states that demographic segmentation is the most widely used base in consumer marketing, and nowadays census data (e.g. age, income, sex, or gender) and other big data sources can be easily accessed to provide this data. Segmentation strategies relying only on demographic variables may produce poor results when identifying homogeneous subgroups in relation to health-related outcomes (Boslaugh et al. 2005). A wider application of segmentation bases is required to form more meaningful segment solutions. Geographical segmentation helps to divide the market into regions, countries, cities or neighbourhoods (Walsh et al. 1993), while psychographic segmentation uncovers the different motivations each segment presents for behaviour change (Wills et al. 2014). Finally, behavioural segmentation groups consumers based upon their use of a product or service (Law 2009).

Similar to commercial marketing, segmentation can help social marketers identify groups of people most in need (Donovan and Henley 2010) or most capable or willing to change their current behaviour and adopt the new behaviour proposed (Lee and Kotler 2015; Lotenberg et al. 2011). A "one size fits all" approach when marketing social change can fail to address the needs of all people (Kolodinsky and Reynolds 2009). Wills et al. (2014) used psychographic segmentation to identify differentiated segments of obese people according to their readiness to change and confidence about tackling obesity. Some studies have employed a combination of bases to undertake segmentation in social marketing, yet they remain in the minority (see for examples Dietrich et al. 2015a, b; Schuster et al. 2015). Mc Leay and Oglethorpe (2013), for example, segmented based on parental purchasing decisions in the context of unhealthy foods in developing countries. Further, Kolodinsky and Reynolds (2009) used knowledge and behavioural variables to segment obese people in the U.S.

Factors affecting the contents of children's lunchboxes Many factors have been identified in the literature relating to children's school lunchboxes and the role that parents play in their preparation. Metcalfe et al. (2008) suggested that the lunchbox is negotiated between children and parents (among various actors) during shopping and in the kitchen while the packed lunch is being prepared. In a study in the UK, a quarter of children aged 11–12 years old reported to have control over the contents packed into their lunchboxes (Douglas 1999). Nutritional value of the food packed into children's lunchboxes appears to be a common concern expressed by parents in some of the studies reviewed (Metcalfe et al. 2008; Bathgate and Begley 2011). One of the parents who participated in Bathgate and Begley's (2011) focus groups reported how, after finding out that muesli bars contained additives and colours, they decided to avoid them in the future. Parents want to provide nutritious meals to their children (Tandon et al. 2010), yet they find themselves having to pack some unhealthy food to make sure that their children will at least eat something (Bathgate and Begley 2011). It is also likely that children who do not like the food brought to school may end up trading it or simply throwing it away. Over time parents become less influential as children approach adolescence and peers become more influential (Moore and Stephens 1975). Hesketh et al. (2005) reported that peer and advertising pressures were the main barriers. Metcalfe et al. (2008) suggested that food is a focus of tension and parents can easily feel conflicted when it comes to juggling a balanced diet and their children's dietary requests. Furthermore, Metcalfe et al. (2008) highlight this difficulty in decision making when feeding their children and suggest that often, compromises are required.

Children from low SES families appear to be consuming less healthy foods from their lunchboxes (Sanigorski et al. 2005). Links between parents' SES and their children's diets have been established (Vereecken et al. 2004). Previous evidence suggests that underprivileged parents have lower nutritional knowledge than privileged parents (Bathgate and Begley 2011). A nutritious diet requires the "knowledge of the contribution of different foods to a healthy and balanced diet" (Douglas 1999, p. 185). People are becoming less competent in nutrition and their knowledge has not matched the rapid increase in scientific knowledge (Oltersdorf 2003). The cost of food can be another important factor affecting the provision of adequate lunches, particularly for those households with lowest income (Bathgate and Begley 2011). Bathgate and Begley (2011) stated that parental concerns about children's nutrition and willingness to do "the right thing" explained their consenting to pay more for healthier foods. A study by Neumark et al. (2003) found a strong positive association between high socioeconomic status households and the frequency of family meals, which appeared to be positively related to the quality of the dietary intake.

The availability of time to prepare lunchboxes may represent a challenge for employed parents, who have previously reported to feel overwhelmed by the responsibilities, causing significant stress (Devine et al. 2006). Bathgate and Begley (2011) found that parents spent on average 15 min daily preparing the food that their children will take to school. This suggests a preference for foods that need little preparation time. Convenience might therefore favour selection of pre-packaged foods at the supermarket.

Finally, parents considered food safety among their biggest concerns, one that can prevent parents from packing healthier foods (Hudson and Walley 2009). Further, Hudson and Walley (2009), found that lunchboxes left at room temperature until lunchtime registered temperatures of up to 20.4 °C (and 17.7 °C for those with an icepack inside), compromising food safety.

Justification of the study Evidence shows that segmentation needs to be used more often (McLeay and Oglethorpe 2013). Against this background, the purpose of the present study is to investigate the existence of segments within carers of children are evident using a Two-Step cluster analysis method. Given the study is regionally-focused in Queensland, segments will be examined on the basis of the remaining segmentation bases, namely demographic, psychographic and behavioural variables. Due to the pivotal role played by parents' attitudes and beliefs in their children's diets, considering psychographic and behavioural variables appears justified. The present study reports an initial segmentation study aiming to determine whether unique homogeneous segments exist. These may then be considered for the design of a tailored social marketing program to improve primary school-aged children's school lunchboxes.

Method

Participants An online survey collected data for this cross-sectional formative research study. Carers/guardians of primary school-aged children in Queensland (Australia) (n = 876) were part of the convenience sample used. Participants had the chance to win a voucher as an incentive. Potential participants were approached through university staff (3600 members), previous university research participants, members of the online parenting website BubHub, fans of the MumBub Connect Facebook page and finally, the researchers' personal networks. Prospective participants received reminder emails eight days after the first wave to increase response rates.

Measures The online survey was created through the web application (LimeSurvey version 1.9×). Carers were questioned about the frequency with which they prepared lunchboxes for their children to carry to school as well as the contents of lunchboxes packed, their attitudes towards lunchboxes, and demographic information. A total of 18 items (two constructs intentions and attitudes towards packing lunchboxes) were utilised for the segmentation analysis. A bipolar scale with eight items was adapted to measure parents' attitudes towards lunchboxes on seven-point rating scales (with values from −3 to +3) (Scott et al. 2007). Semantic differential scales locate respondents' attitudes on a bipolar dimension and result in a score that represents a person's general evaluation of the behaviour in question (e.g. school lunchbox preparation) (Ajzen and Fishbein 1980). Parents and carers' attitudes are polarised (e.g. *Healthy|Unhealthy*; *Pleasant|Unpleasant*;

Expensive|Inexpensive). Intentions to prepare a lunchbox were measured employing a unipolar 7-point scale with three items adapted from Ajzen and Fishbein (1980). Following the process described in Crespo-Casado and Rundle-Thiele (2015), the School Food Checklist (SFC) (Sanigorski et al. 2005; Mitchell et al. 2009) was used as a checklist for carers to record the number of serves (out of 27 food and beverages categories) packed into the school lunchboxes the previous day. To facilitate the analysis, each of the 27 food groups included in the SFC was assigned to one of the six food groups outlined in the Australian dietary guidelines (NHMRC 2013): *vegetables and legumes*; *fruit*; *grain (cereal) foods*; *lean meat and poultry, fish, eggs, nuts and seeds*; *milk, yoghurt, cheese and/or alternatives*; and *discretionary choices* to create convenient categories and facilitate the analysis. Furthermore, a range of demographic measures such as income, education, age, and employment were used to describe the segments. Finally, participants answered one health-related behavioural question regarding smoking.

Analysis TwoStep cluster analysis was used to segment Queensland carers of children that attend primary schools following procedures outlined in Tkaczynski et al. (2010). The TwoStep cluster analysis method has been utilised in a number of different contexts such as segmentation of tourists (Tkaczynski et al. 2010); adolescents' drinking behaviour (Dietrich et al. 2015a, b); and physical activity (Kitunen et al., in press). Following the TwoStep cluster analysis, three distinct segments of carers were identified. Finally, a one-way ANOVA was performed between the three carers' segments obtained and the SFC food groups (reclassified following the dietary guidelines) (NHMRC 2013) to examine group differences.

Results

The majority of participants (98.9 %) reported English as the main language spoken at home, were women (97.6 %), and were between 30 and 44 years old (81.9 %). The study's sample showed a significant income and education difference when compared to the general Australian population (ABS 2013b, c) for the 2011/2012 period and was generally wealthier. Almost two-thirds (65.2 %) of the sample reported an income well over the Australian median, and the sample was more highly educated when compared to the Australian population. The highest percentage of participants reported earnings above AUD$120,000 (27 %) followed by AUD$40,000–60,000.

TwoStep cluster analysis produced a sample (n = 417) with a silhouette measure of cohesion of 0.1, which was high enough to validate the cluster solution. A cross-validating method of the identified segments was carried out by dividing the total data sample (n = 876) in approximate halves and repeating the same analysis on each half of the data sample (Punj and Stewart 1983). Individual carers' ID codes were used to split the data into half and to minimise order effects, and the cases randomly ordered (IBM 2010). After validation of the segments, chi-square tests were performed on all categorical items (8) with statistically significant differences between groups noted for seven of the eight categorical variables (except for the retirement status item). ANOVA testing was conducted on all continuous items (10) representing seven attitudinal items and three intention items. All measures were statistically different between segment groups.

A three-segment solution with 18 segmentation variables was accepted as the final solution (see Table 10.1). Each variable score received an individual predictor importance score (ranging from 0 least important to 1 most important). One attitudinal variable had the highest predictor score of 1 (To me, lunchbox food packed at home is Harmful|Beneficial). Further important predictor variables were the other six attitude items (ranging from 0.64 to 0.90), the carers' education level item (0.83), the carers' reported income (0.56), whether the carers were engaged in home duties (0.24), and all three intentions items (ranging from 0.13 to 0.18). The least important predictor variables were age (0.16), being a student (0.15), smoking (0.07), being retired (0.01), and not employed (0.01).

Segment 1 (*wealthy and less concerned*) was the smallest segment (n = 102) and reported the most negative attitudes towards preparing lunchboxes. For example, across all attitudinal items segment 1 featured the most critical attitudes regarding enjoyment (*Unenjoyable|Enjoyable; M* = 0.90), engagement (*Boring|Interesting;* M = 0.25), importance (*Unimportant|Important;* M = 1.75), and health (*Unhealthy|Healthy;* M = 1.82). This segment was characterised as having a high household income (AUD*$120,000 and over; 33.3 %*) and technical and further education (*TAFE) or trade certificate* was the most commonly reported education level (34.3 %), followed by *undergraduate degree* and *postgraduate degree* (*about 30 % and slightly over 20 %, respectively*). With just 16.7 % being *engaged in home duties*, this was the segment with the lowest proportion of homemakers reported in this category. Interestingly, this segment reported the lowest intentions to increase the number of healthy lunches provided to their children and reported the lowest levels of fruit and vegetable packed in lunchboxes (see Table 10.2). Furthermore, most of the carers in this segment fell into the *35–39 years old* age category (31.4 %), followed by those who belonged to the *40–44 years old* group.

Segment 2 (*concerned with low SES*) was the largest carers′ segment (n = 180) and reported very positive attitudes towards preparing lunchboxes. They also reported the highest intentions to increase the number of healthy lunches provided to their children. The attitudes of this segment were more negative regarding engagement (*Boring|Interesting*; M = 1.95) and for enjoyment (*Unenjoyable| Enjoyable;* M = 2.31), and were more positive for importance (*Unimportant| Important* M = 2.66) and effect (*Harmful|Beneficial;* M = 2.64). This segment was characterised as having the lowest reported household income (most individuals reported *AUD$40,000 and less than AUD$60,000; 33.3 %*) and *TAFE or trade certificate* was the most commonly reported education level (50.0 %), followed by *completed high school* and *some high school*. They majority reported being *engaged in home duties* (53.9 %). Furthermore, most of the carers in this segment fell into the *30–34 years old* age category (37.2 %) which showed a slighter younger demographic than the other two segments.

Table 10.1 Caregivers' segments including importance coefficient, mean/most frequent category and *p*-values for each of the variables

Cluster	1 Wealthy and less concerned (n = 102)	2 Concerned with low SES (n = 180)	3 Concerned wealthy and educated (n = 135)	*p* value
Inputs (importance)	(Mean/most frequent category)	(Mean/most frequent category)	(Mean/most frequent category)	
Attitude 1|To me, lunchbox food packed at home is… Harmful|Beneficial (1.00)	1.2	2.6	2.7	<0.001
Attitude 2|To me, lunchbox food packed at home is… Bad| Good (0.90)	1.3	2.6	2.6	<0.001
Attitude 3| To me, lunchbox food packed at home is… Unpleasant|Pleasant (0.86)	1.0	2.4	2.2	<0.001
Attitude 4|To me, lunchbox food packed at home is… Boring|Interesting (0.84)	0.3	2.0	1.9	<0.001
What is the highest level of education you have completed? (0.83)	TAFE or trade cert diploma	TAFE or trade cert diploma	Postgraduate degree	<0.001
Attitude 5|To me, lunchbox food packed at home is… Unenjoyable|Enjoyable (0.81)	0.9	2.3	2.1	<0.001
Attitude 6|To me, lunchbox food packed at home is… Unimportant|Important (0.76)	1.8	2.7	2.7	<0.001
Attitude 7| To me, lunchbox food packed at home is… Unhealthy|Healthy (0.64)	1.8	2.6	2.7	<0.001
Before tax is taken out, which of the following ranges best describes your household income over the last 12 months? (0.56)	AUD $120,000 and over	AUD $40,000 and less than $60,000	AUD $120,000 and over	<0.001
Which of the following describe your current situation? Engaged in home duties (0.24)	Not selected	Yes	Not selected	<0.001
Intentions 1|I will increase the number of times my child has a healthy lunch (0.18)	5.0	5.9	5.0	<0.001
Which age group do you belong to? (0.16)	25–39 years old	30–34 years old	35–39 years old	<0.001

(continued)

Table 10.1 (continued)

Cluster	1 Wealthy and less concerned (n = 102)	2 Concerned with low SES (n = 180)	3 Concerned wealthy and educated (n = 135)	*p* value
Inputs (importance)	(Mean/most frequent category)	(Mean/most frequent category)	(Mean/most frequent category)	
Intentions 2| I plan to increase the number of times my child has a healthy lunch (0.16)	5.1	5.9	5.1	<0.001
Intentions 3| I intend to provide more healthy lunches for my child (0.13)	0.13 (5.40)	0.13 (6.12)	0.13 (5.70)	<0.001
Do you currently smoke cigarettes, cigars, pipes or any tobacco products? (0.07)	Not at all	0.07 (Not at all)	0.07 (Not at all)	<0.01

Segment 3 (*concerned, wealthy and educated*) was the second largest segment and also reported the most positive attitude scores towards preparing lunchboxes. The most negative attitudes in this segment were for engagement (*Boring|Interesting*; M = 1.87) and for enjoyment (*Unenjoyable|Enjoyable*; M = 2.13), and the most positive attitudes were for importance (*Unimportant|Important*; M = 2.73) and health (*Unhealthy|Healthy*; M = 2.70). This segment was characterised as having the highest reported household income (most individuals reported AUD *$120,000 and over; 54.1 %*) and *postgraduate degree* was the most commonly reported education level (44.4 %), followed by *undergraduate degree* and *TAFE or trade certificate*. About one-third of this segment reported being *engaged in home duties* (29.6 %).

ANOVA tests were undertaken to determine the existence of differences (or not) in lunchboxes packed for children by their parents (see Table 10.2).

A statistically significant difference was observed for packing vegetables and legumes between the three segments. Within the vegetables and legumes, carers in the *concerned, wealthy and educated* segment packed more *vegetables and legumes* (M = 1.0, SD = 1.5) than carers in the *wealthy and less concerned* segment (M = 0.5, SD = 0.9), and more than carers in the *concerned with low SES* segment (M = 0.8, SD = 1.1). The food group *fruit* was significant with a *p*-value of 0.05. Within the *fruits*, carers in the *concerned with low SES* (M = 1.6, SD = 1.0) and *concerned, wealthy and educated* (M = 1.6, SD = 1.2) segments packed more fruit than the *wealthy and less concerned* (M = 1.3, SD = 1.1). No statistically significant differences were observed for *fruit*; *cereal foods*; *lean meat, poultry, eggs and other*; *dairy*; *discretionary choices*; and *water*.

Table 10.2 Mean serves by segment (Australian dietary guidelines classification)

	(1) Wealthy and less concerned	(2) Concerned with low SES	(3) Concerned, wealthy and educated		
	n = 102	n = 180	n = 135		
Food groups	M (SD)	M (SD)	M (SD)	F	*p* value
Vegetables and Legumes	0.5 (0.9)	0.8 (1.1)	1.0 (1.5)	4.409	<0.05
Fruit	1.3 (1.1)	1.6 (1.0)	1.6 (1.2)	2.985	$p = 0.05$
Cereal foods	1.0 (0.7)	1.0 (0.7)	1.0 (0.7)	0.378	n.s.
Lean meat, poultry, eggs and other	1.2 (1.2)	1.2 (1.2)	1.3 (1.1)	0.137	n.s.
Dairy	0.9 (1.0)	0.9 (0.9)	0.9 (1.0)	0.181	n.s.
	Discretionary choices		3.5 (2.5)	3.4 (3.3)	3.0 (2.8)
	1.515	n.s.			
Water	1.2 (1.2)	1.4 (1.2)	1.4 (1.3)	0.938	n.s.

Discussion

The current study employed a large convenience sample of 876 carers/guardians of primary school-aged children to explore whether meaningful segments existed. Three segments were identified within the carers of the present study, namely *wealthy and less concerned* (n = 102), *concerned with low SES* (n = 180) and *concerned, wealthy & educated* (n = 135). All three segments agreed that the preparation of food for children to take to school is considered an important activity by carers given that the item *Unimportant|Important* displays high scores across the three segments. These findings support previous research (Metcalfe et al. 2008) which suggested that parents believe that lunchboxes are an important form of providing healthy nutrition to their children. Extending on earlier research the current study highlights attitudinal differences at a segment level. For example, packing lunchboxes was viewed as a boring and unenjoyable activity by the *wealthy and less concerned* segment, in contrast to interesting and enjoyable in the *concerned with low SES* and *concerned, wealthy and educated* segments. The results for the *wealthy and less concerned* segment are in line with other studies reporting that carers are facing time pressures which make preparing a healthy lunch more challenging and henceforth less enjoyable (Devine et al. 2006; Bathgate and Begley 2011).

When understanding differences between our identified segments, it was interesting to note that carers in the *wealthy less concerned* segment reported the most negative attitudes towards packing lunchboxes and had the most negative intentions to increase the number of healthy lunches for their children. They also reported packing the least serves of vegetables and fruits when compared to the other segments. Although the *wealthy less concerned* had high levels of income and generally high levels of education, it is interesting to see the negative commitment towards providing healthier food options for their children. This is contrary to previous studies which have suggested a positive relationship between parent's education and income with the quality of their children's diet (Vereecken et al. 2004; Neumark-Sztainer et al. 2003). By utilising segmentation we can see this is the case for some high income earners (e.g. the *wealthy less concerned*). These findings are interesting as they may suggest that low SES families do not always consume less healthy foods than their wealthier counterparts (Sanigorski et al. 2005). Also, the findings support the notion that parents with lower SES backgrounds are willing to purchase and pay more to support a better diet of their children (Bathgate and Begley 2011).

Identification of what motivates the audience can assist to design social marketing programs attuned to the target audience's attitudes, motivations and behaviours (Hopwood and Merrit 2011). In line with Lee and Kotler (2015) and Lefebvre (2013), social marketing efforts could focus on those who have higher intentions and offer products and/or services that deliver healthier lunches to their children, contributing to using limited monetary and non-monetary resources available more efficiently (Newton et al. 2013). We argue that this study provides evidence that social marketing product and service offerings may be better directed towards the *concerned with low SES* and *concerned, wealthy, and educated* segments given that the *wealthy and less concerned* segment's intentions to increase healthy eating were the most negative. For example, the *concerned with low SES* segment will need cost-effective alternatives to provide even more healthful lunch solutions for their children while the *concerned, wealthy and educated* segment is likely to be less price sensitive and willing to pay for a healthy lunchbox service within schools. This is wholly consistent with the principle of customising the product and/or service offered to the needs of the audience (Helfert et al. 2002). These findings are particularly insightful for social marketing researchers and practitioners who aim to improve children's nutritional intake. This research suggests that different parental segments exist and that they are likely to require different social marketing programs. For example, while all segments agreed that the preparation of healthy lunchboxes for children is necessary, some segments viewed packing and preparation of lunchboxes as boring and unenjoyable, particularly the *wealthy and less concerned* segment. This segment was also least likely to improve their lunchbox ingredients and currently packed the least amount of vegetables. Given the insights indicating that this segment views packing lunches as boring and that it did not intend to increase healthy food items, policy changes at a school level that require lunches to be packaging-free (thereby precluding convenience foods such as muesli bars, chips and biscuits) may assist to increase the amount of non-processed foods packed into lunchboxes. Alternatively, policies governing food selections in tuckshops/canteens would also help to ensure that the supply of healthier food alternatives is increased.

Limitations and Future Research

This study has limitations. The three-segment solution was identified based upon a convenience sample of Queensland carers. While the solution was supported by splitting the sample in half, more confidence would be gained were segment characteristics similar in a larger and more representative sample, given that low SES was underrepresented in the current study. The study is also limited by analysing only cross-sectional data and there being no possibility of comparing segment response to a social marketing program. A longitudinal approach permits assessment of changes over time (see Dietrich et al. 2015a, b for one methodological approach to considering segments' responses to a social marketing program), and this can be undertaken at a segment level. Further, a controlled design permits an examination of whether segment response is a result of the program implemented. Future research is recommended to extend the study geographically to a nationwide sample. This would allow the fourth segmentation base (geographic) to be included in the segment derivation. We further recommend the additional collection of more behavioural items to provide deeper insights into the segment formation. Up to four segmentation bases (e.g. psychographic, demographic, geographic and behavioural) are available for segmentation researchers and practitioners to identify homogeneous target audience groups in a larger heterogeneous group. To date, empirical exploration hasn't been undertaken in social marketing to determine the optimal base configuration for segmentation purposes. It is possible that one segmentation base is more predictive of behaviour when compared to other bases, and that omission of this base could impact the effectiveness of segmentation. This is an area for future research, and segmentation studies comparing a psychographic-only derived segment to segments arising from all four segmentation bases should be explored. Finally, the current study was limited exclusively to parental responses. Future research needs to examine the packing of lunchboxes with a consumer socialisation lens (Moore and Stephens 1975). Given that the contents of a child's lunchbox are often influenced by a child's preference (Bathgate and Begley 2011), examination of children's choices and their preferences is warranted. It would be particularly relevant to explore the role of peer influences on lunchbox preferences. Research has shown that peers can influence lunchbox preferences and children will pass on these requests to their parents (Bathgate and Begley 2011). Over time, parents become less influential as children approach adolescence and peers become increasingly influential (Moore and Stephens 1975). Furthermore, future research that investigates the power struggles between children and parents, as well as other influence factors (e.g. advertising, school) that determine the packing and contents of lunchboxes, is recommended.

Conclusion

This study demonstrates that market segments can be identified in the carer market, and that these may offer potential to inform social marketing program design and implementation aiming to increase healthful eating for primary school-aged children. Understanding these segments assists to identify product and service opportunities whose feasibility could be explored for the implementation of a comprehensive social marketing program. Different social marketing programs will be required to meet the needs and wants of these three distinct segments.

References

Ajzen, I., & Fishbein, M. (1980). *Understanding attitudes and predicting social behavior*. Englewood Cliffs, NJ: Prentice-Hall.

Australian Bureau of Statistics. (2013a). *Australian health survey: Updated results, 2011–2012,* (Catalogue No. 4364.0.55.003). http://www.abs.gov.au

Australian Bureau of Statistics. (2013b). *Education and work*, Australia, May 2013, cat. no. 6527.0, ABS, Canberra.

Australian Bureau of Statistics. (2013c). *Household income and income distribution 2011–2012*, Australia, cat. no. 6523.0, ABS, Canberra.
Bathgate, K., & Begley, A. (2011). 'It's very hard to find what to put in the kid's lunch': What Perth parents think about food for school lunch boxes. *Nutrition & Dietetics, 68*(1), 21–26.
Bell, A. C., & Swinburn, B. A. (2004). What are the key food groups to target for preventing obesity and improving nutrition in schools? *European Journal of Clinical Nutrition, 58*(2), 258–263.
Birch, L. L., & Fisher, J. O. (1998). Development of eating behaviours among children and adolescents. *Pediatrics, 101*(Supplement2), 539–549.
Boslaugh, S. E., Kreuter, M. W., Nicholson, R. A., & Naleid, K. (2005). Comparing demographic, health status and psychosocial strategies of audience segmentation to promote physical activity. *Health Education Research, 20*, 430–438.
Brennan, L., Miles, C. L., Mitchell, S. A., & Matthews, J. (2010). Changes in the content of children's school lunches across the school week. *Health Promotion Journal of Australia, 21* (3), 196–201.
Crespo-Casado, F., & Rundle-Thiele, S. (2015). Breaking it down: Unpacking children's lunchboxes. *Young Consumers, 16*(4), 438–453.
Croker, H., Lucas, R., & Wardle, J. (2012). Cluster-randomised trial to evaluate the 'Change for Life' mass media/social marketing campaign. *BMC Public Health, 12*(1), 404–417.
De Onis, M., Blössner, M., & Borghi, E. (2010). Global prevalence and trends of overweight and obesity among preschool children. *The American Journal of Clinical Nutrition, 92*, 1257–1264.
Devine, C. M., Jastran, M., Jabs, J., Wethington, E., Farell, T. J., & Bisogni, C. A. (2006). A lot of sacrifices: Work-family spillover and the food choice coping strategies of low-wage employed parents. *Social Science and Medicine, 63*(10), 2591–2603.
Dibb, S. (1998). Market segmentation: Strategies for success. *Marketing Intelligence & Planning, 16*(7), 394–406.
Dietrich, T., Rundle-Thiele, S. R., Leo, C., & Connor, J. (2015a). One size never fits all: Cluster responses to a school based social marketing alcohol program. *Journal of School Health, 85*(4), 251–259.
Dietrich, T., Rundle-Thiele, S. R., Schuster, L., Drennan, J., Russell-Bennett, R., Leo, C., et al. (2015b). Differential segmentation responses to an alcohol social marketing program. *Addiction, 49*, 68–77.
Donovan, R., & Henley, N. (2010). *Principles and practice of social marketing: An international perspective*. London, England: Cambridge University.
Douglas, L. (1999). Contribution of 'packed lunches' to the dietary intake of 11–12 year old children. *Nutrition and Food Science, 4*, 181–186.
Doyle, C. (2011). *A dictionary of marketing* (3 ed.). Oxford: Oxford University Press.
Access Economics. (2008). *The growing cost of obesity in 2008: Three years on*. Canberra, Australia: Diabetes, Australia.
Fine, S. (1980). Toward a theory of segmentation by objectives in social marketing. *Journal of Consumer Research, 7*(1), 1–13.
Gortmaker, S. L., Swinburn, B. A., Levy, D., Carter, R., Mabry, P. L., Finegood, D., et al. (2011). Changing the future of obesity: science, policy, and action. *The Lancet, 378*(9793), 838–847.
Helfert, G., Ritter, T., & Walter, A. (2002). Redefining market orientation from a relationship perspective. *European Journal of Marketing, 36*(9), 1119–1139.
Hesketh, K., Waters, E., Green, J., Salmon, L., & Williams, J. (2005). Healthy eating, activity and obesity prevention: A qualitative study of parent and child perceptions in Australia. *Health Promotion International, 20*(1), 19–26.
Hopwood, T., & Merritt, R. (2011). *The big pocket guide to social marketing* (1st ed.). London: National Social Marketing Centre. www.thensmc.com/sites/default/files/Big_pocket_guide_2011.pdf
Hudson, P. K., & Walley, H. (2009). Food safety issues and children's lunchboxes. *Perspectives in Public Health, 129*(2), 77–84.

IBM. (2010). SPSS Statistics Base 19: SPSS Inc, an IBM Company.

iSMA. (2013). *Consensus definition of social marketing*. http://www.isocialmarketing.org/assets/social_marketing_definition.pdf

Kalwani, M. U., & Morrison, D. G. (1977). A parsimonious description of the Hendry system. *Management Science, 23*, 467–477.

Kelishadi, R. (2007). Childhood overweight, obesity, and the metabolic syndrome in developing countries. *Epidemiologic Reviews, 29*, 62–76.

Kitunen, A, Rundle-Thiele, S., Kubacki, K., & Dietrich, T. (in press). Physical activity patterns of three different 'Melbournian' segments. *Journal of Strategic Marketing*.

Kolodinsky, J., & Reynolds, T. (2009). Segmentation of overweight Americans and opportunities for social marketing. *International Journal of Behavioral Nutrition and Physical Activity, 6*(1), 13–23.

Kotler, P. (1997). *Marketing management: Analysis, planning, implementation and control* (9th ed.). Upper Saddle River, New Jersey: Prentice Hall.

Kotler, P., Armstrong, G., Saunders, J., & Wong, V. (2002). *Principles of marketing* (3rd ed.). London, England: Prentice-Hall.

Law, J. (2009). *A dictionary of business and management* (5th ed.). Oxford, England: Oxford University Press.

Lee, N., & Kotler, P. (2015). *Social marketing—Changing behaviors for good*. Thousand Oaks, California: Sage Publications.

Lefebvre, C. (2013). *Social marketing and social change: Strategies and tools for health, well-being, and the environment*. CA, San Francisco: Jossey-Bass.

Lobstein, T., Baur, L., & Uauy, R. (2004). Obesity in children and young people: A crisis in public health. *Obesity Reviews, 5*(1), 4–85. doi:10.1111/j.1467-789X.2004.00133.x.

Lotenberg, L. D., Schechter, C., & Strand, J. (2011). Segmentation and targeting. In G. Hastings, K. Angus, & C. Bryant (Eds.), *The SAGE handbook of social marketing* (pp. 125–136). London, UK: Sage Publications.

Magarey, A. M., Daniels, L. A., Boulton, T. J., & Cockington, R. A. (2003). Predicting obesity in early adulthood from childhood and parental obesity. *International Journal of Obesity, 27*(4), 505–513.

Mcleay, F., & Oglethorpe, D. (2013). Social marketing, parental purchasing decisions, and unhealthy food in developing countries: A Nigerian typology. *Journal of Consumer Behaviour, 12*, 232–242.

Metcalfe, A., Owen, J., Shipton, G., & Dryden, C. (2008). Inside and outside the school lunchbox: Themes and reflections. *Children's Geographies, 6*(4), 403–412. doi:10.1080/14733280802338098.

Mitchell, S. A., Miles, C. L., Brennan, L., & Matthews, J. (2009). Reliability of the school food checklist for in-school audits and photograph analysis of children's packed lunches. *Journal of Human Nutrition & Dietetics, 23*, 48–53.

Moore, R. L., & Stephens, L. F. (1975). Some communication and demographic determinants of adolescent consumer learning. *Journal of Consumer Research, 2*, 80-92.

Neumark-Sztainer, D., Hannan, P. J., Story, M., Croll, J., & Perry, C. (2003). Family meal patterns: Associations with sociodemographic characteristics and improved dietary intake among adolescents. *Journal of the American Dietetic Association, 103*(3), 317–322.

Newton, J. D., Newton, F. J., Turk, T., & Ewing, M. T. (2013). Ethical evaluation of audience segmentation in social marketing. *European Journal of Marketing, 47*(9), 1421–1438.

NHMRC. (2013). *Australian dietary guidelines* (p. 226). Canberra: National Health and Medical Research Council.

Oltersdorf, U. (2003). Impact of nutrition behaviour research on nutrition programs and nutrition policy. *Appetite, 41*(3), 239–244.

Pettigrew, S. (2015). Pleasure: An under-utilized 'P' in social marketing for healthy eating. *Appetite,*. doi:10.1016/j.appet.2015.10.004.

Portsmouth, L., & Donovan, R. (2012). Television advertising of fruit to children: Promoting anticipation of great taste and constructing memories of great taste to increase consumption and purchase request. In *2012 International Social Marketing Conference (ISM) Proceedings in Griffith University South Bank Campus, Brisbane* (pp. 171–175).

Price Waterhouse Coppers. (2015). *Weighing the cost of obesity: A case for action.* http://www.obesityaustralia.org/files/Weighing-the-cost-of-obesity-Final.pdf

Punj, G., & Stewart, D. (1983). Cluster analysis in marketing research: Review and suggestions for application. *Journal of Marketing Research, 20*(2), 134–148.

Queensland Health (2012). The Health of Queenslanders 2012: Advancing good health. Fourth report of the chief health officer Queensland. Retrieved from http://www.health.qld.gov.au/cho_report/2012/documents/2012-cho-report-all.pdf

Sanigorski, A. M., Bell, A. C., Kremer, P. J., & Swinburn, B. A. (2005). Lunchbox contents of Australian school children: Room for improvement. *European Journal of Clinical Nutrition, 59*(11), 1310–1316. doi:10.1038/sj.ejcn.1602244.

Schuster, L., Kubacki, K., & Rundle-Thiele, S. R. (2015). A theoretical approach to segmenting children's walking behaviour. *Young Consumers, 16*(2), 159–171.

Scott, E. J., Eves, F. F., French, D. P., & Hoppé, R. (2007). The theory of planned behaviour predicts self-reports of walking, but does not predict step count. *British Journal of Health Psychology, 12*(4), 601–620.

Smith, W. R. (1956, July). Product differentiation and market segmentation as alternative marketing strategies. *The Journal of Marketing*, 3–8.

St-Onge, M. P., Keller, K. L., & Heymsfield, S. B. (2003). Changes in childhood food consumption patterns: A cause for concern in light of increasing body weights. *The American Journal of Clinical Nutrition, 78*(6), 1068–1073.

Tandon, P. S., Wright, J., Zhou, C., Rogers, C. B., & Christakis, D. A. (2010). Nutrition menu labeling may lead to lower-calorie restaurant meal choices for children. *Pediatrics, 125*(2), 244–248.

Tkaczynski, A., Rundle-Thiele, S., & Beaumont, N. (2010). Segmentation: A tourism stakeholder view. *Tourism Management, 30*(2), 169–175.

Vereecken, C. A., Keukelier, E., & Maes, L. (2004). Influence of mother's educational level on food parenting practices and food habits of young children. *Appetite, 43*(1), 93–103. doi:10.1016/j.appet.2004.04.002.

Walsh, D. C., Rudd, R. E., Moeykens, B. A., & Moloney, T. W. (1993). Social marketing for public health. *Health Affairs, 12*(2), 104–119.

Wills, J., Crichton, N., Lorenc, A., & Kelly, M. (2014). Using population segmentation to inform local obesity strategy in England. *Health Promotion International, 30*(3), 658–666. doi:10.1093/heapro/dau004.

World Health Organization. (2014). *Obesity and overweight*, May 2014 (Sheet No. 311). www.who.int

World Health Organization. (2015). *Obesity and overweight*, January 2015 (Sheet No. 311). http://www.who.int/mediacentre/factsheets/fs311/en/

Young Adults and Alcohol: An Explorative Audience Segmentation Analysis

Jolanda Mathijssen, Sandra Kuiper and Meriam Janssen

Abstract So far, audience segmentation with respect to alcohol use by young adults has been carried out mainly on the basis of behaviour. In this study we examined the possibility of segmenting young adults (18–24 years) according to their values and attitudes towards alcohol. A random sample of young adults was drawn from the Basic Registration of Persons (BRP) of 21 local authorities in the province of North-Brabant in the Netherlands. By means of an online questionnaire, data were gathered on socio-demographic characteristics, alcohol consumption, and values and attitudes towards alcohol. Factor analysis using principal components with oblimin rotation was conducted to identify alcohol-related values and attitudes. A latent class analysis, using factors found in the factor analysis, was used to identify different segments. We were able to distinguish a total of five segments on the basis of four attitude factors. Moreover, we found that the five segments differed in drinking behaviour independently of socio-demographic variables. Our investigation was a first step in the search for means to segment young adults with respect to alcohol. Further research is required to better understand these results for alcohol policy and practice in more concrete terms.

Background

The prevalence of alcohol consumption and heavy drinking among young adults is higher than in any other age group (e.g. Melchior et al. 2008; Poelen et al. 2005; Naimi et al. 2003). Recent data suggests that in the Netherlands the percentage of

J. Mathijssen (✉) · S. Kuiper · M. Janssen
Tranzo Department, Academic Collaborative Centre Youth, Tilburg University, Tilburg, The Netherlands
e-mail: j.j.p.mathijssen@uvt.nl

S. Kuiper
Community Health Service West-Brabant, Breda, The Netherlands

M. Janssen
Community Health Service Hart voor Brabant, 's-Hertogenbosch
The Netherlands

T. Dietrich et al. (eds.), *Segmentation in Social Marketing*,
DOI 10.1007/978-981-10-1835-0_11

alcohol consumption in the past 12 months increases from 19 % for the 12–16 year olds to 72 % for the 16–20 year olds, and to 89 % for the 20–30 year olds (Statistics Netherlands 2015). Moreover, 18 % of the 16–20 year olds and 20 % of the 20–30 year olds can be defined as a 'heavy drinker', meaning that these young adults drink more than four (women) or six (men) glasses of alcohol a day, at least once a week. Although the percentage of alcohol consumption for adults (until 75 years) is still high (about 85 %), their percentage for heavy drinking is lower (12 %). So, although many young adults will reduce their heavy drinking when growing older, a substantial proportion will continue with problematic drinking.

Heavy drinking is associated with negative consequences such as accidents, injuries, risky sexual behaviour, and high rates of alcohol dependence (Rehm et al. 2006; Hingson et al. 2009; Rubinsky et al. 2013). Due to the negative health consequences, many countries have introduced measures to discourage and prevent alcohol use and/or abuse. In the Netherlands, the minimum legal drinking age was raised from 16 to 18 years in 2014. In addition, the government conducts national campaigns and education at schools to reinforce the social norm of not drinking alcohol before the age of 18 (Government of the Netherlands 2015). As a consequence, prevention and intervention are primarily aimed at those younger than 18 years. However, given the high percentage of (heavy) drinking among young adults, it would make sense for measures to also focus on this older age group.

Research on alcohol use by adolescents has demonstrated that different subgroups can be defined in terms of behaviour (Steinhausen and Metzke 2003) and attitudes (Dietrich et al. 2015; Mathijssen et al. 2012). This so-called audience segmentation, which is one of the eight principles of social marketing, is a method for dividing large heterogeneous populations into separate, relatively homogeneous segments on the basis of shared characteristics known or presumed to be associated with a given outcome of interest (Slater 1996; French et al. 2010). Market research has revealed the importance of tailoring messages and incentives to different population segments. Not every individual is a potential consumer of a particular product, idea or service, so tailoring messages to specific groups will be more effective than broadcasting the same message to everyone (Grier and Kumanyika 2010; Moss et al. 2009; Forthofer and Bryant 2000). Since health messages can be fine-tuned to differences in values, motives, expectancies and attitudes, segments based on these characteristics are expected to be more useful for health communication strategies and interventions (Boslaugh et al. 2005; Moss et al. 2009) than segments based on socio-demographic variables.

Although there are studies on clusters of drinker prototype characteristics in young adults (Van Lettow et al. 2013a, Van Lettow et al. 2013b), segmentation on the basis of attitudes, expectancies, values and motives found in this age group has, to our best knowledge, never been attempted before. Both alcohol expectancies and motives are related to alcohol use. Positive expectancies have been shown to be related to greater alcohol consumption whereas negative expectancies are associated with abstention (Leigh and Stacy 2004). Regarding motives, the review of Kuntsche et al. (2005) demonstrated that most young people reported drinking for social motives, some indicated enhancement motives, and only a few reported coping motives. It appeared that social motives were associated with moderate alcohol use, enhancement with heavy drinking and coping motives with alcohol-related problems. Given the differences in motives and expectancies for alcohol, some young adults will drink for one reason and other young adults for another reason or for a specific combination of reasons. Moreover, it is conceivable that we can define several subgroups which differ among each other in terms of their motives, expectancies, values and attitudes towards alcohol.

We expect a strong association between the different segments and their actual alcohol consumption. Therefore, following on from our study of adolescents (Mathijssen et al. 2012), we have investigated the possibility of defining segments for young adults aged 18–24 years. Furthermore, we examined whether these segments were related to alcohol consumption independent of socio-demographic variables.

Methods

The sample A random sample of 7500 young adults aged 16–24 years was drawn from the Basic Registration of Persons (BRP) of the 21 municipalities in the area of the Community Health Service Brabant Southeast, in the south of the Netherlands. The personal data of each member of the Dutch population are held in the BRP. By means of a letter of invitation, these 7500 young adults were invited to complete a questionnaire, either through the internet with a personal password or on paper. To increase the response rate, two reminders were sent to non-respondents, two and ten weeks after the letter of invitation. As an incentive, one in twenty respondents who filled out the questionnaire received a €15 cinema coupon. For the purpose of the present study, only the data of the 18–24 year olds were used.

Questionnaire We used different sources to compose the questionnaire. Questions concerning demographic variables (gender, age, living arrangements, work status and education) and alcohol consumption were taken from the local and national health monitor (Health Monitor 2011). Alcohol use was measured with three questions: (Q1) *Which alcoholic beverages do you drink?* (Response options: “I have never drunk alcohol”, “I have drunk alcohol, but not in the past 12 months”, and examples of alcoholic beverages), (Q2) *How often did you drink alcohol in the last four weeks?* (recent alcohol use, 1 = “never” to 13 = “20 times or more”), and (Q3) *How often did you drink five or more glasses of alcohol at a single occasion in the last 4 weeks?* (binge drinking, 1 = “never” to 7 = “9 times or more”). Since the last two scores were not measured on a real continuous scale and the distribution was highly skewed, the scores were dichotomised. As there was no validated Dutch questionnaire available to study the attitudes, values and motives of young adults towards alcohol, appropriate questions for this age group were taken from the adolescent audience segmentation study (Mathijssen et al. 2012). To create a more comprehensive questionnaire, we developed extra propositions. These propositions were based on a brief literature study, a workshop with experts, and focus groups with young adults. Health professionals, researchers, health policy officials, and addiction experts participated in the workshop. Together we determined which subjects (in general and related to alcohol) are important for young adults and what the everyday environment of young adults looks like. Four focus group interviews with sufficient spread in alcohol consumption levels, age, gender, and educational level were held among young adults to increase our understanding of the attitudes and experiences of young people regarding alcohol. In total, 31 young adults (18 women and 13 men) participated. This eventually resulted in 42 propositions about alcohol (e.g. *"It is normal to be intoxicated now and then", "Usually I do not even realise that I am drinking alcohol", "Drinking alcohol helps me feel less shy", "If I drink less or no alcohol on an evening, my friends try to persuade me to drink alcohol"*).

Statistical analysis Data were analysed using SPSS 22.0 for windows (factor analysis, ANOVA, chi-square (χ^2) analyses, and multiple logistic regression analyses) and Latent Gold (latent class analysis).

Factor analysis using principal components with oblimin rotation was conducted. The factors retained were based on the following rules: eigenvalues greater than or equal to 1, or factors above the break in the scree plot, and a minimum of 0.40 for factor loadings.

A latent class analysis was then carried out with the factors found in the factor analysis, using the software package Latent Gold (Vermunt and Magidson 2005). In this analysis, a cluster solution was sought according to the following criteria. First, the statistical fit of the latent class model with the data was considered ($p > 0.05$, the null hypothesis is that there is no significant deviation between the predicted data and the observed data). Then the most economical model was chosen from those that fitted, which is the model with the lowest Bayesian Information Criterion (BIC value). This value is higher for more complex, and therefore less economical models.

Analyses of variance (ANOVA) were used to examine differences between the found segments and factor scores and age. With chi-square (χ^2) analyses we investigated whether the segments differed in categorical socio-demographic

Table 1 Socio demographic characteristics

Characteristic	%
Gender female	55.6
Age (mean; SD)	20.11 (2.01)
Living arrangements	
• Living with parents	64.9
• Living with partner and/or child	15.9
• Student dormitory	11.5
• Alone	4.7
• Other form of living	3.0
Work or education	
• Full-time education	54.7
• Part-time education	3.7
• Paid job	31.7
• Unpaid job	0.6
• Jobless	2.8
• Other	6.5

variables (gender, living arrangements, and work/education status) and alcohol consumption (ever drunk alcohol, recent alcohol use and binge drinking).

Logistic regression analyses were performed to determine whether socio-demographic characteristics and the segments were significantly associated with alcohol consumption. Two models were run. In the first model, univariate analyses were conducted including the following independent variables that were expected to be related to alcohol: age, gender, living arrangements, work/education status and the segmentation variable. Second, all variables that showed a significant relationship with the dependent variable on a univariate level ($P < 0.05$) were included in the multivariate logistic regression analysis.

Results

A total of 2599 (35 %) 16–24 year olds completed the questionnaire. For the purpose of this chapter, only the data of the respondents aged 18 years and over (n = 1958) were used. The mean age of these respondents was 20. 11 years, with 56 % female. The majority of this group (65 %) were still living with their parents. More than half of the young adults were following a full-time education program. For more information see Table 1.

Factor Analysis

A first exploratory factor analysis, with oblimin rotation, based on the 42 propositions concerning alcohol, produced nine factors that satisfied the criterion: eigenvalues > 1. On studying the eigenvalues per factor on a scree plot, specifically between the fourth and fifth factor, a fairly large drop in the eigenvalue was observed. Beyond the fourth factor, the eigenvalue gradually decreased further. For this reason, a new analysis was carried out in which the number of factors was fixed at 4. This analysis eventually produced four factors with sufficient reliability (Cronbach's Alpha $\geq$ 0.79). These four remaining factors, consisting of 32 items, together accounted for 45 % of the variance.

These factors were *"means of release"* ($\alpha = 0.91$, 9 items), *"embarrassment about intoxication"* ($\alpha = 0.80$, 5 items), *"peer pressure"* ($\alpha = 0.80$, 10 items), and *"sociability"* ($\alpha = 0.79$, 8 items). The items belonging to the factors are described in Table 2.

Latent Class Analysis

In Table 3, we compare models with one to ten latent classes, presenting the BIC and "*p*" value for each model.

Table 2 Items per factor

	Means of release	Embarrassment about intoxication	Sociability	Peer pressure
'Means of release'				
If I drink alcohol when I go out, I usually have a nicer evening	0.53	−0.07	0.33	0.15
If I drink alcohol, I can just put all my worries aside	0.60	−0.05	0.12	0.14
If I drink alcohol, I find it more easy to talk to someone	0.82	0.00	0.08	−0.15
If I drink alcohol, I feel more relaxed	0.77	−0.03	0.18	−0.09
I drink alcohol in order to release from my busy week schedule	0.52	−0.02	0.02	0.19
Drinking alcohol helps me feel less shy	0.93	0.07	−0.14	−0.11
Drinking alcohol makes me feel happy when I am down	0.66	−0.01	−0.06	0.12
Drinking alcohol makes me feel less tense or nervous	0.74	0.00	−0.09	0.08
Drinking alcohol gives me more confidence	0.87	0.00	−0.09	−0.02
'Embarrassment about intoxication'				
My friends would be embarrassed if I got drunk	−0.02	0.58	−0.06	0.13
I would be embarrassed if I got drunk myself	−0.04	0.75	−0.2	−0.03
I would be embarrassed if one of my friends got drunk	−0.04	0.65	−0.14	0.09
My parents would be embarrassed if I got drunk	0.61	0.83	0.24	−0.01
My friend/partner would be embarrassed if I got drunk	0.08	0.83	0.25	0.04
'Sociability'				
I like alcohol	0.23	−0.24	0.57	−0.13
Alcohol makes me think of having fun	0.19	−0.13	0.63	−0.04
Alcohol makes me think of the weekend	0.03	−0.02	0.56	0.03
Alcohol makes me think of a drink with a meal	−0.12	0.11	0.43	−0.04
Alcohol makes me think of relaxing	0.10	−0.01	0.62	0.00
Alcohol makes me think of letting go	0.15	−0.15	0.37	0.30
Alcohol makes me think: tasty	0.16	−0.14	0.52	−0.33
Alcohol makes me think: sitting on a terrace	0.03	−0.03	0.55	−0.12
'Peer pressure'				

(continued)

Table 2 (continued)

	Means of release	Embarrassment about intoxication	Sociability	Peer pressure
I can imagine that you don't want to be seen with a soft drink when everyone else is drinking alcohol	0.08	0.19	0.02	0.54
It's weird if an adult never drinks alcohol	0.07	−0.08	0.17	0.45
Alcohol makes me think of being drunk	−0.03	−0.18	−0.10	0.60
Alcohol makes me think of being one of them	−0.01	0.15	−0.08	0.62
Alcohol makes me think of a hangover	−0.11	−0.11	−0.02	0.61
It is difficult for me not to drink alcohol when I go out	0.31	−0.06	0.34	0.36
If I drink less or no alcohol on an evening, I feel that I have to defend myself to my friends	0.25	0.11	−0.07	0.50
If I drink less or no alcohol on an evening, my friends try to persuade me to drink alcohol	0.22	0.09	−0.02	0.47
If a friend does not drink when going out, I try to persuade him or her to drink alcohol	0.26	0.01	0.04	0.44
I find it annoying if I am the only one who does not drink alcohol	0.32	0.06	0.07	0.46

Table 3 Model fit statistics for ten latent class models

	BIC(LL)	*p*-value
1-Cluster	17,095	0.00
2-Cluster	16,377	0.00
3-Cluster	16,289	0.00
4-Cluster	16,241	0.00
5-Cluster	**16,217**	**0.40**
6-Cluster	16,231	0.75
7-Cluster	16,245	0.95
8-Cluster	16,229	0.98
9-Cluster	16,281	1.00
10-Cluster	16,309	1.00

BIC Bayesian information criteria; *LL* Log likelihood

The BIC statistic for the five-class model was slightly lower than for the other models. Moreover, the five-class solution was the first model with $p > 0.05$. These findings indicated that the five-class solution offered the best fit (BIC = 16,217, $p = 0.40$). The five clusters were distinguished from each other by differences in the

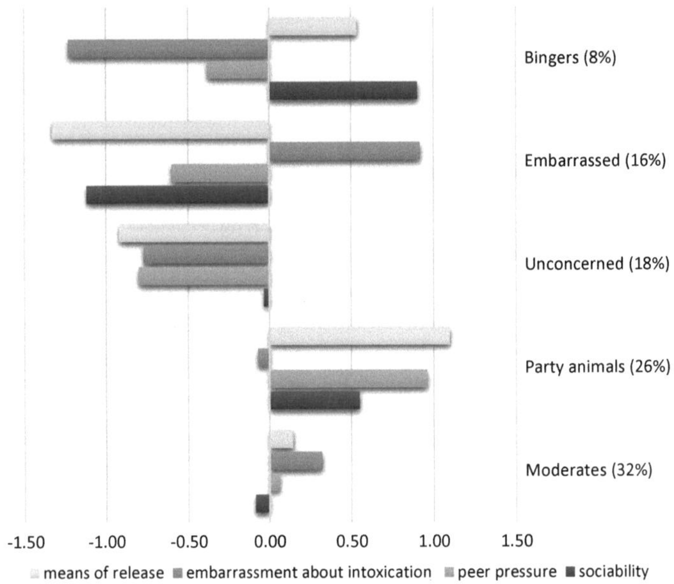

Fig. 1 Standardised factor scores for the five segments

Table 4 Mean scores (SD) on the four factors for the five segments

Segments	Sociability	Means of release	Embarrassment about intoxication	Peer pressure
1. Moderates	3.6 (0.5) [2 4 5]	2.7 (0.4) [2 3 4 5]	3.0 (0.7) [2 3 4 5]	2.1 (0.6) [2 3 4 5]
2. Party animals	4.1 (0.4) [1 3 4 5]	3.6 (0.4) [1 3 4 5]	2.6 (0.8) [1 3 4 5]	2.7 (0.6) [1 3 4 5]
3. Unconcerned	3.7 (0.6) [2 4 5]	1.7 (0.5) [1 2 4 5]	2.0 (0.6) [1 2 4 5]	1.5 (0.3) [1 2 4 5]
4. Embarrassed	2.9 (0.7) [1 2 3 5]	1.4 (0.4) [1 2 3 5]	3.6 (0.7) [1 2 3 5]	1.7 (0.5) [1 2 3 5]
5. Bingers	4.3 (0.3) [1 2 3 4]	3.1 (0.6) [1 2 3 4]	1.6 (0.4) [1 2 3 4]	1.8 (0.4) [1 2 3 4]

[12345] = Statistically significant different from other segments at $p < 0.01$

scores on the four attitude factors. Based on these scores the segments were given the following names: *Moderates* (32 %), *Party animals* (26 %), *Unconcerned* (18 %), *Embarrassed* (16 %), and *Bingers* (8 %), see Fig. 1. The scores in Fig. 1 have been standardised ($\mu = 0$ and SD = 1). In Table 4, the average scores on the five attitude factors are shown for each of the segments. In the figure and the table, it is shown that the segments differ from each other in factor scores. For example, compared to the other segments the young adults in the segment *Embarrassed* score lower on "sociability" and "means of release" and higher on "embarrassment about intoxication". The young adults in the segment *Party animals* score the highest on

Table 5 Differences in socio-demographic variables between the segments

	1. Moderates	2. Party animals	3. Unconcerned	4. Embarrassed	5. Bingers
Gender female	$54.5^{2\ 3\ 4}$	$42.9^{1\ 3\ 4}$	$64.9^{1\ 2}$	$70.1^{1\ 2\ 5}$	54.9^{4}
Age (mean)	20.10	20.11	21.01	21.00	20.11
Living arrangements					
• Living with parents	64.3	68.7	64.1	63.3	62.1
• Living with partner and/or child	13.7^{3}	$10.2^{3\ 4\ 5}$	$24.9^{1\ 2}$	17.7^{2}	19.6^{2}
• Student dormitory	14.0^{3}	13.8^{3}	$5.5^{1\ 2}$	10.5	12.4
• Alone	4.5	4.6	4.1	5.1	4.6
• Other form of living	3.5	2.8	1.4	3.4	1.3
Work or education					
• Fulltime or part-time education	$63.9^{3\ 5}$	62.8^{3}	$47.8^{1\ 2}$	58.6	50.3^{1}
• Paid job	$27.6^{3\ 5}$	28.43^{5}	$41.2^{1\ 2\ 4}$	29.2^{3}	$41.2^{1\ 2}$
• Jobless or unpaid job	3.2	3.4	2.3	2.7	4.6
• Other	5.3	5.4	8.7	9.5	3.9

12345 = Statistically significant different from other segments at $p \leq 0.01$

"means of release" and "peer pressure". In comparison with the other segments, the persons in the segment *Moderates* show average scores on all factors, except for "embarrassment about intoxication". In general, they score relatively high on "embarrassment about intoxication".

Differences in Background Variables per Segment

As Table 5 shows, a significant difference was found for gender ($\chi^2 = 70.0$, df = 4, $p \leq 0.01$). Females were over-represented in the segments *Unconcerned* (65 %) and *Embarrassed* (70 %), and under-represented in the segment *Party animals* (43 %). No significant difference between the segments relating to age was found (F = 0.7, df = 4, $p > 0.05$).

Living arrangements differed between the segments ($\chi^2 = 55.1$, df = 16, p 0.01). The respondents of the segments *Moderates* and *Party animals* more often lived in a student dormitory (14 %). Further, the segment *Party animals* less often lived with a partner (with or without children; 10 %). Finally, the segment *Unconcerned* more often lived with a partner (25 %) and less often in a student dormitory (6 %).

Moreover, we found a statistically significant difference for education/work ($X^2 = 49.4$, df = 20, $p \leq 0.01$). In total, 58 % of the young adults studied full-time or part-time. The segments *Moderates* (63.9 %) and *Party animals* (62.8 %) were over-represented in the education category, while the segment *Unconcerned* (47.8 %) was under-represented. The segment *Moderates* (28 %) was under-represented, and the segments *Unconcerned* and *Bingers* (both 41.2 %) were over-represented in paid jobs (total 32 %).

Alcohol Consumption

We then investigated, with a chi-square (χ^2) test, whether the five segments differed in terms of "ever drunk alcohol", "recent alcohol consumption" (alcohol consumed in the four weeks prior to completion of the questionnaire) and "binge drinking"

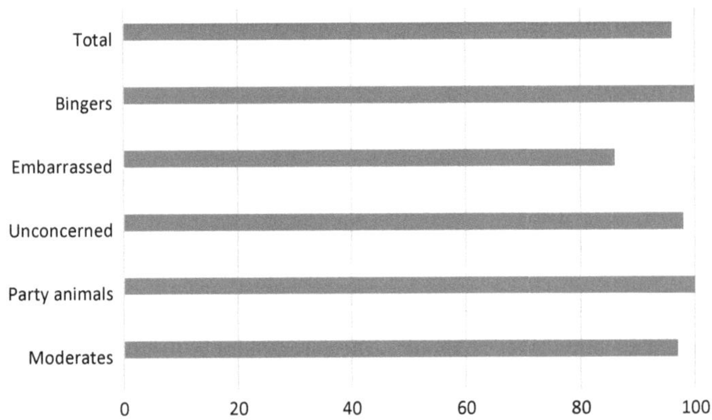

Fig. 2 Ever drunk alcohol (%) per segment

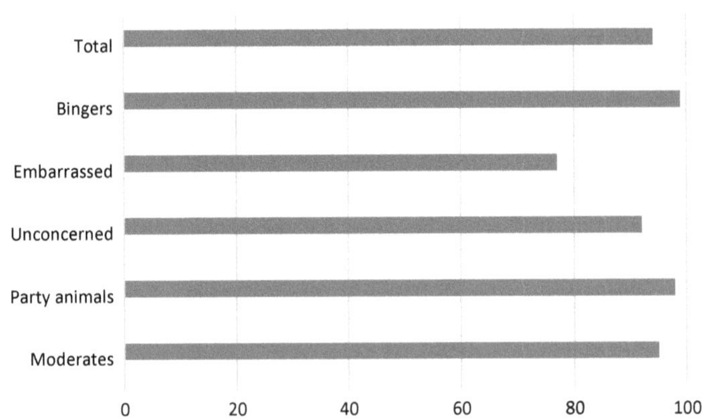

Fig. 3 Recent alcohol consumption (%) per segment

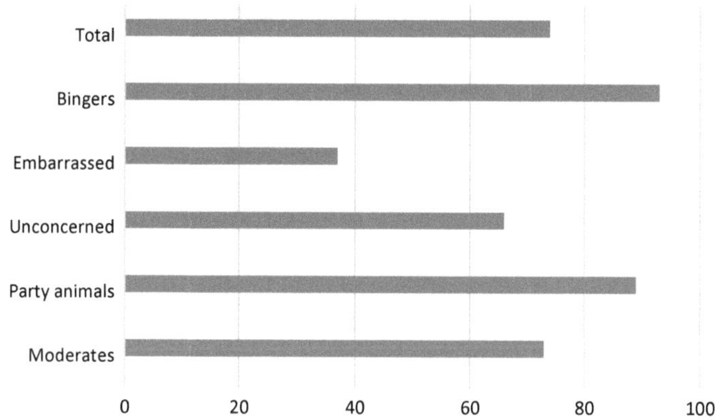

Fig. 4 Binge drinking (%) per segment

(the consumption of five or more glasses of alcohol on a single occasion in the preceding four weeks). All differences were statistically significant ($\chi^2 = 130.0$, df = 4, $p \leq 0.01$ for ever drunk alcohol $\chi^2 = 121.2$, df = 4, $p \leq 0.01$ for recent alcohol consumption and $\chi^2 = 242.5$, df = 4, $p \leq 0.01$ for binge drinking).

On average, 96 % of the young adults had ever drunk alcohol. This percentage was significantly higher for the segments *Party animals* and *Bingers* (both 100 %) and *Unconcerned* (98 %), and significantly lower for the segment *Embarrassed* (86 %), see Fig. 2.

Figure 3 shows that, on average, 94 % of the young adults had recently drunk alcohol. This percentage was significantly higher for the segments *Moderates* (95 %), *Party animals* (98 %) and *Bingers* (99 %), and significantly lower for the segment *Embarrassed* (77 %).

Of the young adults, 74 % can be classified as "binge drinkers" (see Fig. 4). This percentage is statistically significantly higher for the segments *Party animals* (89 %) and *Bingers* (93 %), and significantly lower for the segments *Unconcerned* (66 %) and the *Embarrassed* (37 %).

To examine whether the segments were significantly associated with alcohol consumption, we conducted multivariate logistic regression analyses. Since almost all young adults had ever drunk alcohol we did not run the analyses for this variable. For both recent alcohol consumption and binge drinking we ran two models. In the first model, univariate analyses were conducted including the following independent variables that were expected to be related to alcohol consumption: gender, sex, living arrangements, work/education status and the segmentation variable. Second, all variables that showed a significant relationship with the dependent variable on a univariate level ($P < 0.05$) were included in the multivariate logistic regression analysis. As can be seen in Table 6, both the socio-demographic variables and the segment variable are related to recent alcohol consumption and binge drinking. The multivariate logistic regression analysis demonstrated that the segmentation variable was significantly associated with both recent alcohol consumption and binge drinking, independent of socio-demographic variables. However, some of the

Table 6 Association of the segments and socio-demographic characteristics with recent alcohol consumption and binge drinking

	Recent alcohol consumption		Binge drinking	
	Univariate	Multivariate	Univariate	Multivariate
Age	0.90*	0.91	0.94*	0.93*
Gender				
• Female	Ref	Ref	Ref	Ref
• Male	2.33**	1.74*	2.32**	1.88**
Living arrangements				
• With parents	Ref	Ref	Ref	Ref
• With partner and/or children	0.56*	0.97	0.59**	0.84
• Student dormitory	1.90	1.82	1.11	1.06
• Alone	0.42*	0.55	0.58*	0.63
• Other	0.45	0.98	0.69	0.89
Work/education status				
• Full or part time education	Ref	Ref	Ref	Ref
• Paid job	0.84	1.21	0.92	1.25
• Unpaid job/jobless	0.23**	0.32*	0.42**	0.41*
• Other	0.61	1.13	0.56**	0.78
Segment				
• Moderates	Ref	Ref	Ref	Ref
• Party animals	2.36*	2.23*	3.30**	2.90**
• Unconcerned	0.56*	0.57	0.72*	0.77
• Embarrassed	0.17**	0.17**	0.22**	0.22**
• Bingers	3.64	3.77	4.63**	4.97**
Nagelkerk R^2	–	0.17	–	0.23

$^{*}p \leq 0.05$; $^{**}p \leq 0.01$

socio-demographic variables were no longer statistically significantly associated with alcohol consumption after controlling for other socio-demographic variables and the segments. This was especially the case for living arrangements.

Males scored higher on both recent alcohol consumption and binge drinking. Age was significantly associated with binge drinking only. The older the young adults were, the less they engaged in binge drinking. Compared to the *Moderates*, the *Party animals* scored higher and the *Embarrassed* scored lower on recent alcohol consumption and on binge drinking. The Nagelkerke's R^2 gives an approximation of the level of explained variance.

Discussion

The results of our study demonstrate that it is possible to group young adults into five different and more homogeneous segments on the basis of four different factors concerning values, attitudes and motives in relation to alcohol. The segments found are: *Moderates*, *Party animals*, *Unconcerned*, *Embarrassed*, and *Bingers*. The four factors showed sufficient reliability and were named 'means of release' ($\alpha = 0.91$; e.g. "If I drink alcohol, I can just put all my worries aside"), "embarrassment about intoxication" ($\alpha = 0.80$; e.g. "I would be embarrassed if I got drunk myself"), "peer pressure" ($\alpha = 0.80$; e.g. "I can imagine that you don't want to be seen with a soft drink when everyone else is drinking alcohol"), and "sociability"($\alpha = 0.79$; e.g. "Alcohol makes me think of having fun").

It is important to recognise that the names we gave to the segments are just labels to give a feeling for the characteristics of the five clusters. They are not descriptive names, and are not intended to represent the alcohol consumption of individual members of the clusters.

The segment *Moderates* is the largest (32 %). The respondents in this segment more often than average attend an education program, and more often live in a student dormitory. They score relatively high on "peer pressure" and on "embarrassment about intoxication". In general, they have a higher alcohol consumption than the segments *Embarrassed* and *Unconcerned* and a lower alcohol consumption than the segments *Bingers* and *Party animals.*

About a quarter of the young adults belong to the segment *Party animals*. Males are over-represented in this segment. Like the *Moderates*, the young adults in this segment more often than average attend an education program. They more often live with parents, and less often with a partner. They score highest on "release" and on "peer pressure", and relatively high on "sociability". They have a high alcohol consumption.

The segments *Unconcerned* (18 %) and *Embarrassed* (16 %) are of approximately equal size. In both segments, females are over-represented. The *Unconcerned* score relatively low on "release", "embarrassment about intoxication" and "peer pressure", while scoring average on "sociability". They live less often in a student dormitory and more often with a partner. Further, they less often attend education and more often have a paid job. Almost all have ever drunk alcohol. Their recent alcohol use is average compared to the other segments, and their binge drinking is lower than average. The *Embarrassed* group scores the lowest on "sociability" and "release", the highest on "embarrassment about intoxication" and relatively low on "peer pressure". Their alcohol consumption is the lowest of all groups.

Finally, the group *Bingers* scores highest on "sociability" and lowest on "embarrassment about intoxication", relatively low on "peer pressure" and relatively high on "release". They more often than average have a paid job and show a high level of alcohol consumption.

In our audience segmentation study of 12–18 year olds we also found five segments (Mathijssen et al. 2012). The *Bingers* most resemble the "*High Spirits*" from our earlier study. Like the *High Spirits*, the *Bingers* experience low "embarrassment about intoxication", do not score high on "peer pressure" and have positive associations with alcohol. Moreover, they score highest on binge drinking. No clear similarities with our earlier found segments were apparent for the other segments. In general, the young adults in our study showed high levels of alcohol consumption. Even the *Embarrassed*, who in terms of their attitude are fairly similar to the "*Consciously Sobers*" (Mathijssen et al. 2012), showed a high alcohol consumption (77 % had recently drunk alcohol and 37 % had recently drunk five or more glasses of alcohol). By contrast, the alcohol consumption of the *Consciously Sobers*, who were on average seven years younger, was very low (7 % had recently drunk alcohol and 3 % had recently drunk five or more glasses of alcohol).

A recent synthesis of the literature on alcohol drinking patterns among young people (age range 12–24 years) resulted in six classes of drinkers (Davoren et al. 2015). "*Abstainers*" report no alcohol consumption. "*Light drinkers*" report light levels of alcohol. For the "*social drinkers*" alcohol facilitates social situations. "*Hedonistic drinkers*" are driven by their personal need to feel pleasure. "*Heavy drinkers*" report high levels of alcohol consumption on a regular basis. And finally the "*Problem alcohol users*" also drink high amounts of alcohol. Moreover, they often have a negative mood and wish to improve their mood by drinking alcohol. It seems that the groups *Abstainers* and *Light drinkers* are not present in our study.

Besides the differences in values, attitudes, expectancies, and motives, the segments also differed in drinking behaviour. These differences remained even after controlling for age, gender, living arrangements and work/education status. This association appears to be approximately equal in both the univariate and in the multivariate model. However, for the socio-demographic variables some associations changed. While young adults living with a partner and/or with a child and respondents living alone had a lower alcohol consumption than young adults living with their parents, these significant associations disappeared after controlling for the other socio-demographic variables and the segmentation variable. This suggests that the segmentation variable is more effective in "predicting" alcohol consumption than the living arrangement.

Another striking finding is that young adults following education do not drink more alcohol than other young adults, except with respect to young adults who have a paid job. This seems to contradict what was found in the review by Carter et al. (2010). They found that college students drink more, and more frequently, than their non-college peers. However, on the basis of their results the authors concluded that the found differences were likely the result of factors other than college attendance itself. Possibly it does not matter whether young adults enrolled in an education program or not, but instead it is the network of social relationships to which they belong.

Notwithstanding these promising results, there are of course some reservations concerning the study. First, our study had a relatively low response. Despite two reminders and the incentive (the prospect of a €15 cinema ticket), just over one third of the young adults we approached completed the questionnaire. The percentage of young adults who attend an education program and who have a paid job is more or less the same in our sample as it is in the Dutch population. However, the percentage of respondents who are unemployed is lower (3 %) than in the Dutch population (9 %) (Statistics Netherlands 2015), indicating that our sample is possibly not representative for Dutch young adults. Moreover, the alcohol consumption of the young adults in our study is considerably higher than in the Dutch population. In 2011, 14 % of 20–30 year olds in the Netherlands did not drink alcohol. In our study only 4 % of the young adults did not drink alcohol. Also, compared to the results of the Brabant Health Monitor (GGD 2012) in which young adults of the same age and from the same region were studied, alcohol-consuming respondents are over-represented in our study. In the Brabant Health Monitor, 12 % of the 18–24 year olds did not drink alcohol. As our questionnaire was voluntary, it is possible that only young adults who were interested in alcohol chose to complete the questionnaire, and this may consequently have resulted in self-selection bias.

Second, this was an explorative analysis. Validated questionnaires about values and attitude towards alcohol for young adults were not available. We therefore constructed our own questions, based on a literature study, expert opinions and focus groups with young adults. By conducting a factor analysis we found four different factors. However, it is recommended that these factors and the segments be confirmed in another sample of 18–24 year olds. The segments were significantly associated with alcohol consumption independent of socio-demographic variables. Nevertheless, more research is needed to examine the usefulness of these different subgroups.

Third, since this study was a first step in the process that might lead to a social marketing strategy tackling the alcohol use of young adults, it is too early to conclude which segment(s) should be the target of policy. Based on the results of this study, it seems that the segments *Party animals* and *Bingers* are especially at high risk of developing problematic alcohol use. The focus of an intervention targeting these groups could be to reduce their alcohol consumption on a single occasion to a more responsible/healthy amount. For the *Party animals*, special attention is required to reduce peer pressure (learning to say "no"), and to find ways of release other than through alcohol. For the *Bingers*, the focus should be on finding alternative means of having an enjoyable evening.

Fourth, it is not yet clear how we can identify and reach the different segments in everyday life. Future research should obtain more insight into these subgroups in order to understand which segment should be the target of alcohol policy. Social marketing consists of eight key principles, of which segmentation is one (French et al. 2010). However, the principles of "insight", "exchange" and "competition" are also important when developing a social marketing intervention. This means that insight into what will move and motivate people, insight into what the audience has to give up in order to get the benefits proposed, and insight into the things competing for the audience's time, attention and behaviour are all needed to develop an attractive intervention that is valued by the target group.

Conclusion

The results of this investigation demonstrate that it is possible to group young adults into five different and more homogeneous segments on the basis of four attitude factors. These five segments, moreover, varied in drinking behaviour independent of socio-demographic variables, suggesting that they are meaningful alcohol-related subgroups. Our investigation was a first step towards segmenting the study population on a basis other than socio-demographic characteristics. Further research is required to elaborate the relevance of the results for alcohol policy.

Acknowledgments This study is funded by a grant from ZonMw, the Netherlands Organization for Health Research and Development (204001005).

References

Boslaugh, S. E., Kreuter, M. W., Nicholson, R. A., & Naleid, K. (2005). Comparing demographic, health status and psychosocial strategies of audience segmentation to promote physical activity. *Health Education Research, 20*, 430–438.

Carter, A. C., Brandon, K. O., & Goldman, M. S. (2010). The college and noncollege experience: A review of the factors that influence drinking behavior in young adulthood. *Journal of Studies on Alcohol and Drugs, 71*, 742–750.

Davoren, M. P., Cronin, M., Perry, I. J., Demant, J., Shiely, F., & O'Connor, K. (2015). A typology of alcohol consumption among young people—A narrative synthesis. *Addiction Research & Theory*, 1–13.

Dietrich, T., Rundle-Thiele, S., Leo, C., & Connor, J. (2015). One size (never) fits all: segment differences observed following a school-based alcohol social marketing program. *Journal of School Health, 85*, 251–259.

Forthofer, M., & Bryant, C. (2000). Using audience-segmentation techniques to tailor health behavior change strategies. *American Journal of Health Behavior, 24*, 36–43.

French, J., Blair-Stevens, C., McVey, D., & Merrit, R. (2010). *Social marketing and public health: Theory and practice*. New York: Oxford University Press.

GGD. (2012). *Gezondheidsmonitor, Brabantse Volwassenmonitor*, 19–65 (Online). http://ggd-hvb.buurtmonitor.nl/

Government of the Netherlands. (2015). https://www.rijksoverheid.nl/onderwerpen/alcohol

Grier, S. A., & Kumanyika, S. (2010). Targeted marketing and public health. *Annual Review of Public Health, 31*, 349–369.

Health Monitor. (2011). https://www.monitorgezondheid.nl/

Hingson, R. W., Zha, W., & Weitzman, E. R. (2009). Magnitude of and trends in alcohol-related mortality and morbidity among U.S. college students ages 18–24, 1998–2005. *Journal of Studies on Alcohol and Drugs*, 12–20.

Kuntsche, E., Knibbe, R., Gmel, G., & Engels, R. (2005). Why do young people drink? A review of drinking motives. *Clinical Psychology Review, 25*, 841–861.

Leigh, B. C., & Stacy, A. W. (2004). Alcohol expectancies and drinking in different age groups. *Addiction, 99*, 215–227.

Mathijssen, J., Janssen, M., Van Bon-Martens, M., & Van De Goor, I. (2012). Adolescents and alcohol: An explorative audience segmentation analysis. *BMC Public Health, 12*, 742.

Melchior, M., Chastang, J. F., Goldberg, P., & Fombonne, E. (2008). High prevalence rates of tobacco, alcohol and drug use in adolescents and young adults in France: Results from the GAZEL youth study. *Addictive Behaviors, 33*, 122–133.

Moss, H. B., Kirby, S. D., & Donodeo, F. (2009). Characterizing and reaching high-risk drinkers using audience segmentation. *Alcoholism, Clinical and Experimental Research, 33*, 1336–1345.

Naimi, T. S., Brewer, R. D., Mokdad, A., Denny, C., Serdula, M. K., & Marks, J. S. (2003). Binge drinking among US adults. *Journal of Amercian Medical Association, 289*, 70–75.

Poelen, E. A. P., Scholte, R. H. J., Engels, R. C. M. E., Boomsma, D. I., & Willemsen, G. (2005). Prevalence and trends of alcohol use and misuse among adolescents and young adults in the Netherlands from 1993 to 2000. *Drug and Alcohol Dependence, 79*, 413–421.

Rehm, J., Taylor, B., & Room, R. (2006). Global burden of disease from alcohol, illicit drugs and tobacco. *Drug and Alcohol Review, 25*, 503–513.

Rubinsky, A. D., Dawson, D. A., Williams, E. C., Kivlahan, D. R., & Bradley, K. A. (2013). AUDIT-C scores as a scaled marker of mean daily drinking, alcohol use disorder severity, and probability of alcohol dependence in a U.S. general population sample of drinkers. *Alcoholism: Clinïcal and Experimental Research, 37*, 1380–1390.

Slater, M. D. (1996). Theory and method in health audience segmentation. *Journal of Health Communication*, 267–283.

Statistics Netherlands. (2015). http://statline.cbs.nl/Statweb/

Steinhausen, H. C., & Metzke, C. W. (2003). The validity of adolescent types of alcohol use. *Journal of Child Psychology and Psychiatry, 44*, 677–686.

Van Lettow, B., De Vries, H., Burdorf, A., Norman, P., & Van Empelen, P. (2013a). Associations between abstainer, moderate and heavy drinker prototypes and drinking behaviour in young adults. *Psychology and Health, 28*, 1407–1423.

Van Lettow, B., Vermunt, J. K., De Vries, H., Burdorf, A., & Van Empelen, P. (2013b). Clustering of drinker prototype characteristics: What characterizes the typical drinker? *British Journal of Psychology, 104*, 382–399.

Vermunt, J., & Magidson, J. (2005). *Latent Gold 4.0. User's Guide.* Belmont, Massachusetts: Statistical Innovations Inc.

Using Segmentation and Theory to Design Better Promotion and Prevention Campaigns: A RECYC-QUÉBEC Case Study

Maxime Boivin, Emmanuelle Gagné and Valériane Champagne Saint-Arnaud

Abstract Theory-based interventions aiming to change behaviour can help overcome diverse social issues more efficiently. However, theory is often disregarded by social marketing practitioners. Hence, an important gap lies between theory and practice, leading to potentially important shortfalls in social marketing campaigns. Through a practical case study, we intend on demonstrating how theory can be effectively, and easily, used throughout the conception of such campaigns. Using a large-scale segmentation study among the Quebec population from RECYC-QUÉBEC (RQ), a public organisation promoting responsible waste management behaviours, our goal is to suggest viable avenues for the promotion of composting. Working with the Theory of Planned Behaviour's main psychological variables (Fishbein and Azjen 2010), we analysed and interpreted the study's seven market segments in order to suggest targeting and positioning strategies that could lead to more effective interventions. Our theory-informed approach led us to better understand the various factors surrounding composting and its adoption. Finally, we formulated limits and recommendations that should prove particularly useful to practitioners. Our research's practical implications relate namely to the use of theory, segmentation, and the conception of data collection tools, as well as behavioural and methodological limits.

Background

Literature points out the importance of theory and research in designing and implementing social marketing campaigns (i.e. Blair-Stevens et al. 2009; French and Gordon 2015; Frenette 2010). Indeed, according to many authors, theory-informed interventions relating to behavioural change can help address social issues more effectively, whether for the promotion of health, road safety, environmental awareness, and so on. However, research and theory are not systematically called upon by practitioners, consequently resulting in a significant and inauspicious gap

M. Boivin (✉) · E. Gagné · V. Champagne Saint-Arnaud
Université Laval, Quebec City, QC, Canada
e-mail: maxime.boivin.4@ulaval.ca

T. Dietrich et al. (eds.), *Segmentation in Social Marketing*,
DOI 10.1007/978-981-10-1835-0_12

between theory and practice in social marketing (i.e. Coffman 2002; Webb et al. 2010; Campo et al. 2012).

Similarly, research shows that promotion and prevention campaigns should adopt a customer-oriented perspective (Frenette 2010; French et al. 2011). In fact, the knowledge that had been acquired over the years demonstrated the importance of taking into account the diversity of needs and desires within the population. Consequently, segmentation rapidly became a central element of marketing (Wedel and Kamakura 2000). Based on the opinions, needs, fears, aspirations and concerns of the target audience, this useful insight into people's lives leads to better suited campaigns (i.e. Andreasen 2006; Campo et al. 2012). Increasing cultural and social relevance for the targeted audience, segmentation raises a campaign's chances of success (Lotenberg et al. 2011), notably by increasing the likelihood of reaching the target audience, a renowned challenge in social marketing (Evans et al. 2008). Finally, from a practical standpoint, the use of segmentation also allows for a more efficient and effective allocation of resources (McVey and Walsh 2009).

Regardless of its recognised impact, segmentation remains, as theory is, under-used. Indeed, the mindset, priorities and understanding of the advertiser or sponsoring organisation often work against the implementation of segmentation or theory-based approaches (Atkin and Freimuth 2013). For instance, studies suggest that the complexity related to existing models and theories, coupled with time and financial pressures, can hinder the use of theory and research in practice (i.e. Frenette 2010; Michie et al. 2011).

Hence, we intend on demonstrating how accessible and propitious using theory and research can be for practitioners. More explicitly, we will illustrate how theory and research can lead to more effective goals and strategies in social marketing campaigns through a practical case study. Based on a large-scale segmentation of Quebecers' opinions, attitudes, and behaviours regarding various environmental issues conducted by RECYC-QUÉBEC (RQ), a public organisation promoting responsible waste management behaviours among the Quebec population, we organised the significant data according to the Theory of Planned Behaviour (TPB)'s three main psychological variables (behavioural beliefs, normative beliefs, and control beliefs) (Fishbein and Azjen 2010). The sound and simple structure provided by the TPB served as canvas, facilitating the analysis and interpretation of the compiled data.

Study Overview

RQ is the recycling and resource recovery corporation in the province of Quebec (Canada). Aiming to reduce waste from year to year, it relies, in part, on social marketing campaigns to reach its objectives. In an effort to develop more grounded and efficient campaigns, RQ mandated a survey firm to conduct a large-scale quantitative study. The study compiled data regarding attitudes towards the environment and behaviours such as recycling and composting (RECYC-QUÉBEC 2015). The study led to a segmentation of behaviours and psychosocial characteristics with regard to waste management. Armed with this newfound, thorough understanding of influential factors, RQ's goal was then to develop well-adapted campaigns on various environmental issues, tailored to each of the market segments that were found.

RECYC-QUEBEC Study and Methodology

To divide the sample population into homogeneous groups, the survey firm mandated by RQ used a sequential mixed methods design, relying firstly on focus groups before conducting a quantitative survey. In this case, a mixed methods approach was deemed relevant since neither qualitative nor quantitative methods were sufficient in themselves to provide a deep examination of the citizens' behavioural and psychosocial characteristics.

Qualitative data collection and analysis Six focus groups were held among Quebecers aged 18 years and over (n = 54) in three cities (Montreal, Sherbrooke, and Quebec), with the aim of obtaining greater insight into opinions, attitudes and behaviours regarding waste management. These observations were then used to build the quantitative questionnaire.

Quantitative data collection and analysis The survey was conducted in November and December of 2014, among Quebecers aged 18 years and over (n = 2068), and who were responsible (in part or solely) for the waste management in their households. A mixed data collection (48 % by telephone and 52 % by internet) was used. Respondents were questioned regarding four types of behaviours: (1) recycling, (2) visits to drop-off depots, (3) composting, and (4) yard waste management.

Two statistical analyses were conducted to produce a segmentation of the sampled population:

- A factor analysis using principal components produced five factors regarding opinions and attitudes towards the environment. The five factors consisted of 35 items and accounted, together, for 58 % of the variance.
- A clustering analysis was then conducted, based on the above-mentioned five factors plus three additional behavioural variables. It produced six to nine cluster solutions. In the end, the seven cluster solution provided the best fit for the data, as it accounted for 80 % of the variance ($R^2 = 0.8$).

Figure 1 shows the seven segments and their weight in the sampled population.

Behaviour of Interest: Food Waste Composting

Among the four possible behaviours included in the study, we chose to focus on composting because of the growing interest surrounding its practice, both from individuals and organisations. Composting is notably the next behaviour targeted by Quebec's public administration in an effort to improve waste management. More

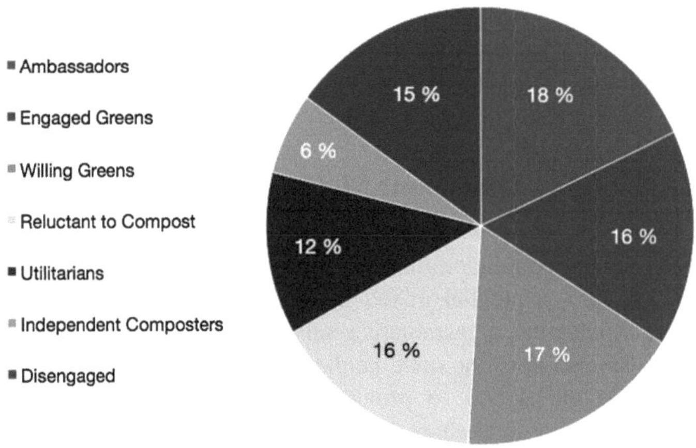

Fig. 1 RECYC-QUÉBEC's segmentation regarding opinions, attitudes, and behaviours towards waste management (adapted from RECYC-QUÉBEC 2015)

precisely, a legislative project was put forward, planning to ban organic waste from landfill sites (MDELCC 2012). Although the new legislation was supposed to enter into force as of 2020, the target was recently pushed back to 2022, because municipalities and citizens were not deemed ready for such a project (MAMROT 2015). For instance, only about 10 % of all municipalities had started establishing a compost collection service. However, for composting to be adopted by the population, it is essential that a compost collection service be available, and that citizens be willing to participate (Communauté métropolitaine de Montréal 2015). In order for the new target to be viable, work has to start now. Indeed, municipalities have to start planning their new compost collection service. In addition, we have to start raising awareness and informing people as of now in order for a significant portion of the population to start adopting composting once collection is made available to them. To that effect, social marketing campaigns will come as a great help.

Behaviour Change Pathway: The Theory of Planned Behaviour

Using Fishbein and Azjen's TPB (2010), a leading model in the field of social marketing, we analysed RQ's segmentation and suggested targeting and positioning strategies based on our results. Multiple meta-analysis demonstrated real impact on efficacy of social campaigns when using the TPB (i.e. Armitage and Conner 2001; Webb et al. 2010), hence supporting our use of this model. More specifically, the TPB guided us in the selection, the organisation and the interpretation of the data. Through the model's three main psychological variables, we methodologically grouped the significant data for each segment in order to offer a clear portrait of their needs and positions regarding composting.

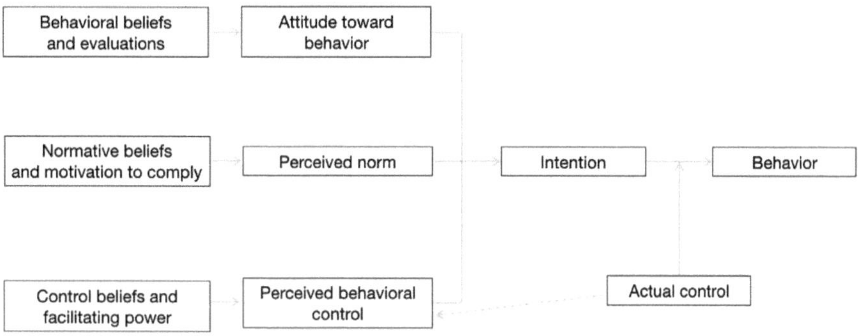

Fig. 2 Theory of planned behaviour (adapted from Yzer 2013). *Note* Fishbein and Ajzen (2010) published a more recent version of the TPB under a new name: the Reasoned Action Approach (RAA). Its main difference from the 2006 version relates to the addition of background and environmental factors that can influence one's behaviour, attitude and beliefs. We opted for the prior model for very pragmatic reasons. As our approach focuses on the TPB's psychological variables, which remain identical in the RAA, the changes in the newer version have no incidence on our results. Hence, we favoured the TPB as it is more widespread and recognised

This model tries to explain and help predict behaviour change through (1) behavioural beliefs, (2) normative beliefs, and (3) control beliefs (see Fig. 2). These variables are believed to influence behavioural intention, which is considered to be the most reliable predictor of behaviour (Fishbein and Azjen 2010). Consequently, they should indicate the most effective strategies and arguments to adopt.

The **behavioural beliefs** refer to one's perceptions of the likelihood that performing a particular behaviour will have positive or negative consequences (i.e. "*Composting is useful to protect the environment*"). The **normative beliefs** refer to the way one perceives the judgment of others (friends, family, society, etc.) (i.e. "*I believe my friends think composting is important and I want to meet their expectations*" or "*I don't think composting is a valued behaviour in society so there is no need to adopt it*"). Finally, the **control beliefs** refer to how much control one believes they have over performing a behaviour, how easy or difficult they believe performing the behaviour will be, or how confident they are that they can perform the behaviour (i.e. "*I won't be able to prevent my compost from smelling bad or attracting flies*") (Yzer 2013). Generally speaking, the intention to modify a behaviour should become higher the more behavioural beliefs and normative beliefs are favourable towards the suggested behaviour, and the more control one believes to have over it.

All in all, the TPB can help professionals in the conception and implementation of social marketing campaigns. As French and Gordon (2015, p. 218) indicated, it can serve as a "diagnostic tool" when trying to understand a behaviour and its components. The use of this model by social marketers can shed light on key aspects for developing successful behaviour change interventions. For example, a study by Schultz et al. (2007) found that when residents were informed that most of their neighbours engaged in specific behaviours to reduce their energy use at home, they subsequently started adopting these energy saving behaviours themselves. A social marketing practitioner could have used this information to design a successful campaign using normative beliefs.

Results: Segmentation Through the Theory of Planned Behaviour

As exposed previously, the RQ study suggested a seven segment typology of the respondents (see Fig. 1). Of all included behaviours, we chose to focus on composting, illustrating each segment's characteristics regarding this behaviour through the TPB.

When looking at the seven segments, we find, at one end of the spectrum, the *Ambassadors*; the greenest, most engaged group. One of the first things we notice when looking at Fig. 3 is the important proportion of *Ambassadors* who compost in comparison with the other segments. They are the only segment to compost widely regardless of access. At the other end of the spectrum, we encounter the *Disengaged*, the least engaged and also least interested segment. Among the other five segments,

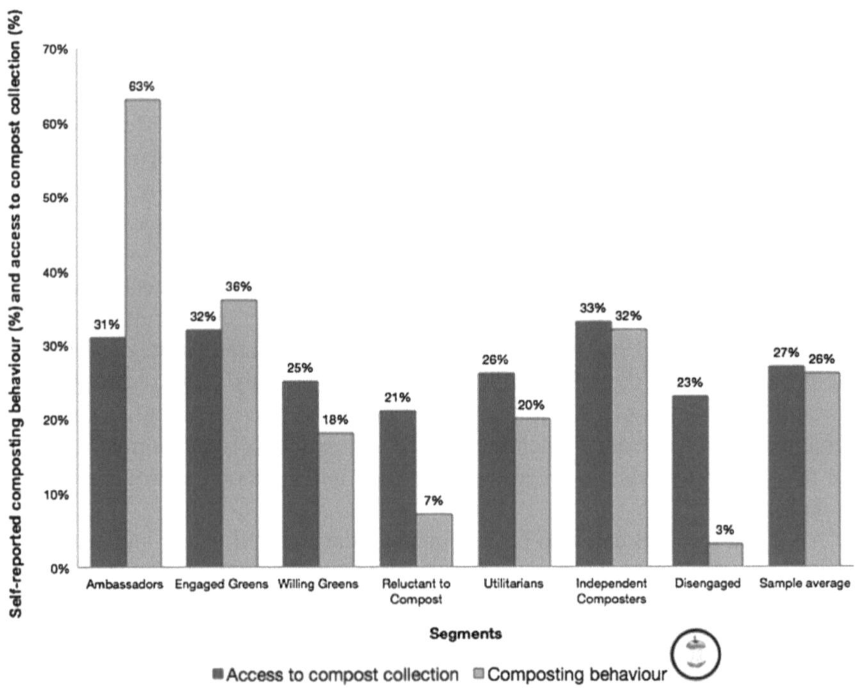

Fig. 3 Self-reported composting behaviour and access to compost collection

behaviours, attitudes, and opinions vary greatly, though generally in a descending fashion (from most environmentally friendly to least environmentally friendly). A first look at self-reported composting behaviours for each segment confirms this global trend (see Fig. 3). Interestingly, we quickly notice in Fig. 3 that this trend does not apply to the *Utilitarians* and the *Independent Composters*, who compost to the levels of more environmentally prone groups such as the *Willing Greens* and the *Engaged Greens*. This can be attributed to the fact that RQ's segmentation is not based solely on composting, but rather on general environmental behaviours and attitudes, including recycling, visits to drop-off depots, composting, and yard waste management, without distinctions. The segmentation may thus be ill-suited for specific behaviours, as their particularities can go unnoticed (this issue will be discussed in greater detail in the section Limits of the RQ Study).

It is important to point out that the *Ambassadors* are the only segment where people seem to compost regardless of access to a collection service. For the six other groups, access remains a crucial barrier to composting. Furthermore, although all segments share a relatively similar access to compost collection services (ranging approximately between 20 and 30 %), composting behaviour varies greatly across the segments. For example, while the *Willing Greens* and the *Disengaged* share almost identical access to composting services (25 % vs. 23 %), the former composts much more than the latter (25 % vs. 3 %). This shows that, although we found access to a collection service to be a critical condition of behaviour adoption, it is not sufficient to influence composting behaviours alone.

Since access alone is not enough, what are the other significant factors that influence composting behaviour and its adoption? Using data from the aforementioned RQ study, we put together a portrait of each segment regarding composting based on the TPB.

Ambassadors

 63 % vs. 26 %[1]

Behavioural beliefs We find in the *Ambassadors* people who are the most enthusiastic towards composting. As a matter of fact, they are the most concerned and motivated about environmental issues in general, perceiving a direct link between green behaviours and positive consequences for the environment and society. Regarding composting per se, almost all *Ambassadors* believe the benefits of composting are well worth the time and effort (97 % vs. 72 %).[2]

---

[1]This symbol, the apple core, stands for "composting behaviour". Next to it, we present each segment's self-reported composting behaviour (%) in comparison with the sample average (%).

[2]Statistical data from the RQ study is used throughout this section to support or illustrate our interpretation. Unless otherwise mentioned, statistical data related to our interpretations are presented in comparison to the sample average (e.g. in the sentence "Regarding composting per se, almost all *Ambassadors* believe that the benefits of composting are well worth the time and efforts (97 % vs 72 %)," 97 % represents the percentage of *Ambassadors* who believe that the benefits of composting are worth the time and efforts and 72 % represents the sample average from the RQ study).

Normative beliefs Although *Ambassadors* perceive people who compost as examples to follow (94 % vs. 79 %), they do not believe that it is useless to compost before the majority adopts the behaviour (4 % vs. 22 %).
Control beliefs *Ambassadors* perceive few, if any, barriers to composting. As a matter of fact, a strong majority thinks that composting is rather easy or very easy (79 % vs. 42 %).
Engaged Greens

36 % vs. 26 %

Behavioural beliefs Similar to the *Ambassadors*, the *Engaged Greens* also show a very favourable environmental attitude. As in the previous group, they believe that it is urgent to act on environmental issues (87 % vs. 81 %), and do not think that environmental concerns hinder economic development (74 % vs. 67 %).
Normative beliefs More *Engaged Greens* (15 %) than *Ambassadors* (4 %) say it is useless to compost before the majority adopts the behaviour. However, only a small portion of that segment shares this belief. They also believe those who compost are examples to follow (85 % vs. 79 %).
Control beliefs Although very similar to the *Ambassadors*, the *Engaged Greens* do not compost as much. This is likely due to their more negative perceptions of composting barriers, including mostly flies (29 % vs. 60 %) and odours (19 % vs. 59 %). Regardless, they assert that they would compost if their municipalities offered a collection service (95 % vs. 78 %).
Willing Greens

18 % vs. 26 %

Behavioural beliefs The *Willing Greens* also have a very favourable attitude towards the environment. They also feel a moral obligation to do more for the environment (even higher than for the *Engaged Greens*). Moreover, they strongly believe their everyday actions may have a positive impact on the environment. With regard to composting, 82 % (vs. 72 %) believe it is well worth the time and effort.
Normative beliefs Although still more likely than the *Ambassadors* (4 %) to think that it is useless to compost before the majority adopts the behaviour, the *Willing Greens* (10 %) are less likely to believe so than the *Engaged Greens* (15 %).
Control beliefs Sensitivity to the barriers of composting is greater again in this segment. Notably, three quarters of the *Willing Greens* indicated that odours (vs. 59 %) and flies (vs. 60 %) are important downsides to composting. Interestingly, we notice that as sensitivity to barriers grows through the segments, composting behaviour tends to drop. This prompts us to wonder whether the barriers originate from personal experience or perceived fears and myths surrounding composting. Access to a municipal collection service is also of importance to this group (73 % vs. 62 %).

Reluctant to Compost

7 % vs. 26 %

Behavioural beliefs Regardless of their reluctance towards composting, the *Reluctant to Compost* still have a favourable environmental attitude, similar to that of previous groups. They even show a certain openness to composting, since 55 % of them (vs. 72 %) think that it is worth the time and effort. However, this does not translate to reported composting behaviour.

Normative beliefs As one of the two segments least favourable to composting, the *Reluctant to Compost* are significantly more likely to believe it is useless to compost until the majority does (40 % vs. 22 %). They are also less likely to believe people who compost are examples to follow (72 % vs. 79 %). However, these numbers also tell us that a majority of the *Reluctant to Compost* might be open to composting.

Control beliefs The respondents in this segment were very sensitive to the barriers of composting—almost all of them mention odours (99 % vs. 59 %), flies (98 % vs. 60 %) and hygiene (91 % vs. 46 %) as important downsides. In addition, although more than half of them (64 %) say that they would be inclined to compost if a collection service was available, they are much less likely to say so than the rest of the respondents (78 %). Similarly, less than half of them think that it is important for the municipality to offer such services (43 % vs. 62 %). Finally, the *Reluctant to Compost* are more likely to perceive composting as bringing more disadvantages than benefits (52 % vs. 30 %).

Again, although this segment's portrait is a lot bleaker than that of previously presented segments, it is important to keep in mind that more than half of those who are *Reluctant to Compost* show important signs of openness towards composting. From this point of view, the portrait does not seem so gloomy. It merely shows that more efforts will be needed in order to bring this group closer to adopting composting behaviour.

Utilitarians

20 % vs. 26 %

Behavioural beliefs As with previous segments, the *Utilitarians* show positive attitudes towards the environment. However, like the previous group, they are more likely to perceive composting as having more costs than benefits (40 % vs. 30 %).

Normative beliefs A significant proportion of *Utilitarians* believe it is useless to compost until the majority does (24 % vs 22 %). However, the vast majority (84 % vs. 79 %) believes people who compost are examples to follow.

Control beliefs Here is where the *Utilitarians*' distinctive characteristic mostly arises. As in many other groups, they seem very favourable to the establishment of a collection service (91 % vs. 78 %), yet are sensitive to the barriers of composting, e.g. 78 % mention odours (vs. 59 %) and flies (vs. 60 %). However, they also say they would be significantly more inclined to do more with an economic incentive

(66 % vs. 40 %). They seem strongly motivated by personal gain ("what's in it for me?"). In order to get them to adopt composting, it would be crucial to show *Utilitarians* that the personal benefits are worth the effort, an idea with which 40 % of them (vs. 30 %) disagree at present.

Independent Composters

32 % vs. 26 %

Behavioural beliefs Although they represent only 6 % of the population sample, the *Independent Composters* reveal interesting features. On the one hand, they are less engaged towards environmental issues and are more sceptical of the benefits of recycling. For example, a majority doubts that what is put in the recycling bins is actually recycled (52 % vs. 37 %). Regarding composting, they are less likely to think it is worth the time and effort (62 % vs. 72 %). On the other hand, at the same time they are already among the biggest composters (32 %), after the *Ambassadors* (63 %) and the *Engaged Greens* (36 %).

Normative beliefs This segment strongly believes that people who compost are examples to follow (74 % vs. 79 %). A small but significant portion believes it is useless to compost until the majority does (18 % vs. 22 %).

Control beliefs Surprisingly, the *Independent Composters* are less sensitive to the barriers of composting in comparison with the sample average (though still burdened by odours (43 % vs. 59 %), flies (32 % vs. 60 %), space required in the kitchen (22 % vs. 47 %), etc.). Accordingly, they seem more inclined to adopt the behaviour if the municipality offered a collection service (85 % vs. 78 %).

The Disengaged

3 % vs 26 %

Behavioural beliefs Even though their attitude towards environmental issues is relatively favourable (though in lesser proportion than the other groups), most of the *Disengaged* do not compost and are less motivated to do so. In other words, they are less likely to think it is urgent to act on environmental issues (70 % vs. 82 %), less likely to wish to do more (30 % vs. 48 %), and more likely to think environmental preoccupations are barriers to economic development (55 % vs. 33 %). They also tend to believe the costs of composting outweigh its advantages (63 % vs. 30 %).

Normative beliefs The *Disengaged* are much less likely to think people who compost lead by example (49 % vs. 79 %). Trying to reach them through normative beliefs will thus prove much harder than with other groups. They are also much more likely to believe it is useless to compost until the majority does (42 % vs. 22 %), which indicates they will most likely be late adopters.

Control beliefs Finally, the *Disengaged* seem very sensitive to the downsides of composting, almost all of them mention odours (99 % vs. 59 %), flies (96 % vs. 60 %), hygiene (93 % vs. 46 %), and the space needed in the kitchen (92 % vs. 47 %) as important downsides. In addition, only a fifth of them think providing a municipal compost collection service would be important (22 % vs. 62 %), and only 45 % of them (vs. 78 %) say they would be likely to compost if such a service was offered (smallest proportions of all segments).

Targeting and Positioning

Following segmentation is targeting. Through this process, we evaluate the segments in order to determine which ones to address in a campaign. This evaluation is based on factors related to the issue at hand, but also on pragmatic factors. Hence, the segments are firstly evaluated based on the incidence of the issue within the population, its severity, and the difficulty for the population to resolve the issue itself. The segments are also evaluated according to their size, ease of access, and sensitivity towards the issue at hand. Once the targets are selected, we have to orientate our messages according to their preferences and characteristics. Through positioning, we determine the best way to reach the targeted audience, with the help of research and theory.

Following our analysis of the seven segments, we will now suggest targeting and positioning strategies, in which we establish what segments to target and how. Because some segments shared similar composting behaviours, barriers and motivations, we grouped some of them together (the shared similarities are explained more thoroughly in the following sections). Main targets were thus formed, regrouping five of the seven segments: *Target A* (*The Motivated*) and *Target B* (*The Late Composters*). At this stage, only the *Ambassadors* and the *Disengaged* were put aside, for reasons that will be explained later on. In keeping with our goal of paving the way for new legislation regarding organic waste planned for 2022 in Quebec, we suggest communication strategies to help raise awareness regarding composting and bring Quebecers towards the adoption of the behaviour.

Target A: The Motivated (*Engaged Greens, Willing Greens* and *Independent Composters*)

The *Motivated* are comprised of the three most engaged segments after the *Ambassadors*. These segments do not need to be convinced of the relevance of composting: they already believe in its relevance and its use. However, they also perceive downsides to composting, in particular odours and flies.

A campaign targeting the *Motivated* should offer tips, tools, and advice to help make their experience with composting more successful and less stressful. The main barrier inhibiting composting for this target group relates to their control beliefs. Addressing this barrier to composting should give them a greater sense of control, help them feel more at ease with composting. For example, by giving concrete and easy tips on how to maintain the right level of humidity to allow the organic waste to decompose rather than rot (a useful tip for avoiding flies and bad odours), the *Motivated* could gain confidence in their ability to properly compost.

As they view composting as a socially desirable behaviour, relying in part on normative beliefs could also engage them. For instance, opinion leaders might be of positive influence in this matter, working to increase this group's interest in composting, and adding to its perceived value. Although the *Ambassadors* would seem to be ideal opinion leaders at first glance, we would tend to advise against such a strategy. Indeed, their behaviour and their positions regarding the environment might come off as unreasonable or excessive to the *Motivated*, and their divergent postures and behaviours might lead to a strategy that quickly backfires. Instead, we would suggest using either *Engaged Greens* or *Willing Greens* as opinion leaders.

The *Motivated* hence need to be accompanied, either on their way to adopt the behaviour, or in maintaining it. Ultimately, the goal for this target would be to get them ready to test the behaviour once compost collection is available. We believe, at that point, an additional form of support should be offered in order to make sure the experience is a positive one. Such support might be presented in the form of explanatory pamphlets or, ideally, ground teams who would be better able to cater to the needs of the people they visit. Indeed, reinforcement through interpersonal interactions tends to be highly successful and effective (McKenzie-Mohr et al. 2012).

Target B: The Late Composters (*Utilitarians* and *Reluctant to Compost*)

The *Late Composters* are comprised of the two least motivated and engaged segments after the *Disengaged*. These segments are not yet completely convinced of the relevance and utility of composting. They are also much more unlikely to have tested the behaviour, yet are much more sensitive to its barriers. Consequently, the barriers they perceive will most likely be based on preconceptions or myths relating to composting rather than on personal experience. Hence, the *Late Composters* will need greater help and guidance than the previous group. Messages for this target could try to demystify the perception that composting requires a lot of work, exposing how easy it is to compost in an urban setting.

More precisely, a campaign targeting these segments should focus on building awareness and knowledge concerning composting. Considering their strong negative views of the practicality of composting, such a campaign should concentrate particularly on control beliefs, addressing the perceived barriers and myths that make the *Late Composters* so reluctant to compost. Again, control beliefs present the greatest barrier to composting. However, the goal here would be to make composting appear as more feasible and relevant to these groups.

Since the *Late Composters* are not convinced of the relevance and usefulness of composting, working to improve this perception will also be fundamental. Subsequently, we suggest relying specifically on normative beliefs because this segment seems sensitive to their influence. By presenting the social acceptability of composting, in the numbers of people who compost or want to do so, for example, the *Late Composters* might grow more acceptant of composting and its importance. The *Motivated* can become leaders in that matter; however, treading lightly is crucial. Such a strategy, if not well implemented, may miss its target and seem to be patronising. Patronising, authoritative and condescending tones should be avoided in social marketing efforts, as they may result in adverse reactions from the recipients (Frenette 2010).

Finally, because of their sensitivity to financial incentives, it would be relevant to raise the economic relevance of composting for the individuals and their community. This aspect suggests that external incentives such as contests or gifts might help to get *Late Composters* closer to adopting the behaviour. However, we keep in mind that the effects of such incentives only last as long as their presence. Once the incentive is taken away, the behaviour tends to disappear (McKenzie-Mohr et al. 2012).

Ultimately, the goal for this target would be to increase receptiveness and interest about composting. Subsequent efforts should then focus on their trying the behaviour successfully (i.e. having a positive composting experience).

The Ambassadors We chose not to target the *Ambassadors* specifically. We believe that the possible behavioural gains would be marginal since a high proportion already composts. Implementation of a compost collection service would be the most realistic way of getting more *Ambassadors* to compost. In the meantime, we still believe that with their sensitivity and awareness towards the issue, messages about composting will still have a positive impact on this segment. Accordingly, campaigns targeted to the *Motivated* and *Late Composters* should reinforce their beliefs in the relevance and importance of composting.

The Disengaged We also chose not to target the *Disengaged*. We believe the possible gains made by a campaign would be marginal due to their negative attitudes towards composting and their lack of motivation to do more on this issue. Unfortunately, the *Disengaged* do not seem to be at the stage where they are receptive to information about composting or its value. However, we believe the campaigns, and especially that of the *Late Composters*, should activate the adoption process by raising the group's awareness towards the issue. As the *Disengaged* tend to believe it to be useless to compost until the majority does, exposure to messages about composting in the media should increase their awareness of the issue.

Limits of the RECYC-QUEBEC Study

Segmentation Because RQ's study provides a general segmentation regarding waste management behaviours and attitudes, no distinction is made regarding specific behaviours such as recycling or composting. Had a segmentation been developed specifically for each behaviour, the results of the statistical analysis would probably have been different. For instance, the *Independent Composters* were described as uninterested and unmotivated people with regard to environmental issues. Nonetheless, we saw great promise among this segment regarding composting. Originally named as *Passives* in the RQ study, we chose to rename them, during studying composting, for greater consistency. This example illustrates the possible differences between a global segmentation and a specific one. Adapting the segmentation to each behaviour would have led to a more relevant and precise portrait.

Measures Although RQ's study was, altogether, well designed, we found some gaps, notably in the information that was gathered. For instance, despite the fact that RQ's goal was ultimately to study specific environmental behaviours (i.e. recycling, composting, etc.), the study only inquired about general environmental attitudes.

However, measuring people's general attitudes towards the environment cannot successfully predict a specific behaviour such as composting. This refers to the principle of correspondence, according to Fishbein and Azjen (2010). In addition, it would have been interesting to inquire about the respondents' past behaviour through the quantitative portion of the study, to find out whether or not they had ever tried composting in particular. We could have learned more about the motivations and barriers related to composting by distinguishing people who compost, those who have abandoned composting, and those who have never composted. This information would also have likely modified the segmentation, and influenced the manner in which we approached the segments.

It is also important to note that RQ's study, as with any other survey, is based on self-reported responses. Even though self-reports are very practical, they are subject to limitations such as the social desirability bias (Paulhus and Vazire 2007). For example, a respondent who feels embarrassed by his attitude towards composting might paint a slightly more socially acceptable portrait of himself. Notably, this could explain the overall positive attitude towards the environment.

Also apparent in RQ's study were seeming inconsistencies in the study's results. For example, while 78 % of the respondents said they would be likely to compost if such a service was offered, only 25 % of them mentioned that the offer of this service would be an incentive to get them to compost. Such discrepancies between similar questions might be rooted in a faulty understanding of, or ambiguity in, some questions. These issues could also be related to the length of the questionnaire, with respondents becoming less attentive over time. To avoid such issues, it is crucial to carry out a pre-test.

It is also important to remember that composting is not yet a widespread behaviour. Only a minority of respondents had composted before being surveyed. Therefore, it is possible that many of the respondents' answers were based upon hypothetical conceptions of composting.

Global Recommendations

Referring to theory and research As shown through this case study, using theory and research to analyse and interpret data is essential. In fact, according to Donovan (2011, p. 15), "*such thinking results in the identification of a variety of factors that may influence [the targeted] behaviour.*" Because the targeted behaviours are generally complex, trying to influence them can prove to be quite a challenge (Stead and McDermott 2011). Hence, a theory-based strategy founded on a good understanding of the issue at hand and the people it is targeting is crucial to designing and implementing effective social marketing campaigns (Atkin and Freimuth 2013). Here, we exclusively presented the TPB, but using a combination of models would be beneficial (i.e. French and Gordon 2015; Frenette 2010).

Developing a detailed segmentation We believe RQ's segmentation to be a good example to follow, although we would suggest adding theory to help shape it.

Unlike many existing segmentation efforts, its main focus is not on demographic and geographic variables, as is often the case, but rather on psychographic and behavioural variables, as it should be. Relying primarily on needs, behaviours, beliefs and barriers, it ensures a more adapted segmentation and a better chance of success for social marketing campaigns. Indeed, psychographic and behavioural variables, structured according to theory, should yield better predictive and explanatory value than demographic and geographic variables, which, although useful to paint a segment's portrait, do not determine individual behaviour. For example, people with a certain lifestyle, similar beliefs regarding some issues, and similar desires, might also share the same behaviours regarding a social issue. However, not all 45 year old men living on a particular street with a similar bachelor's degree and work experience will demonstrate the same behaviours towards the environment. Demographic and geographic variables are more suited to guiding strategic decisions, such as determining the best way to reach the segment. Moreover, demographic and geographic variables are not relevant to every segmentation, since they cannot always significantly describe a segment. In our case, we found very little applicable information regarding the various segments. For example, the only distinctive characteristic regarding the *Ambassadors* related to their real estate ownership (70 % were home owners). No other significant information could have helped us.

Combining multiple approaches Although we focused on communication strategies, we would like to stress the importance of employing a combination of approaches to achieve behavioural changes (French et al. 2011). Indeed, social marketing encompasses a broad variety of interventions. For instance, with regard to composting, the implementation of a compost collection service would have a limited impact on behaviour adoption without the help of a communication campaign (and vice versa). The combination of these mutually reinforcing interventions is what renders a large-scale adoption of composting feasible.

Conclusion

This case study highlights the importance of theory, and detailed segmentation, in designing social marketing campaigns. In doing so, it proves useful for social marketing practitioners. By demonstrating how to effectively and efficiently define targeting and positioning strategies with reference to the theory of planned behaviour, we tried to create a helpful and practical guide for practitioners to follow in their personal endeavours. The theory-based approach we favoured to guide our analysis of empirical data also provides a rich opportunity to bridge the gap between research and practice in the field of social marketing.

References

Andreasen, A. R. (2006). *Social marketing in the 21st century*. Thousand Oaks, CA: Sage Publications.
Armitage, C. J., & Conner, M. (2001). Efficacy of the theory of planned behaviour. *British Journal of Social Psychology, 40*, 471–499.
Atkin, C. K., & Freimuth, V. S. (2013). Guidelines for formative evaluation research in campaign design. In R. E. Rice & C. K. Atkin (Eds.), *Public communication campaigns* (pp. 53–68). Thousand Oaks, CA: Sage Publications.
Blair-Stevens, C., Reynolds, R., & Christopoulos, A. (2009). Behavioural theory: Understanding the key influences on human behaviour. In J. French et al. (Eds.), *Social marketing and public health: Theory and practice* (pp. 45–66). Oxford University Press.
Campo, S., Askelson, N. M., Carter, K. D., & Losch, M. (2012). Segmenting audiences and tailoring messages: Using the extended parallel process model and cluster analysis to improve health campaigns. *Social Marketing Quarterly, 18*, 98–111. doi:10.1177/1524500412450490.
Coffman, J. (2002). *Public communication campaign evaluation: An environmental scan of challenges, criticisms, practice, and opportunities*. Cambridge: Mass.
Communauté métropolitaine de Montréal. (2015). Collecte et valorisation des matières organiques. Projet de plan métropolitain de gestion des matières résiduelles 2015–2020. http://cmm.qc.ca/fileadmin/user_upload/pmgmr/fiches/20150303_collecte-matieres-organiques.pdf. Accessed March 10, 2016.
Donovan, R. (2011). Theoretical models of behaviour change. In G. Hasting, K. Angus, & C. Bryant (Eds.), *The SAGE handbook of social marketing* (pp. 15–31). Thousand Oaks, CA: SAGE Publications.
Evans, W. D., Blitstein, J., & Hersey, J. (2008). Evaluation of public health brands: Design, measurement, and analysis. In W. D. Douglas & G. Hastings (Eds.), *Public health branding: Applying marketing for social change* (pp. 43–72). Oxford University Press.
Fishbein, M., & Azjen, I. (2010). *Predicting and changing behavior: The reasoned action approach*. New York, NY: Psychology Press.
French, J., & Gordon, R. (2015). *Strategic social marketing*. London, UK: Sage Publications.
French, J., Merritt, R., & Reynolds, L. (2011). *Social marketing casebook*. London, UK: SAGE.
Frenette, M. (2010). *La recherche en communication: un atout pour les campagnes sociales*. Sainte-Foy: Presses de l'Université du Québec.
Lotenberg, D. L., Schechter, C., & Strand, J. (2011). Segmentation and Targeting. In G. Hasting, K. Angus, & C. Bryant (Eds.), *The SAGE handbook of social marketing* (pp. 125–135). Thousand Oaks, CA: SAGE Publications.
McKenzie-Mohr, D., Lee, N. R., Schultz, P. W., & Kotler, P. (2012). *Social marketing to protect the environment*. Thousand Oaks, CA: SAGE Publications.
McVey, D., & Walsh, L. (2009). Generating "insight" and building segmentations—moving beyond simple targeting. In J. French et al. (Eds.), *Social marketing and public health: Theory and practice* (pp. 97–122). Oxford University Press.
Michie, S., van Stralen, M. M., & West, R. (2011). The behaviour change wheel: A new method for characterising and designing behaviour change interventions. *Implementation Science, 6*, 42. doi:10.1186/1748-5908-6-42.
Ministère des Affaires municipales et de l'Occupation du territoire (MAMROT). (2015). Accord de partenariat avec les municipalités pour 2016–2019. http://www.mamrot.gouv.qc.ca/pub/grands_dossiers/entente_signee_accord_partenariat_municipalites.pdf. Accessed March 10, 2016.
Ministère du Développement durable de l'Environnement et de la Lutte contre les Changements Climatiques (MDELCC). (2012). Banissement des matières organiques de l'élimination au

Québec: état des lieux et prospectives. http://www.mddelcc.gouv.qc.ca/matieres/organique/bannissement-mat-organ-etatdeslieux.pdf. Accessed March 10, 2016.

Paulhus, D. L., & Vazire, S. (2007). The self-report method. In R. W. Robins, R. C. Fraley, & R. F. Krueger (Eds.), *Handbook of research methods in personality psychology* (pp. 224–239). New York, NY: Guilford Press.

RECYC-QUÉBEC. (2015). Portrait des comportements et attitudes des citoyens québécois à l'égard des 3RV. https://www.recyc-quebec.gouv.qc.ca/sites/default/files/documents/etude-portrait-comportements-citoyens.pdf. Accessed November 1, 2015.

Schultz, P. W., Nolan, J. M., Cialdini, R. B., Goldstein, N. J., & Griskevicius, V. (2007). The constructive, destructive and reconstructive power of social norms. *Psychology Science, 18*, 429–434.

Stead, M., & McDermott, R. J. (2011). Evaluation in social marketing. In G. Hastings, K. Angus, & C. Bryant (Eds.), *The SAGE handbook of social marketing* (pp. 193–207). Thousand Oaks, CA: SAGE Publications.

Webb, T. L., Joseph, J., Yardley, L., & Michie, S. (2010). Using the Internet to promote health behavior change: A meta-analytic review of the impact of theoretical basis, use of behavior change techniques, and mode of delivery on efficacy. *Journal of Medical Internet Research, 12*, e4. doi:10.2196/jmir.1376.

Wedel, M., & Kamakura, W. (2000). *Market segmentation: Conceptual and methodological foundations* (2nd ed.). Norwell, MA: Kluwer Academic Publishers.

Yzer, M. (2013). Reasoned action theory: Persuasion as belief-based behavior change. In J. P. Dillard & L. Shen (Eds.), *The SAGE handbook of persuasion: Developments in theory and practice* (pp. 120–136). Thousand Oaks, CA: Sage Publications.

Why We Need Segmentation When Designing Social Marketing Programs

Sharyn Rundle-Thiele, Timo Dietrich and Krzysztof Kubacki

Abstract Evolving from the marketing discipline, social marketing operates with a customer focus that involves designing programs around the satisfaction and needs of customers while ensuring that offered alternatives are more attractive than the competition. Given that social marketers are outgunned by competitors operating with larger budgets and reach, optimisation of scarce resources is critical to deliver maximum effect. This chapter presents a competitively minded view proposing that social marketers need to embrace marketing thinking and apply segmentation. Application of segmentation to understand response to programs at a segment level, use of theory to inform segmentation and application of personas to simplify complex multivariate data output generated from segmentation approaches are detailed. By applying personas, social marketers will be able to more easily understand segments and in turn plan and design programs that meet the needs and wants of more people in segments targeted. Use of the same toolkits, timeframes and thinking allows social marketers to become the enemy delivering programs, products and services that people want at a convenient time and place and price.

S. Rundle-Thiele (✉) · T. Dietrich · K. Kubacki
Menzies Health Institute Queensland, Griffith University, Nathan, Australia
e-mail: s.rundle-thiele@griffith.edu.au

T. Dietrich
e-mail: t.dietrich@griffith.edu.au

K. Kubacki
e-mail: k.kubacki@griffith.edu.au

S. Rundle-Thiele · T. Dietrich · K. Kubacki
Department of Marketing, Griffith University, 170 Kessels Road, Nathan, QLD 4111, Australia

T. Dietrich
Faculty of Medicine and Biomedical Sciences, Centre for Youth Substance Abuse, University of Queensland, Herston, QLD 4029, Australia

T. Dietrich et al. (eds.), *Segmentation in Social Marketing*,
DOI 10.1007/978-981-10-1835-0_13

Are We Playing on the Same Field?

If social marketers were to compare themselves to the industries potentially causing the health, environmental and social harms they are engaged to fix, they would realise they are thinking the same way. Commercial entities have been competing in marketplaces delivering the products and services that customers need and want for decades and even centuries. Commercial firms are able to meet customer needs and wants through market intelligence derived from cutting edge technologies (e.g. big data) and rigorous methodologies (e.g. multivariate data analysis techniques). This intelligence is then applied to gain further market share and financial advantage in an ever increasingly competitive and globalised world. Commercial employees are incentivised to deliver revenue growth along with saving costs, ensuring they will please shareholders, beat targets and maximise bonuses. Together, the many corporations that are competing in the one marketplace continue to sell more products, on more occasions, at rates exceeding population growth. This is the commercial and business mindset or way of thinking that social marketers are up against.

Social marketers are outgunned when it comes to competing with industries that have long-term, sustainable budgets permitting heavy promotion of the very goods and services that are contributing to the problem social marketers are tasked to overcome. Consider statistics from the alcohol industry. UK Statistics reported in Hastings and Angus (2011) demonstrate that industry-funded efforts to promote safer drinking ($US104 million) are greatly outgunned by alcohol advertising ($US4.9 billion). As a result, young people are 239 times more likely to see an alcohol advertisement than an advertisement promoting safe drinking (moderate drinking or abstinence). It has been suggested the public health sector cannot compete for 'share of mind' obtained by industries who can intensively use promotion and distribution strategies to ensure their products are well known and widely available (Pettigrew and Jongenelis 2016). In a world where social marketers are reliant on donations and grant funding this may be true.

Now, let's take a moment. Imagine a world where social marketers offer programs, products and services that people want. Instead of reaching for a bottle of Coca Cola, a bottle of water is chosen, or a person decides to meet up with a group to walk instead of sleeping in or watching TV. Choices are made and behaviours are performed many times every day-day in and day out. By applying marketing thinking, consumers can be persuaded to choose one alternative over another, or to replace behaviours. Moreover, they are willing to give up money to get what they want, which in turn delivers revenue allowing further investment to occur to achieve change. Many social enterprises are operating across the globe with this thinking.

A product that meets the unique wants and needs of a target audience will increase uptake (sales). If focus is narrowed to a unique segment, less promotional expenditure is needed to achieve adequate reach and frequency. Moreover, if the features of the product or service can be increased, perceived value increases permitting higher prices to be charged, therefore increasing revenue. For example, Purdy (2011) reported a social marketing program implemented by DKT International to increase condom usage in Turkey, where withdrawal was the most common form of contraception reported. DKT International, a social marketing enterprise, implemented segmentation and built two brands Fiesta and Kiss. Fiesta condoms were targeted at more affluent consumers at a higher price point (10 Turkish lira or US$6.70 for 12) and with more variants and wider market availability than Kiss condoms (US$3.30 for 12). Fiesta, the premium condom brand, was promoted using a wide range of digital platforms to sexually active young people (more men than women) achieving sales of 4.3 million condoms (of which 8 % were sold online) in the first 18 months. In contrast, Kiss, a far more inexpensive DKT condom, which was not promoted due to the lower pricing and was only available in low-cost outlets, sold 2.6 million condoms. The DKT International example outlined in Purdy (2011) provides a clear case where social marketers can clearly gain revenue which can be re-invested into the program in future to further extend reach. The tools, techniques and thinking that are used in commercial marketing need to be used in social marketing.

Time to Get in the Game

When Alan Andreasen outlined six key social marketing benchmark criteria in 2002 he stated that when one or more of the six criteria are used, it is social marketing. Fast forward to 2016 and this is not enough for social marketers to effectively compete. Firstly, evidence indicates that social marketing is more effective when more of Andreasen's (2002) social marketing benchmark criteria are used (Carins and Rundle-Thiele 2014). Second, given that commercial competitors are delivering attractive exchange offerings catering to the unique needs and wants of targeted segments, social marketers operating with communication-only campaigns are simply not in the game, in strictly competitive terms, given the absence of attractive alternatives to induce a target to change their behaviour for the better. As noted by Hastings (2007) in 'Why should the Devil have all the best tunes?' it is asking a lot to counter multinational corporations without access to the same toolkit and timeframes. Moving forward, social marketing programs need to operate with a commercial marketing mindset. Rather than implementing a social advertising campaign emphasising health benefits or raising awareness for an issue across a population, social marketers need to partner with commercial companies, or operate social enterprises ensuring an ongoing revenue stream can be delivered over time to sustain a program, and each effort needs to be aimed at one or more target audiences.

Commercial marketers have long understood that a market is comprised of a sum of individuals. In measurement terms each and every individual in the market can be characterised by a broad range of demographic, psychographic, geographic and behavioural variables. Commercial marketers view each customer as an individual, understanding that each individual is driven by a unique set of needs and wants, and technologies are emerging permitting one-to-one marketing to occur. Despite technology shift permitting one-to-one marketing, for most marketers cost economics prevent individual customised products and services from being delivered and consequently, strategies and ways of thinking are needed to find ways to maximise our ability to reach the most consumers as cost efficiently as possible. Segmentation is one strategy that has been employed over time by commercial marketers to maximise return on investment in marketing. As noted earlier in Chap. 2 of this book, segmentation is rarely used in social marketing, with reasons for the lack of use outlined in Chaps. 3 and 4.

Recent reviews of social marketing interventions guided by Alan Andreasen's (2002) six social marketing benchmark criteria indicate that social marketing is not being implemented to its full extent (see Carins and Rundle-Thiele 2014; Fujihira et al. 2015; Kubacki et al. 2015a, b, c). Chapter 2 presented an overview of segmentation use across 93 social marketing interventions reported in peer reviewed literature. The umbrella review identified restricted use of segmentation in social marketing interventions (16 %). Given that segmentation is mentioned as one of the core social marketing benchmark criteria in the most widely accepted frameworks (Andreasen 2002; French and Blair-Stevens 2005), social marketers need to adopt segmentation practice. This chapter continues with a case study outlining how the NSW Fire Service worked with Experian, a global market intelligence organisation, applying segmentation to more directly communicate to households with lowered communication costs. The chapter then continues by outlining the importance of applying segmentation in the social marketing strategic tool kit.

Breaking it All Down (Experian Marketing Services Fire and Rescue New South Wales/Client Case Study, Fire and Rescue News)

Fire and Rescue New South Wales (FRNSW) FRNSW is one of the world's largest urban fire and rescue services. FRNSW's goal is to prevent household fires from occurring, reduce the need to fight fires and to enhance overall community safety and quality of life across New South Wales (NSW). Having observed strong positive change in the United Kingdom (UK) where fire services had embraced segmentation practice FRNSW decided it was time to break it all down.

Thousands of fire incident records from FRNSW were matched to Experian reference data using household addresses. Once matched, each incident was attributed into one of 49 different Mosaic Types (i.e. Australian household and neighbourhood types) which are aggregated in 13 segments. The Mosaic Types are highly reflective of the differences between households in NSW with data drawn from national census and other sources. Experian is able to draw on a broad range of data including financial spending data and demographic data such as income, wealth, housing type and tenure (see illustrative USA mosaic below).

This ability to link national databases enabled Experian to deliver a fire risk profiling tool which FRNSW then applied to understand neighbourhoods and households (Mosaic types) that were most at-risk.

Results By employing segmentation FRNSW was able to obtain an in-depth understanding of the NSW neighbourhood segments that were most at risk of experiencing house fires with details down to the fire station area and household level.

By understanding which segments were most at risk of household fires FRNSW was able to more precisely deliver its fire prevention efforts through targeted communications and the delivery of segment-specific messages. For example, FRNSW delivered a trial home visitation project to at-risk members of the community. FRNSW was able to save costs by ceasing to run expensive TV advertisements promoting fire prevention. Instead, they are now using more cost efficient and targeted marketing tactics, such as online advertising and local community newspapers, to communicate to at-risk segments directly.

What's Good for the Goose Must Be Good for the Gander

The NSW Fire Service worked with Experian, a global market intelligence organisation, applying segmentation to more directly communicate to households at fire risk saving communication costs in the process. DKT International was able to sell 4.3 million condoms at a price premium by applying segmentation. Together, these cases demonstrate that selected social marketers have embraced marketing thinking. The time has come for the remaining 84 % of social marketers to apply segmentation in practice and to do so, they need to embrace (commercial) marketing thinking.

Commercial marketing is centred on the consumer and is focused on delivering a competitive value offering that is superior in some way to the competition. Accordingly, the (commercial) marketing concept suggests *a customer focus that involves designing organisation operations around the profitable satisfaction of customers* (Pettigrew and Jongenelis 2016, p. 62). Markets are evolving and as a result consumer choices change constantly in response to market offerings (competitor actions and reactions) with consumers choosing the most attractive alternatives. At a practical level, assessment of the competition needs to be made to understand how to effectively combat commercial market offerings. As market sizes have grown, products have proliferated in the marketplace, suggesting it is not commercially viable to produce one product or service to meet the needs and wants of an entire population. Think about how Coca-Cola Amatil offers a family of Coke-branded (and many other) products. Coca Cola Amatil's vision is *to create millions of moments of happiness and possibilities* (CCA Annual Report 2015). To achieve this vision Coca Cola Amatil aims to *'delight consumers with an exceptional portfolio of brands, always within an arm's reach'* (ibid.). Coca Cola Amatil achieves this by targeting different groups in the overall population. Consider the Coke family of products which is distributed as follows:

- Coke
    - 2 l bottle
    - 1.25 l bottle
    - 1 l glass and plastic bottle
    - 600 ml bottle
    - 385 ml glass bottle
    - 375 ml bottle launched in 2012
    - 330 ml can and glass bottles
    - 300 ml mini bottles
    - 250 ml slim line can launched in 2013 at 105 calories
    - 200 ml mini cans
    - 12 × 300 ml cans
- Diet Coke—Launched in 1983 and targeted towards women
- Coke Zero—A low-calorie (0.3 kcal per 100 ml) variation specifically marketed to men who were shown to associate *diet* drinks with women
- Coke Life—A 35 % reduction in sugar and calories including natural Stevia sweetener for the more health conscious consumer

- Vanilla Coke
- Diet Coke Caffeine free

In addition to the Coke family Coca Cola Amatil offers an extensive range of beverages for the Australian market manufacturing, selling, distributing and marketing 26 non-alcohol beverage brands via thousands of retail outlets across the country. Coca Cola Amatil's portfolio includes Sprite, Fanta, Lift, Kirks, Deep Spring, Mount Franklin, Pump, Powerade, Barista Bros and Zico Coconut Water. By offering variants Coca Cola Amatil is always within an arm's reach of its target audience(s), and its Australian arm is earning AUD$514M in a calendar year (CCA Annual Report 2015). Each variant is strategically planned to target a specific target group within the Australian population.

Whether a social marketing program is delivering one or many of the Ps in marketing's toolkit (product, place, price, promotion, processes, physical evidence, people), the principles and processes of segmentation offer considerable opportunity to more effectively target an attractive offering to meet audience needs and wants. If some of the most successful marketers of our time can offer a broad array of variants to extend their reach as far as it is economically viable, then surely social marketers can finally embrace a commercial mindset?

Social marketers need to work within their budget parameters and, as noted in Chap. 3 by Jeff French, in some cases this will necessarily involve focusing on one single attractive market segment. This chapter is not alone in suggesting that social marketers need to embrace marketing thinking. In Chap. 4 Sally Dibb indicated the need to bridge the gap between commercial marketers and social marketers and other behaviour change fields given the recent step-change in technology which permits more sophisticated segmentation models to be undertaken.

Given that approximately one-third of managers have difficulties interpreting segmentation solutions (see discussion in Chap. 3) considerable training within the sector is needed. This book offers a first step towards encouraging the wider adoption of segmentation in social marketing. As noted in Chap. 3, experiments indicate that unstructured approaches to selecting target segments lead to significantly worse choices. In contrast, when asked to select the best target segments and given guidance on which criteria to consider, significantly better decisions can be made. It is our hope that this book can assist to raise segmentation's prominence in social marketing and behaviour change practice.

Embrace Marketing Thinking: Apply Segmentation

The results of the umbrella review presented in Chap. 2 suggest there is ample opportunity to extend segmentation's use in social marketing with less than one in five social marketing programs currently reporting use of segmentation. Moving forward social marketers need to become comfortable operating with a more commercial mindset and as such need to consider that groups of people are different, and often want different things or will respond differently to social marketing programs in terms of engagement and interaction.

Not only can segmentation be used to identify different motivations to inform program planning and design, consideration of segments in outcome evaluation can guide subsequent planning. Consider the following example from Dietrich et al. (2015) that was undertaken to assess segment response to an early pilot alcohol social marketing program delivered in a school setting. A sample of 371 Year 10 students (aged 14–16 years; 51.4 % boys) who had participated in a prospective (pre-post) multisite (3 schools participated in the program pilot) alcohol social marketing program. *Game On: Know Alcohol* (GO:KA) aimed to deliver a suite of strategies adolescents could use to abstain from or moderate their alcohol drinking through a series of six student-centred modules. Baseline demographics, drinking attitudes, drinking intentions, and alcohol knowledge were cluster analysed using the Two-Step cluster analysis procedure outlined in Chap. 8 to identify segments. Next, a repeated measures design was used to assess key program outcomes at the segment level and satisfaction with program components was assessed in a process evaluation.

Three segments were identified: (1) *Sceptics*, (2) *Risky Males*, (3) *Good Females* (see Dietrich et al. 2015 for a detailed segment level description). Segments 2 and 3 showed greatest change in drinking attitudes and intentions (see Figs.1 and 2).

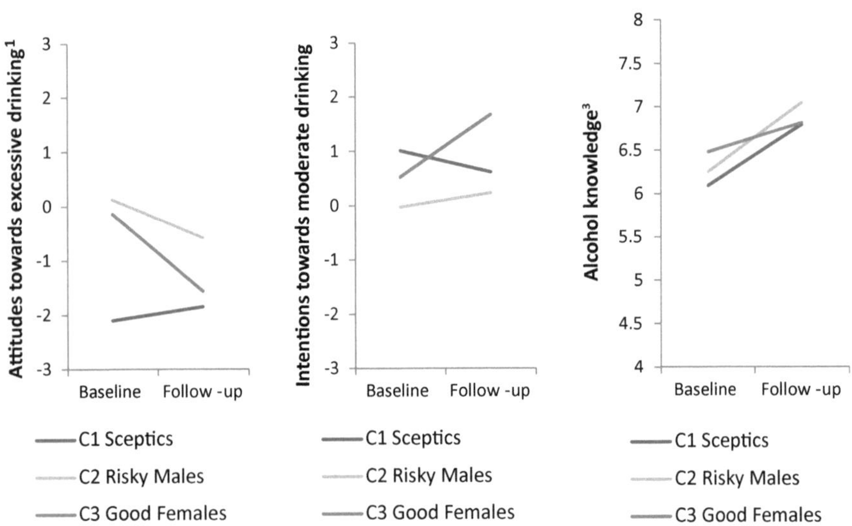

[1] Bipolar items (-3 negative to positive 3)

[2] Average total of the individual attitudes (intentions) items

[3] Knowledge score (0 to 10)

Fig. 1 Segment response to an alcohol program delivered in a high school setting. Attitude change[1], Intention change[2], Knowledge change[3]

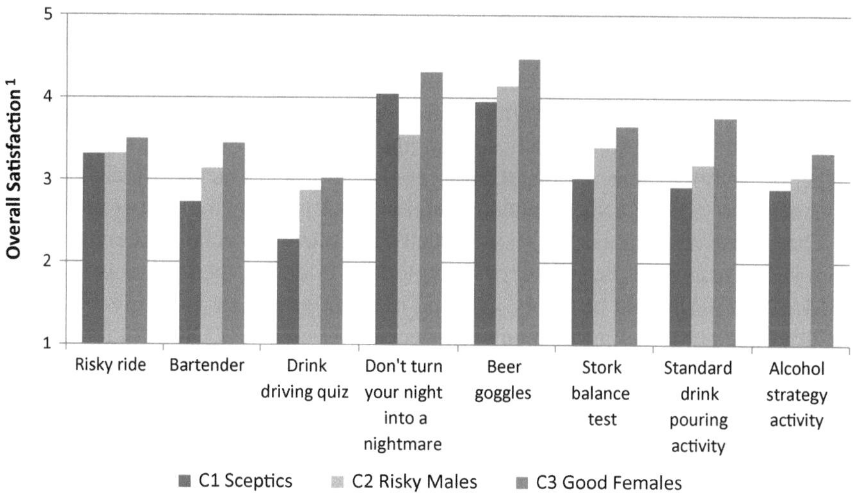

[1]Likert-scale (1 very dissatisfied, 5 very satisfied)

Fig. 2 Segment response to an alcohol program delivered in a high school setting. Segments by individual component satisfaction

The Dietrich et al. (2015) outcome assessment indicated that *Good Females* showed the largest positive attitude shift along with the most favourable satisfaction ratings for the GO:KA program. On the contrary, GO:KA received the lowest satisfaction scores from the *Sceptics* who did not resonate with the program content. These segment differences indicate that one size does not fit all and that it is important to think about more tailored program solutions to engage the wider target audience. The insights gained from this study indicated that differential delivery should be explored given that technology can provide the opportunity to deliver unique program components catering to the unique needs and wants of the different segments. Insights from the outcome evaluation suggest that satisfaction with the program components is likely to impact change in the key outcome variables, and therefore understanding how to satisfy the *Sceptics* would in turn assist improvements in the outcomes delivered.

Using Theory to Guide

As outlined in Part II of this book there is no universally best market segmentation method and more importantly, the data analysis techniques will always deliver an answer requiring the analyst to be highly skilled in identifying segments that offer validity. One means to enhance the effectiveness of segmentation may involve the use theory to guide segmentation.

According to Sutton and Staw (1995), good theory 'explains, predicts and delights'. Theory encapsulates what we know about the way things are, the way they work, and the way they interact or fit together. A theory seeks to answer questions of how, when (if longitudinal data are available), where or why, which is distinct from description, which simply answers the questions of what or who (Whetton 1989). In other words, theories consist of a set of factors which should be considered to explain a social phenomenon and outline how the factors are related.

Theory use is recognised as an important component of social marketing with 61 % of social marketing experts across the globe considering theory use as important (iSMA 2016). The role of theory in social marketing practice is also recognised in the third Social Marketing Benchmark criterion offered by the UK's National Social Marketing Centre (see http://www.snh.org.uk/pdfs/sgp/A328466.pdf), which states:

> *Social Marketing uses behavioural theories to understand behaviour and inform the intervention:*
>
> *The theory, or theories used, are identified after conducting the customer orientation research*
>
> *Appropriate behavioural theory is clearly used to inform and guide the methods mix (Benchmark 8)*
>
> *Theoretical assumptions are tested as part of the intervention developed by pre-testing.*

Given the importance of theory use in social marketing, the application of theory within the segmentation process can deliver actionable behavioural insights to inform planning at the segment level. A recent study by Schuster et al. (2015) applied the principle of theory to market segmentation to gain insight into changing the physical activity behaviour of children in the context of walking to/from school behaviour. The utility of employing theory (Theory of Planned Behaviour) in addition to other variables (demographic, geographic, and behavioural) was examined in the Schuster et al. (2015) study. A total of 512 caregivers of primary school aged children (5–13 years old) were surveyed online. First, structural equation modelling was undertaken to examine the theoretical model. According to Schuster et al. (2015) model fit supported the Theory of Planned Behaviour suggesting that together attitudes, social norms and perceived behavioural control influenced intentions to increase walking to/from school. Next, the two-step cluster analysis procedure, outlined in Chap. 8, was used to identify segments. A total of 14 geographic, demographic, psychographic and behavioural variables formed the base for analysis. The analysis revealed three distinct segments of caregivers, each with unique beliefs about their children walking to/from school: Segment 1—short-distance frequent walkers, Segment 2—middle-distance sporadic walkers and Segment 3—long-distance non-walkers (see Schuster et al. 2015 for segment descriptions). Four variables were found to be highly important in distinguishing these segments: distance to school, current walk to/from school behaviour, subjective norms and intentions to increase their child's walk to school behaviour indicating theory's prominence in this context. Given that social norms influence intentions which in turn are related to behaviour, application of the Theory of

Planned Behaviour in this context can further improve walking to and from school behaviour.

Theoretically derived segments assists to understand the commonalities between people within a segment along with differences between segments. Further, application of theory shows how change can be achieved. For example, in the walking to and from school study, distance lived from school impacted walking, with Segment 1 walking twice as often (N = 4.9 times) compared to Segment 2 (N = 2.4 times) (see Fig. 3). Armed with this insight, social marketers understand the need for tailoring the program offering to deliver services that are relevant to each segment. This thinking allows the needs of more people in the target audience to be met. In the Schuster et al. (2015) study, consumer insights gained during the research assisted to understand that the distance lived from school was the most distinguishing factor in segmentation analysis, and that social norms are a driving influence in walk to school rates (see Fig. 3). Therefore, social marketers can offer a walking school bus from one or more designated drop-off zones to effectively target one segment (long-distance non-walkers) while focusing communication efforts to improve social norms for segments living within a 2 km radius of schools.

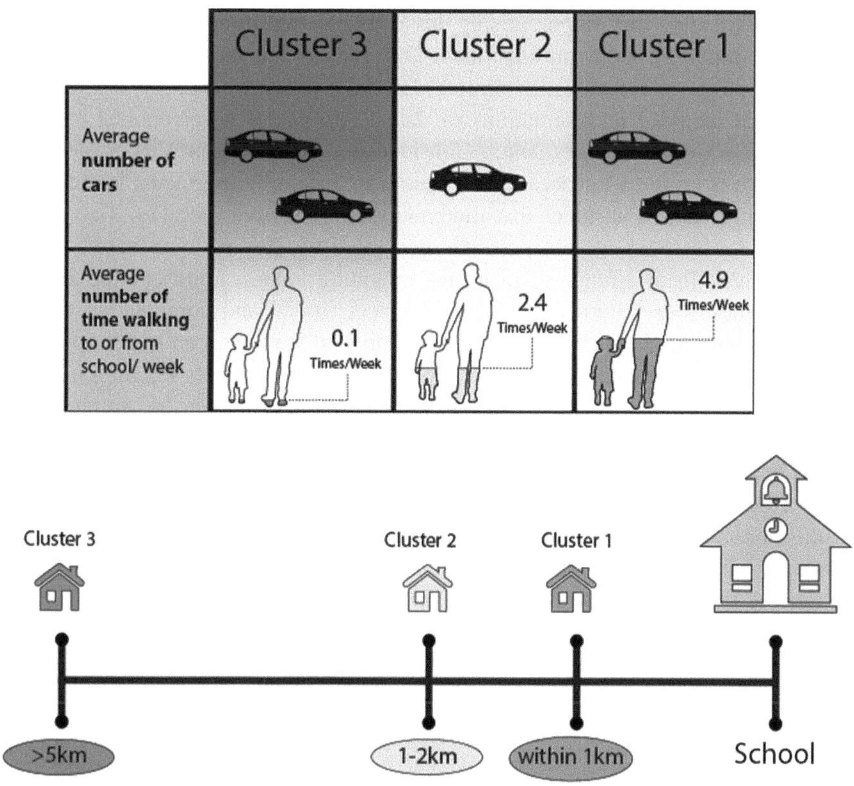

Fig. 3 Walk to and from school segments

The Schuster et al. (2015) study demonstrated the usefulness of incorporating theory (Theory of Planned Behaviour) in distinguishing segments to gain insights that could be used to change walking to and from school behaviour. By understanding the different types of segments, program developers (or social marketers) can then start to understand the competing forces that either motivate each segment to behave in a certain way (current behaviours) or inhibit each segment from taking up the desired behaviour. Understanding segment differences is extremely important in the process of developing a robust understanding of the means that can be successfully employed to encourage the target audience to change for the better. In the absence of an attractive offering that overcomes distance (e.g. a walking school bus, morning activity program or Bike Buses), communications (alone) encouraging parents to allow their child to walk to and from school would be less effective.

Simplifying the Presentation

In many cases segmentation employs complex multivariate statistical techniques and consequently, the output arising involves the reporting of many measures across the range of segments identified. One means that has been used commercially over time to simplify descriptions for the segments generated is the use of personas or pictorial representations of data to assist the non-technical reader to more clearly understand segments. Consider the Roy Morgan Values segments, which have been used for decades in Australia to describe segments based on the values, mindsets and attitudes that motivate their behaviour (see Fig. 4).

Figure 4 illustrates the ten personas generated by Roy Morgan based on segments derived from a range of measures including values, mindsets and attitudes and how these can be considered by marketers (social and commercial) alike to inform decision making. For example, according to Roy Morgan's description the 'Socially Aware' segment believes strongly in the concept of 'learning a living' rather than earning a living, always seeking new opportunities for training, education and knowledge. They tend to seek detailed information about their options and consider the consequences of each choice carefully before making a decision. With a strong sense of social responsibility and a propensity for convincing others of their opinions, they often become involved in lobby groups. Common occupations are public servants, politicians and researchers. 'Socially Aware' refers to a pattern of responses mostly offered by people who are community minded and socially active. Being 'information vacuum cleaners', this segment is always searching for new things to learn, something new and different. In 2013 'Socially Aware' consumers could be targeted in Australia using any radio platform, given that 90 % of socially aware consumers listen to radio—a considerably higher level than other segments.

The use of personas can be employed for all segmentation studies. Consider Chap. 10, which provided a case study that sought to understand whether segments

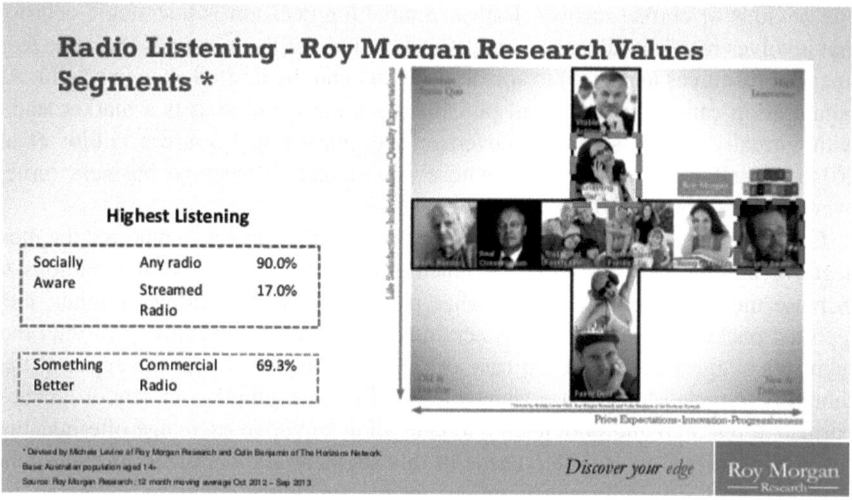

Fig. 4 Roy Morgan value segments and radio usage—2013 (http://www.slideshare.net/RoyMorganResearch/state-of-the-nation-spotlight-on-the-australian-media-landscape)

existed within the Queensland carers of primary school-aged children market. A Two-Step cluster analysis method was used drawing on a sample of 876 carers across three commonly used segmentation bases. A combination of 15 demographic (education, age, income, occupation), psychographic (attitudes and intentions towards healthy eating) and behavioural (smoking status) variables were used to distinguish between carers. Three different carer segments emerged: (1) wealthy and less concerned, (2) concerned with low socioeconomic status and (3) concerned wealthy and educated. For detailed descriptions of the segments see Chap. 10. These segments are displayed graphically in Fig. 5.

Following determination that three segments existed, a decision would need to be made about which segment(s) to target for the social marketer. Both segment 2 (Concerned with low SES) and 3 (Concerned, wealthy and educated) held favourable attitudes towards healthy eating and reported packing healthier lunches than segment 3 (Wealthy and less concerned). This leaves a social marketer deciding whether to target one segment only, two segments or all three segments—an issue that was discussed extensively in Chap. 3. It is important to note there is no

Fig. 5 Lunchbox study personas

one obvious or correct answer. Rather, a targeting decision is a strategic decision that involves resource allocation and is made in light of the resources available (e.g. financial resources and time) to social marketers and the desired change sought. An organisation cannot market to all potential customers, unless it is a market leader with virtually limitless market coverage and marketing resources (Elliot et al. 2014). Recall Coca Cola Amatil whose non-alcoholic beverage business turned over $514 million in 2015 in Australia.

Carers in the wealthy and less concerned segment (Segment 1) reported the most negative attitudes towards packing lunchboxes and had the lowest intentions to increase the number of healthy lunches provided to their children. Further, they reported packing significantly less servings of vegetables and fruit than the other segments suggesting that in the case of a limited budget, this is the segment that should be targeted to increase vegetable and fruit consumption in school lunches. Formative research and pilot testing to determine attractive exchange offerings that could be delivered to meet the needs of this segment are warranted to understand how fruit and vegetable consumption via the lunchbox could be increased for children in this segment. It is possible this segment (Wealthy and less concerned) would be attracted by a fun lunchbox sold at school where contents packed deliver the level of fruit and vegetables children need, given any emphasis on health would not attract this segment.

The Segmentation Process: A Way to Organise and Think About the Market

The segmentation process (see Chap. 6) provides a means to organise a complex market comprised of a broad array of individuals who are each unique into groups that can be characterised by their similarities. The grouping of individuals who are similar permits thinking to be focused, ensuring that resources can be allocated effectively and efficiently, thereby maximising the return on investment (see Chap. 5). By employing personas (see Fig. 3, 4 and 5 for an array of persona examples) social marketers can think of a segment as a person and use the data gathered to make decisions catering to the needs and wants of people in one or more segment (s). By understanding the types of people being targeted social marketers can ensure:

- Program offerings such as products and services are designed to meet the preferences of the segment(s) being targeted (Product)
- The offering meets the cost expectation of the segment (Price). Recall that differential prices were charged by DKT International for Kiss and Fiesta condoms.
- The offering is available at a time and location that is convenient for the segment (s) (Place). Recall that different outlets were used by DKT International to distribute Kiss and Fiesta condoms.

- Advertisements and other promotions are placed in media that the segment(s) frequent, which can in turn assist to increase the number of times each selected segment is exposed to the program (and/or messages) thereby increasing message recall.

Segmentation permits resources to be maximised by placing a preferred offering in a time and place convenient for the target audience, who can be reached effectively within the budget constraints faced by the marketer. Different segments may have different needs and wants and for this reason, offering variants (e.g. DKT International and Coca Cola Amatil examples highlighted in this Chapter) allows marketers to set different prices and distribution channels for different products, thereby delivering to more customers.

Improving Our Technical Ability

As mentioned previously, the data analysis techniques used to determine segments will always produce a solution. Highly trained statisticians experienced in segmentation analysis have evolved a range of procedures to assess the stability and reproducibility of cluster results. They suggest that solutions which can be obtained repeatedly across independent calculations (with slight changes in the algorithm or the data) are preferable to solutions that cannot be repeatedly obtained. Procedures used to validate segmentation solutions were discussed in Section II of this book.

In the age of big data social marketers need to be adept at understanding data in order to monitor rapidly evolving and large markets. Ideally, moving forward, improvements in the social marketing profession need to occur, ensuring that all social marketers can interpret the segmentation solutions presented to them, since the available data can inform marketing mix decisions, communication focus and program formulation. In the meantime, the data analysts who serve the social marketing profession need to be able to clearly communicate the segments derived through use of personas and other means that assist to summarise large volumes of data into a more consumable form, ensuring that clear segment descriptions are delivered to assist intervention design, implementation and evaluation.

Segmentation techniques provide marketers with the means to arrange complex multivariate data into a more simplified form to assist managerial decision making. For some time commercial marketers have been using segmentation to gain an in-depth, accurate and up-to-date understanding of the needs and buying behaviours of potential customers and how those needs and behaviour might be changing. With limited reported application of segmentation (16 % of 93 interventions) the social marketing profession has yet to embrace marketing tools such as segmentation. Segmentation needs to become a social marketing competency that all practitioners will be able to confidently apply and interpret.

Optimising Outcomes: Maximising Financial Resources Through Targeted Thinking

This book has outlined the importance of using segmentation to optimise outcomes and in some cases clear examples of how segmentation has been used in practice have been provided. The DKT International example at the beginning of this chapter provided a clear example of pricing differences for products in a social marketing program aimed at improving contraception methods, while the FRNSW program demonstrates how communication was more narrowly targeted to reach the group most at risk of house fires. Segmentation provides a means for social marketers to maximise scarce financial resources by concentrating limited resources to achieve a maximum outcome.

In market research it is widely understood that measurement needs to be optimised as measurement levels enhance precision of estimates. At one level, social marketers should seek to gain objective data wherever possible. Commercial firms routinely gather transactional customer data as part of their daily operations. Consider retailers such as Woolworths in Australia who ask customers to scan their 'Rewards' cards providing Woolworths dollars as a benefit in exchange for access to data for all products purchased in store form every recorded transaction at an individual customer level. Many social marketers combatting the obesity epidemic may not have access to this information and have to resort to partnerships, or paying data suppliers to gain access to this data. Access to rich data is needed to develop insights to design and implement social marketing programs, products and services. As noted by Dibbs in Chap. 4, while commercial firms have capitalised on technological advances that have increased data availability and state-of-the art analytics to create more sophisticated segmentation schemes, most social marketers remain more reliant on simple approaches. Ideally, social marketers need objective measures of the behaviours and people they are trying to change.

With survey data, consideration of measurement optimisation is also a focus. Metric measures that have true numeric properties permit more precise estimates to be obtained than their categorical counterparts. It is worthwhile to note that segmentation techniques that utilise metric measurements do not always yield data in a form that is easy to interpret for the novice users. Segmentation data analysis techniques such as Two-Step cluster analysis offers one means to use survey data given its ability to cope with both numeric and categorical data. Two-Step cluster analysis has been validated across studies and over time, giving confidence to the personas derived from this technique. Data driven segmentation techniques may give investors more confidence when evaluating budget requests when compared to a priori segmentation approaches, and it is worth bearing this in mind when making decisions about which segmentation tool to employ.

Conclusions

'To know your enemy, you must become your enemy.'

Attributed to Sun Tzu—a Chinese general, highly influential military strategist and philosopher—this quote embodies the philosophy that needs to underpin social marketing practice moving forward. Social marketers need to embrace a way of thinking permitting them to exploit situations to change the behaviour of the targeted individual. To do this, intelligence needs to be highly accurate and segmentation provides one means to increase accuracy. The time has come for social marketers to think in the same way that commercial marketers do.

This book has provided a range of methods that have been widely used in both commercial and social marketing practice. Some methods outlined can be used regardless of budgetary constraints, overcoming one of social marketing's biggest weaknesses—a limited budget. How many social marketers do you know fortunate enough to have an annual turnover of $514M? If you decide to apply segmentation, take confidence in knowing there is no one best method for segmentation. Segmentation is a process that is applied acknowledging that markets are complex, made up of many individuals, and that marketers need to take differences into account during the design and planning phases to understand where, when and how they can reach different consumers in their target market. Moving forward, social marketers can embrace marketing thinking regardless of their budgets.

Ignoring differences that inherently occur within a market and delivering one program based on a market average misses the mark for too many. Segmentation provides a means to think about a complex market filled with unique people more economically. By breaking a market into groups, each of which are distinguishable from each other, social marketers are better placed to cater to some differences, helping to reach more customers in a more direct and meaningful manner. Consideration of segments or personas during social marketing program design ensures that needs and wants can be met, satisfying more customers, which, in turn, delivers improved behavioural outcomes—the desired end goal for social marketers.

References

Andreasen, A. R. (2002). Marketing social marketing in the social change marketplace. *Journal of Public Policy & Marketing, 21*(1), 3–13.

Carins, J., & Rundle-Thiele, S. R. (2014). Eating for the better: A social marketing review (2000–2012). *Public Health Nutrition, 17*(7), 1628–1639.

CCA Annual Report. (2015). https://www.ccamatil.com/-/media/Cca/Corporate/Files/Annual-Reports/2015/CCA166-CCA-Annual-Report-2015-WEB_final.ashx. Accessed May 17, 2016.

Dietrich, T., Rundle-Thiele, S. R., Leo, C., & Connor, J. (2015). One size never fits all: Cluster responses to a school based social marketing alcohol program. *Journal of School Health, 85*(4), 251–259.

Elliot, G., Rundle-Thiele, S. R., & Waller, D. (2014). *Marketing* (3rd ed.). Brisbane, Australia: Wiley.

French, J., & Blair-Stevens, C. (2005). *The big pocket guide to using social marketing for behaviour change*. London: The NSMC. www.thensmc.com/sites/default/files/Big_pocket_guide_2011.pdf. Accessed February 21, 2015.

Fujihira, H., Kubacki, K., Ronto, R., Pang, B., & Rundle-Thiele, S. R. (2015). Social marketing physical activity interventions among adults sixty years old and older: A systematic review. *Social Marketing Quarterly, 21*(4), 214–229.

Hastings, G. (2007). *Social marketing: Why should the devil have all the best tunes*. Oxford: Elsevier.

iSMA. (2016, p. 3). Available online at http://www.i-socialmarketing.org/assets/social_marketing_definition.pdf. Web site last accessed June 4th, 2016.

Kubacki, K., Rundle-Thiele, S. R., Pang, B., & Buyucek, N. (2015a). Minimising alcohol harm: A systematic social marketing review (2000–2014). *Journal of Business Research, 68*(10), 2214–2222.

Kubacki, K., Rundle-Thiele, S. R., Parkinson, J., & Lahtinen, V. (2015b). A systematic review assessing the extent of social marketing principle use in interventions targeting children (2000–2014). *Young Consumers, 16*(2), 141–158.

Kubacki, K., Rundle-Thiele, S. R., Schuster, L., Wessels, C., & Gruneklee, N. (2015c). Digital innovation in social marketing: A systematic literature of interventions using digital channels for engagement. In W. Wymer (Ed.), *Innovations in social marketing and public health communications: Applying quality of research* (pp. 49–66). Switzerland: Springer International Publishing.

Pettigrew, S., & Jongenelis, M. I. (2016). promoting public health: Understanding the limitations of marketing principles and the need for alternative approaches. In C. Plewa & J. Conduit (Eds.), *Making a difference through marketing: A quest for diverse perspectives* (pp. 61–72). Singapore: Springer.

Purdy, C. H. (2011). Using the Internet and social media to promote condom use in Turkey. *Reproductive Health Matters, 19*(37), 157–165.

Schuster, L., Kubacki, K., & Rundle-Thiele, S. R. (2015). A theoretical approach to segmenting children's walking behaviour. *Young Consumers, 16*(2), 159–171.

Sutton, R. I., & Staw, B. M. (1995). What theory is not. *Administrative Science Quarterly, 40*(3), 371–384.

Whetton, D. A. (1989). What constitutes a theoretical contribution? *Academy of Management Review, 14*(4), 490–495.

MIX
Papier aus verantwortungsvollen Quellen
Paper from responsible sources
FSC® C105338

If you have any concerns about our products,
you can contact us on
ProductSafety@springernature.com

In case Publisher is established outside the EU,
the EU authorized representative is:
Springer Nature Customer Service Center GmbH
Europaplatz 3, 69115 Heidelberg, Germany

Printed by Libri Plureos GmbH
in Hamburg, Germany